Dropshipping And Facebook Advertising

Discover How To Make Money Online,

And Create Passive Income Streams

With Dropshipping and Social Media Marketing

By

Michael Ezeanaka

www.MichaelEzeanaka.com

Copyright ©2019

Disclaimer

This publication is designed to provide competent and reliable information regarding the subject matter covered. However, it is sold with the understanding that the author is not engaged in rendering investment or other professional advice. Laws and practices often vary from state to state and country to country and if investment or other expert assistance is required, the services of a professional should be sought. The author specifically disclaims any liability that is incurred from the use or application of the contents of this book.

This Book Bundle Consist Of:

Dropshipping – Discover How to Make Money Online, Build Sustainable Streams of Passive Income and Gain Financial Freedom Using The Dropshipping E-Commerce Business Model (Part I)

&

Facebook Advertising – Learn How to Make $10,000+ Each Month With Facebook Marketing (Part II)

Answer Booklet

How would you like to download a booklet that neatly summarizes, all the answers to the end of chapter questions in the Facebook Advertising section of this book? If you want it, a PDF version of the card is hosted on my website and can be downloaded for free. However, a password is required to unlock the download. Follow the steps below to retrieve the password!

Steps to take

1. The password consists of 8 characters (all lower case)
2. Here is the incomplete password: p-z-b-y-
3. The second, fourth, sixth and eight character of the password is missing and is located in random pages of this book.
4. Read this book carefully to locate and retrieve them (they're so obvious you can't miss them).
5. Once you have the complete password then go to www.MichaelEzeanaka.com > Free Stuff > Ebooks/audiobooks > Facebook Advertising Answer Booklet, enter the password, download the Answer Booklet and enjoy!

Books In The Business and Money Series	
Series #	**Book Title**
1	Affiliate Marketing
2	Passive Income Ideas
3	Affiliate Marketing + Passive Income Ideas (2-in-1 Bundle)
4	Facebook Advertising
5	Dropshipping
6	Dropshipping + Facebook Advertising (2-in-1 Bundle)
7	Real Estate Investing For Beginners
8	Credit Cards and Credit Repair Secrets
9	Real Estate Investing And Credit Repair (2-in-1 Bundle)
10	Passive Income With Affiliate Marketing (2nd Edition)
11	Passive Income With Dividend Investing
The kindle edition will be available to you for FREE when you purchase the paperback version from Amazon.com (The US Store)	

Download The Audio Versions Along With The Complementary PDF Document For FREE from

www.MichaelEzeanaka.com > My Audiobooks

Table of Contents

Introduction

The internet has opened a lot of doors for aspiring online entrepreneurs. Anyone with an idea and the resolve to pursue such an idea can start and build a successful online business. It so happens that one of the most lucrative business ideas today is dropshipping. Dropshipping is popular for the simple reason that it follows a business model which is perfect for the digital age. There are numerous definitions for dropshipping that are being thrown out there. But in the simplest of terms, it's a type of business that follows the traditional buy-and-sell model. Only this time, you don't need to get your hands on the inventory. You simply act as the middleman between the product manufacturer or supplier and the consumer.

The business model looks simple on paper. However, without the right information, it can be difficult to execute. This is why I have decided to write this book to help you fully understand how dropshipping works and how you can create your own successful dropshipping business. There are so many factors involved in setting up a dropshipping business. I will be discussing every single one of these factors in this book.

Be that as it may, I need to emphasize here that this book is not a blueprint for some get-rich-quick scheme. If you are looking for a get-rich-quick business model, then this book is not for you. You don't get instantly rich after starting a Dropshipping business. Sure, there are some who get lucky and earn a ton of money from the get-go. But these are few and far in between. Moreover, building a sustainable business requires the right knowledge, mindset and perseverance - not luck. This is why before you continue reading this book, I need you to have *realistic expectations*. Just like any form of business, dropshipping requires time and efforts to be profitable. It can take weeks or months before you see any meaningful profits going your way. That's the reality.

I'm not saying this to discourage you or downplay the merits of dropshipping. I'm telling you this to make sure that you get started with the right mindset, realistic goals and actionable plans. **These are the keys to achieving success in dropshipping.** You have to come up with goals that are achievable based on your current knowledge, skillset, and experience. To reach these goals, you also need a comprehensive plan which describes in detail the steps that you are going to take. If you have these, then you are off to a good start. You have a good foundation that will be of great help to you in the long run.

A very common question among beginners in the dropshipping industry is this: "Is the business model sustainable?" My answer is yes, it is indeed sustainable. However, you shouldn't confuse the term sustainable with the term profitable. Just because a business model is sustainable doesn't necessarily mean it's profitable. You have to always keep that in mind. Building a sustainable and profitable dropshipping business requires the *right knowledge*, time and effort. There are no shortcuts to success here. You have to focus on improving and building the business day in and day out.

I want this book to serve as your guide as you navigate through the complicated world of dropshipping. Whether you are a complete beginner or someone who has some experience in the industry, there's a ton of information in this book that you are going to find valuable. Even after finishing this book, you can always use it as a reference for questions and problems you might encounter in the future. With that said, I suggest that you always keep a copy of this book in your files for easy access and reference.

How much you earn from your dropshipping business depends on a lot of factors. But I'm here to tell you right now that it's possible to make five figures each month from your business. Thousands of other people are doing it. So why can't you? Yes, you can reach $10,000 a month or even go beyond that amount with the right products coupled with a great marketing strategy. The icing on the cake is the possibility that you can earn this amount on autopilot. That is not an exaggeration. You definitely can earn thousands of dollars a month through dropshipping after setting things up the right way. That is the beauty of dropshipping. You can automate most of the processes involved in the business.

Before you dig into this book, there's one last tip I want to tell you. Don't rush! This is something I always tell people who wish to start their own dropshipping business. Majority of those who rush their businesses skip a couple of crucial steps and eventually fail. Don't make the same mistake. What you need to do is build your business one day at a time. Make a detailed plan for everything that you want to accomplish. Before you make any decision, make sure that it's backed up by good data and information. Don't make decisions on instincts alone. Relying solely on our instincts is risky and a common cause of failure.

Without further ado, lets get right into it!

Did You Know

71% of shoppers believe they will get a better deal online than in stores.
Are you aware of what campaigns your competitors are running both in-store and online?

Congratulations!

The second character of the password required to unlock the Answer Booklet is letter l (l for letter).

Chapter 1

Understanding Dropshipping

Dropshipping is not exactly a brand new concept. The business model has been around for decades even before the arrival of the internet. Some enterprising people would put up ads in local newspapers, in the radio, or on television informing consumers that they are selling this or that product. But they don't actually own or have these products on hand. If a customer calls to buy a product, what these entrepreneurs do is get in touch with a supplier or a manufacturer, buy the product, and instruct the supplier to ship the product directly to the customer. The entrepreneurs make money on the difference between the product's advertised price and the supplier's price.

This is basically the precursor to today's version of dropshipping. The internet has completely revolutionized the business model. It made it very easy to move products from anywhere in the world. All you need to do is set up a website, install a piece of dropshipping software, and you are good to go. You can literally do everything from the comfort of your home. You don't hold any inventory. You don't do the shipping. Your responsibilities only involve running the website and making deals with suppliers and manufacturers.

The online dropshipping model rode on the back of online retail sites. When the internet first came about, most people used it merely for research and entertainment. Then businesses and enterprising individuals saw the internet's potential as a marketplace for products and services. Ecommerce quickly boomed and grew at a very fast pace. Businesses would build websites and sell their products and services there. For a while, ecommerce only had people and businesses selling their own products and services. But there soon came a shift when ecommerce concepts like affiliate marketing were introduced. People who don't have their own products and services now have the chance to make money through ecommerce.

In a way, online dropshipping is an offshoot of affiliate marketing. You are basically promoting and selling someone else's products. However, in the dropshipping model, you have the option of rebranding the products as if they are your own. You can make a deal with a supplier or manufacturer who produces the products then marks them with your customized labels. You purchase the products at cost basis (i.e. original cost) then resell them with a marked up price (i.e. original cost + your profit). In short, as a dropshipper, you are not a product developer or manufacturer. You are merely a marketer.

As I've mentioned earlier, online dropshipping has revolutionized online commerce. And it continues to evolve as we speak. In fact, dropshipping has become so big that it can be aptly considered as an industry on its own. Online dropshipping registers billions of sales a year. This will only grow in the coming years as more and more people get involved in the business. Almost every product today can be sold using the dropshipping model. You just have to find and approach the right suppliers and manufacturers.

It also does not matter where you are located. As long as you have a reliable internet connection, you can build and run an online dropshipping operation. You can be in Antarctica and still run a successful dropshipping business that ships products from China to the United States. Or you could be vacationing in Thailand and still run a business that dropships products from Brazil to Australia. My point here is that this business model offers time and location freedom. You can run your business from anywhere and at any time.

Another good reason why now is the time to be involved in dropshipping is the availability of tools and resources that make the process so much easier. In the early days, online entrepreneurs had to build everything from scratch. This meant that you had to be a programmer or you needed to hire a team of programmers to help you set up your website. Today, you can build a fully-functioning dropshipping website in minutes by just clicking on a few buttons and following step-by-step, beginner friendly instructions. There are all sorts of software that you can download and install on your dropshipping website. Some of these software programs automate your website so that you don't have to do anything else. The website will run itself with you doing very minimal work. This is one of the reasons why this business model was awarded a simplicity and passivity score of 80% in the book Passive Income Ideas: 50 Ways To Make Money Online Analyzed.

Before we proceed to the next chapter, let's make sure that you fully understand how online dropshipping works. Basically, here are the main steps involved in dropshipping:

- **Step 1**: You build a website that's specifically designed for dropshipping.
- **Step 2**: You get into a deal with a supplier or manufacturer to produce the products you are going to sell.
- **Step 3**: Promote the products on your website.
- **Step 4**: If someone orders a product from your website, you order the product from your supplier or manufacturer.
- **Step 5**: Your supplier is automatically informed about the order.
- **Step 6**: Your supplier or manufacturer ships the product to the buyer.
- **Step 7**: Rinse and repeat.

Chapter Summary

The business model for online dropshipping is pretty straightforward. You build the website, make a deal with a supplier, promote the product, and instruct the supplier to ship the product directly to customers. It's basically buying and reselling products but this time, you don't hold any inventory. You simply do the marketing and selling. Your supplier handles product development, manufacturing, and shipping. It's a business model that is perfect suited to today's digitally connected world. The barriers to setting up a dropshipping business are very minimal. Remember that you are not going to hold inventory. This zero inventory benefit drives down your startup costs. In a nutshell, all you need to get started is a deal with a supplier or manufacturer, a functioning dropshipping website, and a reliable internet connection.

Did You Know

70% of E-Commerce traffic is from smartphones. Is your website and your products being represented on a retailer's website optimised for mobile? Watch out for truncated product descriptions.

Chapter 2

Benefits Of The Dropshipping Model

Why would you build a dropshipping business instead of other alternative online business models? This is a very important question which we will address in this chapter. One of the reasons why some people tend to downplay the merits of dropshipping is that they aren't fully aware of the benefits that it offers. On paper or through the definition alone, dropshipping seems like a simple business that can only earn you spare change. That isn't the case at all. As I've said in the Introduction, you can earn as much as $10,000 a month from dropshipping if you do it right.

Anyway, let us go back to the question. Why would you spend your time and efforts in building an online dropshipping business? Well, lets see.

1. Dropshipping Requires Very Little Capital Investment

This is without a doubt the most important benefit of starting a dropshipping business. Dropshipping won't cost you an arm and a leg. Always keep in mind that in dropshipping, you are not holding any inventory. Unlike a traditional business model wherein you buy products then resell them, dropshipping involves purchasing the product only when a customer makes an order. You only make some sort of expense when a customer buys from you. But that expense basically means nothing because you are turning a profit from every sale you make.
The costs associated with starting a dropshipping business are mostly related to setting up the dropshipping website; like web development costs, web hosting costs, domain registration costs, and other technical expenses related to creating and maintaining the website. You also have to spend money in order to drive traffic to your website via Google ads, Facebook ads, Instagram etc.

Furthermore, you may also have to pay for the tools, software programs, plugins, and add-ons that you are going to use in your dropshipping website. Some of these are one-time costs. Others are recurring costs (i.e. plugins that require you to pay a monthly subscription fee).

As far as inventory costs are concerned, your expenses will depend on the negotiations and deals that you enter into with your supplier or manufacturer. For sure, there will be inventory costs especially if you are going to customize or rebrand a product and sell it as if you've made it yourself. With this practice, you will have to have a sample batch developed and manufactured. Needless to say, this isn't going to be free. You have to pay for the sample batch of products. Even with these expenses, they are still very minimal compared to the costs you would have incurred if you follow a traditional buy-and-sell business model.

My main point here is that no matter what angle you look at it, dropshipping requires relatively little capital investment from you. Your finances are easily manageable right from the start. With just a few hundred dollars, you can start a fully-functioning dropshipping website and business. With that said, there aren't much financial barriers when it comes to starting and building an online dropshipping business.

2. It's Super Easy to Get Started

Would you believe me if I tell you that you can get a dropshipping business fully running within an hour? It's probably hard to believe, but it's definitely possible. That's how easy it is to get started with dropshipping. I have mentioned earlier the availability of tools, plugins, and pieces of software that are *specifically designed for dropshipping processes*. These tools make it hassle-free to start and run a dropshipping business. These can also be used to automate the business so you don't have to do everything on your own.

You don't need much to launch a dropshipping business. A website and the product, these are the two most important things you need. Getting the website isn't difficult. There are tons of pre-made templates out there for dropshipping websites. Feel free to check out the options available at ThemeForest, Shopify and plenty other vendors out there. Just get one of these templates, customize it depending on your specific needs and preferences, and upload the products you are promoting and selling. If you have programming or coding skills, doing these should be a breeze. If you are not that technically proficient, you can always outsource the responsibilities to a freelancer or contractor. Freelancers can be hired from sites like upwork, fiverr etc.

When getting started, my advice for you is that you decide first on the types of products you are going to promote before you begin building the website. The reason why you should follow this strategy is that it's easier to build a website if you know the products that you are going to sell. You will know which features you need and what kind of content you are going to publish on the site. If you are outsourcing the website-building process, the web developer will have an idea of the direction you want to take.

3. There's Less Overhead Costs

For a lot of traditional online businesses, overhead costs are a huge problem. You don't have this problem if you are running a dropshipping operation. Since you are not keeping any inventory of the products you are selling, and let's keep in mind that overhead costs are usually related to inventory management, you don't have inventory so there's nothing to manage. That's a significant chunk of overhead costs that you take off your plate. These include:

- **Cost of space** - facility in which the inventory is housed i.e. warehouse depreciation, insurance, utilities, warehouse staff, storage racks etc.
- **Cost of money** - Interest cost associated with the cost of borrowing money to pay for inventory e.g. bank loans, credit cards etc.
- **Cost of obsolescence** - Some inventory item may never be used or will be damaged while in storage, and so must be disposed of at a reduced price, or at no price at all. Depending on how perishable the inventory is, or the speed with which technology changes impact inventory values, this can be a substantial cost.

Another great thing about the dropshipping model is that your overhead costs usually go down as time goes by. A huge portion of your overhead costs are spent on your first weeks and months. As you build your business, these overhead costs normally decrease with time. Why is this the case? In the first stages of your business, you are basically still learning the ropes so you are prone to risks and mistakes. These risks and mistakes often result to overhead expenses. But as you refine your business and find more efficient ways to run things, these risks and mistakes eventually go away. Fewer risks and fewer mistakes mean you will have less overhead expenses.

4. Access to a Wide Selection of Products

If a product can be shipped whether domestically or internationally, you can market and sell it via dropshipping. There are literally hundreds of thousands of products out there that you can sell through the dropshipping model. All you have to do is choose. A common misconception about dropshipping is that you can only sell one or two products through a dropshipping website. This is not true. You can sell dozens or even hundreds of products in your online store and dropship every single one of them. For sure, as you add more products to your selection, the harder it gets to manage the varying orders. But that's not the point. The point here is that there is no ceiling to the number of unique products that you can promote and sell through a dropshipping website.

However, if it's your first time starting a dropshipping business, I would recommend that you start with just one or two products. You are new so you are still learning the ropes. With a few products in your plate, it's going to be much easier to run and manage the business. As you gain more experience, you can then start introducing additional products into the mix. The lesson here is that you shouldn't bite more than what you can chew.

5. It's Not That Difficult to Scale

With the dropshipping model, all you need to do to scale your business is add more products to your selection or you start another dropshipping website that offers a new selection of products. Setting up another website will only require a small amount of time and efforts from you especially if you are utilizing a ready-made template. With a dropshipping template, all you have to do is customize the look of the website, upload your product images and descriptions, add information about your business, and install any needed plugins or software programs.

It's definitely possible for you to start and run several dropshipping businesses at the same time. As I have said in an earlier chapter, there's nothing to stop you from starting as many dropshipping websites as you can. If you can manage and run all of them, then by all means, go for it. I know of some online entrepreneurs who manage dozens of dropshipping websites so it can definitely be done. This is why you should learn everything you can about online business automation. You have to take advantage of all the tools and resources that allow you to automate your business processes.

And just so you know, this was one of the most scalable businesses analyzed in the book Passive Income Ideas: 50 Ways to Make Money Online Analyzed, with a scalability score of 90%!

6. Access to a Global Market

With the dropshipping model, you can promote and sell products to anyone in the world provided that your supplier or manufacturer has the means to ship the products there. That is the beauty of online commerce. With just a simple website, you have the ability to reach out to millions of potential customers. However, before you offer global shipping, make sure that you are fully aware of the associated costs. You have to look into the costs of shipping a product to every country. These costs often vary so you need to be careful.

I personally know of a few dropshippers who made the mistake of not learning about shipping costs per country before offering global shipping for their customers. They ended up losing a lot of money because of this simple mistake. You have to understand that shipping costs per country are always different. For example, let's say that your supplier ships products from China. The cost of shipping a product from China to the United States is different to the cost of shipping the same product to Brazil.

So how do you solve this glaring problem? What most dropshipping entrepreneurs do is **price their products based on the geographical location of the buyer**. A person from Brazil sees a different price point compared to a person from the United States. For example, the price for United States customers may be $15 while the price for Brazil customers is $10. The price all depends on the shipping costs associated with that country. If the shipping cost is higher, the price of the product will reasonably be higher as well.

For this to work, you need to **build a dynamic website** wherein a visitor from the United States sees $15 while a visitor from Brazil sees $10. It's all about catering to the customer based on where he or she is located. This enables you to offer your product to a global market. A tool that can potentially help with this is an app called Multi Country Pricing. As of writing, it's currently available in the Shopify app store. There could be plenty other resources like this to assist you!

7. It Can Be Easily Automated

Advances in online commerce have made it very easy to get things done. With just a few clicks of the mouse button, you are able to build a fully-functioning website. With just a simple plugin, the customer service feature on your website can be managed by a chatbot that runs on artificial intelligence (AI). By installing a piece of software, anyone can order and pay for products on your website. These are just some of the instances where you can see automation in action. All of these are applicable in the dropshipping industry.

Automation allows the business to run and manage itself with very minimal intervention from you. This is every online entrepreneur's dream. The business runs itself and continues to process orders and sales even when you are sleeping or if you are vacationing in the Virgin Islands. As long as there are no bugs or errors in the system, you continue making money. In short, dropshipping is one of the few businesses that can help you earn a consistent stream of passive income. You keep on earning money with very little work. You don't even have to keep inventories of your products. You don't even ship the products. All you do is drive customers to your website, accept the orders, process them, and forward them to your supplier or manufacturer who handles the rest of the transaction cycle.

8. There's No Shortage of Suppliers and Manufacturers

Do something for me, will you? Go to Google and search for Alibaba. Visit the website and browse there for a bit and get an understanding of what the website is and what it does. Are you done? It's an immense marketplace, is it not? Almost every product you can conceive of is available there for sale and for bulk purchase. Hundreds of thousands of merchants, traders, suppliers, and manufacturers strut their wares on the site. This is why Alibaba is one of the biggest sources of dropshipped products in the world today. This is not an exaggeration. You have access to very cheap products that you can customize, rebrand, and resell at premium prices.

And here's the thing. Alibaba is just the tip of the iceberg. It's just one of dozens of online marketplaces where you can find products to promote and dropship in your own store. Alibaba is based in China and it's by far the go-to marketplace for a lot of dropshippers. What makes Alibaba so popular among dropshippers is that the marketplace offers the cheapest prices in the industry. If for some reason you can't do business with Alibaba, worry not, because you have a lot of other options. You just have to look for them. It all depends on the types of products that you plan on dropshipping.

Chapter Summary

The bottom line here is that dropshipping is an ultimately viable business opportunity which offers a lot of benefits to both aspiring and established online entrepreneurs. The barriers to entry are very minimal so anyone can start a dropshipping business. You don't need a thick wallet to get started. In a lot of cases, just a few hundred dollars will do. Furthermore, there is no ceiling to how much you can scale the business. You can start a dozen dropshipping sites if you want to as long as you have the time and the manpower to run all of them. In a nutshell, the dropshipping model offers a variety of benefits that make it very appealing to those looking to make money online.

Did You Know

38% cite social media interaction as their reason for visiting a retailers website. Does your brand have a strong social media strategy to drive traffic?

Chapter 3

Disadvantages of The Dropshipping Model

Since we have discussed the benefits and rewards of engaging in a dropshipping business, it's important that we also discuss its possible drawbacks. I will be the first to tell you that the dropshipping model is not a perfect business model. Just like any business opportunity, it has its own flaws. And that's what we are going to discuss in this chapter. That being said, these drawbacks should not in any way discourage you. I'm telling you these so that you will know what to expect and what kinds of risks you will be facing when you finally embark in your dropshipping journey. This way, you'll be able to make an informed decision.

1. Sudden Stock Shortages

This is one of the most common problems with the dropshipping model. There are always huge ups and downs with the way product orders are made. Let's say for instance that in one given week, you receive a few orders a day. What if in the next week, orders suddenly balloon to hundreds of orders a day? In most of these scenarios, the supplier or manufacturer won't be able to fulfill the orders as fast as you would want them to. Stock availability is really something that you don't have complete control over. This can be very problematic if there's no consistency in the way customers order products from your dropshipping website. That being said, this problem can be managed by using Google Trends website to monitor the seasonality of a product, anticipate periods of large demands e.g. during festive periods and having multiple suppliers capable of matching the demand.

2. Higher Cost of Goods Sold

The cost of goods sold is higher in the sense that you pay more for the goods if you are a dropshipper compared to the price being paid by a stocking retailer. A stocking retailer is someone who buys the products before reselling them (i.e. direct retailers, supermarkets, grocery stores). It's understandable why suppliers and manufacturers offer lower prices to these stocking retailers. This is something you must take seriously especially if you are going to dropship products that are already available in supermarkets and other retail outlets. Since your cost of goods sold are higher, your prices will often be higher compared to other retailers.

3. Higher Fulfillment Costs

Here's something you need to understand about the dropshipping process. You are not only paying for the cost of the goods. You are also paying for the costs associated with stocking, picking, packing, packaging, and shipping. This means you are dealing with a huge mark-up. Of course, you can cut down the costs by negotiating with your supplier and manufacturer but the fulfilment costs will still be high.

4. More Customer Service Issues

The shipping aspect of the business may be under the control of your supplier but customer service is still your responsibility. It's not that difficult to see why this can cause a lot of headaches to you. You are not the one handling the packaging and shipping duties so you are often clueless how and when the products get to your customers. This is a recipe for disaster as far as customer service is concerned. There are so many factors that you have to know about the shipping process in order to be able to provide answers and solutions to disgruntled customers. You have to know when the product was shipped, what the tracking details are, and the estimated arrival time of the product. To know these things, you have to be communicating with your supplier and manufacturer.

5. You Don't Have Full Control Over the Business

This is a no-brainer but a lot of aspiring dropshippers tend to ignore it until it hits them in the head. Letting a separate entity take charge of your product handling and shipping process is very risky, to say the least. It's great if your supplier or manufacturer does a great job. But what if it keeps delaying its shipments or if it doesn't ship the products the right way such that a lot of the products get damaged or even lost along the way? You know that when this happens, the customers will be blaming you, not the supplier. Your brand (if any) will suffer the consequences. This is why I always advise aspiring dropshippers to make sure that a supplier is trustworthy and reliable before making a deal with him/her.

6. Reliance on Stocks

This is very similar to stock shortages. You are relying on the good faith of the supplier that the stocks will always be available. Let's be honest here. 100% of your business relies on the stocks being held by your supplier. If you get orders from customers and your supplier tells you that stocks aren't available for now, that's not good. If this happens too often, you might as well close your shop. So I need to repeat my advice above. Only enter into deals with suppliers and manufacturers who have proven themselves to be reliable. Your business literally stands on their reliability. To avoid being over reliant on one supplier build relationships with multiple suppliers.

7. Potential Quality Control Issues

Again, you are not developing, manufacturing, and handling the products you are selling. In short, you have very little control on the products including their quality. Quality control is one of the things that you have to sacrifice if you engage in a dropshipping business. You can try to agree on quality issues with the supplier but this doesn't always mean that the quality standards will remain the same. You just have to hope that the supplier delivers his other end of the deal. Since you don't hold any of the inventory, you will only hear about a decrease in product quality if you start receiving an uptick in customer complaints and product returns. By this time, the damage has already been done. You have to rebuild once again a positive relationship between you and your customers. In a nutshell, if you plan on starting a dropshipping business, keep in mind that product quality is something that you have very minimal control over.

8. Overcrowded Markets

In many ways, dropshipping has gone mainstream and the competition among sellers is growing tougher by the day. A lot of the markets being targeted by dropshippers are overcrowded already. It's easy to set up a dropshipping store so anyone who knows how online commerce works can start his own dropshipping operation. The competition will only get worse in the coming months and years as more and more people attempt to get a piece of the action. I guess what I'm trying to say here is that you have to be ready to compete with hundreds or even thousands of other sellers when you set up your own dropshipping business. You can minimize this by conducting good product research and niching down to product categories that have good demand but not as much competition. Later in this book, you'll discover how to go about doing that.

9. No Guarantee of Profits

There is this common misconception that it's easy to be profitable in dropshipping because you don't hold any inventory. People often assume that you are reaping huge rewards from every sale because you didn't have anything to do with the production and shipping of the products. But just like any business, there's no guarantee of profits here. There are various factors that can cause things to go wrong. You might suddenly lose the deal with your supplier. Your manufacturer might produce a product that's subpar. You may have overestimated your potential market. Or the products just don't sell. Any of these problems can occur. Not only won't you be profitable, you will likely lose some money as well. In other words, don't expect dropshipping to be a 100% guaranteed easy route to business profitability. There is no such thing.

10. Requires *Basic* Technical Skills

In a lot of ways, online dropshipping is a very technical business. Always remember that many aspects of the business involves building and managing a website. This means you should at least have *basic* knowledge of web development and coding or access to freelancers with the knowledge. This is especially important if you are running the business on your own. You must have the technical knowledge and skills to keep the website running smoothly without major glitches.

You should also have the capability to fix technical problems. What if the website suddenly goes down? What if a customer can't place an order? What if the customer's payment is not going through? What if the website takes forever to load? These are just a few of the potential problems that your website might encounter. It's important that you have what it takes to fix them as soon as possible. If you are not confident with your technical skills, then you should hire someone who is. Dropshipping requires a lot of technical work. There's no other way around this. Either you do the technical work yourself or you get a skilled and experienced professional to do it for you.

11. More Products or More Suppliers Means More Work

Scaling a dropshipping business is very doable but you have to be aware that if you double your list of products, you are also doubling the amount of work that you have to do. This is why many online dropshippers are often not that enthusiastic to add more products to their listings because they are adding more work upon themselves. It gets even more complicated if you are working with more than one supplier. There may be instances wherein one product comes from one supplier and another product comes from a different supplier. Tracking and managing different products and different suppliers can be challenging.

My advice for you is that you shouldn't bite off more than you can chew. Start with a single product. If you can easily manage the work it demands, then you should probably add another product in your listings. If you can manage the two products, then you can add a third product. My main point here is that you add products to your business in a slow and gradual way. Don't add too many products at the same time. Doing so might overwhelm you. Your best strategy is to add the products one at a time.

Be that as it may, much of this task can be outsourced to freelancers who will help you handle customer service and other menial tasks associated with this business.

12. Low Margins

This often flies under the radar when it comes to newbies starting a dropshipping business. A lot of beginners tend to assume that dropshipping always comes with high profit margins. Again, this is mostly because of the fact that they neither handle nor keep the products. This often makes beginners think that they will be dealing with very low product costs. That's not the case at all. As I've mentioned earlier, it's actually more expensive to dropship a product than purchase them in bulk and sell them as a direct retailer.

Since you are buying the products at higher costs as a dropshipper, this means that you will be left with lower profit margins. This will always be the case if the dropshipping model doesn't go through major changes. Another thing you should always remember is that you are not just competing with other sellers online, you are also competing with offline sellers. You have to put a price tag on your products that's reasonable in the context of both your online and offline competition.

13. Inventory Issues

There are a lot of things that can go wrong with the products you are selling. The problem is that you usually don't have any control of these issues. If something goes wrong with the inventory, it's usually the fault of the supplier or manufacturer. But the problem will still be reflected upon your business. Your customers will be looking at you for answers. Keep in mind that your customers don't know that you are the middleman. They think that you make and ship the products yourself. With that said, every problem they see in the products will be blamed upon you.

Problems with inventories are without a doubt one of the biggest drawbacks of online dropshipping. Making matters worse is the fact that these problems are often way beyond your control. The most effective way of avoiding these problems is to only deal with suppliers and manufacturers who are reliable. You should be able to trust them. They should have a good track record. Always check their backgrounds and their ratings before you enter into any deals with them. Most online marketplaces these days have rating systems for suppliers and manufacturers. If a supplier has **been around for a long time and has a lot of good ratings** from entrepreneurs they've worked with in the past, then that supplier is most likely a good bet. If it's the other way around, then you are better off looking for another supplier.

14. Shipping Complexities

Shipping a product to a customer is never an easy task. The good news is that this responsibility lies not in you but in your supplier or manufacturer. However, this doesn't mean that you can ignore the complexity of the process. There must be a smooth connection between your sales process and the supplier's shipping procedures. In this way, when a customer orders a product from your dropshipping website, your supplier is immediately informed about the order. The faster the supplier is informed about the sale, the quicker he will be able to ship the product to the customer. If there isn't an efficient communication line between your business website and the supplier, this is where shipping complexities arise and cause havoc to the business.

15. Supplier Errors

Your supplier or manufacturer will be making errors. This is something you have to take into account. No supplier or manufacturer is perfect. They all have their flaws and they are not immune to making errors. A supplier error can be anything. It could be the wrong product being sent to the customer. It could be the right product but it was sent to the wrong customer. Products with the wrong specifications being sent to customers are a common occurrence in the dropshipping industry. It happens all the time and it can be very frustrating because as a dropshipper, you don't have control over these errors. If a customer complains about receiving the wrong product, then you have to work to ensure that the product is recalled and that the right product is resent.

Chapter Summary

As you can see, the dropshipping business model has a lot of inherent flaws. There are so many things that can go wrong. **Being aware of these potential problems can help prepare you in dealing with them.** The gist of this chapter is that dropshipping isn't a perfect business model. It's easy to get into the business but it can be complicated if you're not adequately prepared. What's frustrating is that a lot of these problems are often not under your control. They are usually not your fault, to put it simply. However, don't let these drawbacks discourage you from starting and building an online dropshipping business. Let these drawbacks serve as reminders why you need to be smarter and more careful in running your business. Also, knowing about these drawbacks enable you to come up with solutions when you encounter any of the problems discussed in this chapter.

What's more? Having acquired this book and the information it contains, you've given yourself a considerable edge over your competitors who intend to start a dropshipping business without adequate knowledge or preparation – they just hope to wing it.

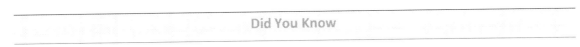

Did You Know

70% of online shoppers prioritize zooming in on images before purchasing. Are your images all optimized for web and easy to see?

Chapter 4

How to Start Your Own Dropshipping Business

Alright, now that you know what you are getting into, let's now discuss how you can actually start your own dropshipping business from scratch. I'll need you to pay close attention because we'll be discussing the basic framework with regards to starting a dropshipping business. I suggest that you read every word in this chapter if you are a complete beginner. When you look into the dropshipping business model, it seems so simple. It's almost too simple to a fault. But don't let that trick you into thinking that the journey is going to be easy. Underestimating the journey ahead is one of the biggest mistakes that aspiring entrepreneurs often mistake.

Before You Even Begin

I need you to do me a favor. Before you start building your own dropshipping business, I need you to make a promise to yourself that you are in it for the long run. As I have said a few times already, dropshipping is not a get-rich-quick scheme. So I need you to get rid of this type of thinking. I want you to be in it because you want to build something that is going to be sustainable in months and years to come. I'm telling you this out of my personal experience. When I first started dropshipping, I was in a hurry to find success and I wanted to make as much money as I could then move on to something else.

Needless to say, I wasn't successful in my first attempts at dropshipping. I made so many mistakes. Looking back, it's so clear to me now how those mistakes caused me to fail numerous times. Hopefully, with this book, I'll be able to teach people how to avoid those mistakes. I don't want you making the same mistakes I made. I don't want you to lose money the way I lost money because I was blinded by promises of instant profits. I just want you to start with a good business foundation.

The Mindset Required to Succeed

When it comes to mindset, you should be focused on achieving your goals no matter what. It doesn't matter how big or small your goals are, you should laser-focus your efforts and attention on them. Everything you do should be about taking steps toward those goals. Before you do anything, you ask yourself the following question: will this take me a step closer towards achieving my goal? If the answer is yes, then keep doing it. If the answer is no, then you should stop whatever you're doing and refocus. With regards to commitment, it's helpful if you are as committed as you are focused. Commitment means putting all your effort into the business. You go the extra mile if you have to. Never ever procrastinate. Don't put off for tomorrow what you can do today.

Where Do You Start?

To begin your dropshipping business, you have to do your assignment and that is to educate yourself about the business and the industry. Learn everything you can about dropshipping. That includes reading this book from page one to the last. I want you to read other books on dropshipping if necessary. I am not that self-centered to think that I have the answer to every question you have. Please do your assignment. Read blogs on dropshipping. Read websites on dropshipping. Browse through forums that tackle dropshipping topics. Dropshipping is just like any business. You have better chances in succeeding if you are knowledgeable about the industry's ins and outs.

After Educating Yourself, What's Your Next Move?

Okay, so you've done your assignment. You've done your research on how dropshipping works and how the model operates. Your mind is full of ideas, data, statistics, and other necessary information. Now what? Well, it's time to jump into the bandwagon and get started. It's time to get your hands dirty. To make this chapter easy to read and digest, I've decided to write it in the form of a step-by-step guide. Simply follow the steps and you will always be on the right track. So here we go!

Step 1: Make Sure That You Have Everything You Need

So the obvious question is this: what are the things you need to start a dropshipping business? There is no definitive answer to this question because every dropshipping business is unique. This means that different dropshipping businesses have different needs and requirements. However, there are the main requirements that should be present in every dropshipping business. These are as follows:

> The product or products.
> Capital.
> Website.
> Supplier or manufacturer.
> An ordering and payment system specifically designed for the dropshipping model.
> A method of receiving money (i.e. PayPal, Payoneer, money transfer, credit cards, or direct bank transfer)

These are the most basic things you need to get started. Each of these are discussed in more depth in other chapters in this book so I'm not going to expand on them in this particular chapter.

Step 2: Decide on the Products That You Are Going to Sell

What's great about the dropshipping business model is that you can sell almost every type of product. As long as it can be safely and legally shipped, it's up for grabs. The two most important factors you need to consider when deciding which products to sell are demand and competition. There should be enough online demand for the product for your business to be profitable. And the competition shouldn't be too tough in the sense that it won't be very difficult for you to take a piece of the market. So the formula in deciding what products to sell is as follows:

High Demand + Low Competition = Profitable Product

But how will you know if there's high demand or if there's low competition surrounding a product. This is where your research skills come into play. You have to do a lot of researching to determine the profitability of a product. Fortunately, there are a lot of tools and resources online that can help you with your research. You should not take this step lightly. Many aspiring online entrepreneurs go with their instincts and most of them will fail. Don't make the same mistake. Every decision you make should be backed up by data and statistics. This is why I keep on reiterating the importance of doing research and finding out as much as you can about the products that you are going to sell.

You need to focus your attention on a specific niche. Finding a niche and selecting the products to sell are discussed in more detail in Chapter Seven. The biggest reason why you should focus your efforts on a particular niche is that it's easier to compete which means you have better chances of being successful. It's also easier to get an accurate measurement of the demand for products in a niche.

Again, to determine demand and competition for a product, you should make use of online tools like keyword tools, trend spotters, and search metrics. So far, the best keyword research tool out there is Google's Keyword Tool. It offers much more accurate information and data. This is not surprising given the fact that Google controls more than 60% of the search market. The keyword tool is free to use so you there's absolutely no reason why you shouldn't use it. If you have a Gmail account, that's all you need to log into the keyword tool and start using its various features and functions. Other notable keyword tools are Merchant Words and KeywordTool IO

When doing your research, keep an eye on keywords that get a lot of searches but with very little competition. These keywords don't have to be product-related. If they are popular enough, maybe you can think of a product that you can tie into it. That's why using a keyword research tool is very important. It opens doors and introduces you to product ideas that you normally wouldn't think of on your own.

Step 3: Decide on the Business Structure That You Want to Pursue

In order to maximize your revenue and protect yourself from lawsuit, it can be advantageous to run your business with a company. You have several options. You can either register your business as a sole proprietorship, a limited liability company (LLC), or a C corporation. These are the three most commonly used business structures. It's important that you are completely aware of the differences between these business types - their pros and cons, so to speak. There are a lot of factors that you must take into account in deciding whether it would be better to register your new business as a sole proprietorship or as any of the other business types. Such factors include your business plan, business model, the possible tax advantages, the level of structure and formality, your business goals, your sources of investment, and where you want to conduct your business.

Most experienced dropshippers will tell you that it's best for you to choose between sole proprietorship and limited liability company (LLC). Although a C Corporation is still a great choice depending on the nature of your planned business. Below is a quick rundown of these three business structures.

➤ **Sole Proprietorship** – This business structure is the easiest to implement but you have to always keep in mind that it does not offer you much protection against personal liability. You are in danger of losing your personal assets in the event that your business get sued. Many dropshippers choose the sole proprietorship business structure because it has very minimal filing requirements. When it comes to reporting your earnings from the business, all you have to do is report the earnings under your personal taxes. That's it. No other federal or state business filings are required from you.

➤ **Limited Liability Company (LLC)** – This business structure establishes your business as a separate legal entity from you. This means that it provides better protection for all your personal assets. Simply put, it offers much better protection compared to that offered by a sole proprietorship. However, you should take note that this protection is neither foolproof nor absolute. Furthermore, in most instances, you will be required to comply with additional filings. You will also be paying for incorporation fees and ongoing fees.

➤ **C Corporation** – When it comes to protection against liabilities, a C Corporation business structure offers the most comprehensive protection. But this increased protection comes at a cost. First of all, it is much more expensive to start a business with this structure. The business will also likely be subjected to double taxation. This is because income from the business does not pass directly to the shareholders. Instead, they can be accessed via dividends, which are taxed separately after corporation tax.

I highly advise that you consult with a lawyer, accountant or a business consultant to help you decide which structure is *best suited to you* and your business needs. Get their thoughts and recommendations before you make any incorporation decisions. Majority of small businesses go with either an LLC or a sole proprietorship. Many go with an LLC because it provides a good trade-off with regards to personal liability protection, costs, and autonomy from personal finances.

What You Need to Know About Incorporating Outside of the United States

What if you are located outside the United States but you still want to create a Limited Liability Company or a C Corporation under US laws and jurisdiction? Here's how you should go about it. It's not as difficult as you might think. These are the core steps you should follow:

1. Choose your business structure.
2. Choose a state to incorporate or file your LLC in.
3. Get a registered agent.
4. Get an employer identification number (EIN).
5. Open a U.S. business bank account (e.g. via Payoneer)
6. Get the advice of a business consultant or any knowledgeable professional.
7. Stay compliant with the rules and regulations.

Step 4: Get Your Finances in Order

The amount of money you need to invest in the business depends on several factors. These factors include the size of your planned business, the overall price of the products you are selling, the location of your supplier or manufacturer, the software and programs you use on your dropshipping website, and projected overhead costs. Take all of these factors into account to ensure that you come up with a realistic estimate for your finances. You need to make sure that you have enough funds to get started. You also need to make projections of your costs and expenses in a time period of at least one year.

Ways to Finance Your Dropshipping Business

1. **Self-Funding**: You finance the business yourself. That is all business expenses will be covered by you alone.

2. **Crowdfunding**: This is a good option if you don't have enough savings to cover the projected costs of starting and building your business. Crowdfunding sites you can consider include:

   - Kickstarter,
   - Indiegogo,
   - Crowd Supply,
   - Crowdfunder,
   - Experiment,
   - Chuffed,
   - Patreon,
   - Fundable,
   - Wefunder,
   - SeedInvest,
   - Fundly,
   - LendingClub,
   - StartSomeGood,
   - Crowdcube, and
   - Funding Circle.

3. **Small Business Loan**: Applying for a loan with the Small Business Administration or SBA is a great choice if you have a good personal credit rating. Your credit rating is among the things that the SBA will take into consideration. It is also required that you present clear copies of your business plan and financial projections. If your application is compelling, the SBA might grant you with a low-interest loan. I highly recommend that you go over your presentation numerous times. You should also consult with a business advisor to ensure that your talking points and data for the presentation are accurate and correct.

4. **Bootstrapping**: This refers to the practice of funding your business operations from money you have at hand and from the profits you make from the business. Every dollar that your business earns is put back into the business. You don't incur debts and you get to build your business at a balanced and controlled pace.

5. **Local Investors**: These are prominent people in your area who have a knack for investing in local businesses. They usually provide you with the funds you need in exchange for a share of the profits or some equity in the business.

It is also important that you learn how to separate your personal expenses from your business expenses. You do this by opening new accounts under the name of your business. Your business should always be a separate entity from your personal life. There should be a clear boundary between the two especially during the early stages of your business. There are a lot of reasons why your personal expenses should be completely separate from your business expenses. One, it's easier to account for the expenses and costs that are related to your business. Two, it's much easier to track where your funds are going. Three, it will be easier for the IRS to audit your documents. And last but not the least, it protects you from liability on business debts. If there is no clear distinction between your personal and business finances, then your creditors have a better position in going after your personal assets to offset the debts.

Your business should have separate accounts for the following:

- ✓ **Business Checking Account** – When creating a checking account for your business, your ultimate goal should be to use it for all your business finances. All you really need is one primary checking account. All of your expenses should be withdrawn from the account. It also follows that all your profits will be deposited back into the account. One obvious benefit of this setup is that it makes accounting much easier for your business. The trails of your expenses and revenues are much clearer thus easier to follow and track.

- ✓ **PayPal Account** – When you sign up with PayPal, you have three types of accounts to choose from. These are Personal, Premier, and Business. If you are going to use PayPal for cash inflows and outflows in your dropshipping business, then you should sign up using a Business account. Don't worry, you can always create a Personal account that's completely separate from your Business account. Just make sure that you don't mingle your finances using the two accounts.

- ✓ **Business Debit/Credit Card** – It's never a good idea to use your personal debit/credit card for business expenses and for purchasing inventories from a supplier. So what you need to do is set up a business credit card or debit card that is used *solely* for your business expenses. If you want recommendations about which credit cards are best for dropshipping businesses, I suggest that you consider Capital One, American Express, and Fidelity Visa.

How Much Money Are You Going to Need to Start a Dropshipping Business?

Good question. Unfortunately, there is no definitive answer. There are a lot of factors that determine how much funds you need to start your business. These include the selling price of your products, the number of products you expect to move, the location of your supplier, the cost of acquiring the necessary sales software for your business, the cost of building your website, the cost of hiring a web designer and developer, the cost of hiring a customer support operator, the cost of registering your business, the expenses you spend on consultants, and so on and so forth. The expenses and costs associated with these factors vary greatly. This means that the funds you need to start your business could be as low as $500 or as high as one million dollars.

It can be very difficult to track all of your expenses and costs especially if you do not have a background or experience in accounting or bookkeeping. For this reason, I highly recommend that you hire an accountant to keep track of your cash inflows and outflows. You don't have to hire him to work as a full-time employee. There are thousands of freelance accountants and bookkeepers out there so this shouldn't be a problem. Aside from keeping records and making your finances easy to understand, the accountant can also help you in making major business decisions based on the financial health of your business. Furthermore, there are plenty of online accounting software you can get to help you with bookkeeping e.g. Quickbooks.

Step 5: Request for an EIN Number

The Internal Revenue Service or IRS requires all types of businesses with principal operations in the United States or U.S. Territories to apply for an EIN (Employer Identification Number). The EIN serves as a social security number for your dropshipping business. You are going to use this number when filing your taxes, opening a bank account, applying for wholesale dropshipping accounts, and pretty much anything that's related to the operation of your business. You have to keep in mind that majority of reputable dropship suppliers will ask you for an EIN if you want to do business with them. If you don't have an EIN number, it will be difficult for you to find good dropship suppliers.

To start requesting for an EIN number, you need to get a copy of the application form which is the IRS Form SS-4. You can download this form from the official website of the IRS. Just print out a copy of the application form then answer all the questions therein. If you need help in completing the application form, you should get in touch with a lawyer or a business adviser.

4 Ways to Request for an EIN Number
1. **Apply Online** – You can only apply online if you have a valid tax identification number. Go to the official IRS website and look for the section called EIN Assistant. This is where you input and submit your data. After completing and submitting the form online, the system will verify and validate the information. If the form is deemed correct and error-free, you can receive an EIN immediately.

2. **Apply by Fax** – After completing your IRS Form SS-4, you send it via fax to your state fax number. Don't forget to include your own fax number in your submission. You should be able to get a response within four business days. Receiving your EIN number this way is slower compared to when you apply online.

3. **Apply by Snail Mail** – Although I don't recommend this method of requesting for an EIN number, it's still a good method especially if it's the only option you have. You fill up the form then send it to the appropriate IRS office depending on the state where you are located. Your EIN number will also arrive at your place via snail mail within four weeks. That's a whole month.

4. **Apply by Telephone** – To get an EIN number via phone, all you have to do is call the Business and Specialty Tax Line at (800) 829-4933. You can call them on weekdays from 7:00 am until 10:00 pm. An IRS representative will ask you for all your information and if things go smoothly, the representative should be able to assign you a EIN number at the end of the phone conversation.

Step 6: Get Your Sales Taxes in Order

Because of its business model, paying taxes for goods sold via dropshipping is more complicated than you might expect. The process is made complicated by issues of dropshipper location, customer location, product sourcing, and sales tax nexus. Nexus is a legal term which refers to the requirement for businesses conducting business in a state to collect and pay taxes on sales originating from the same state. For instance, if you sell goods in Houston, then you must file and pay state taxes in Texas. It's not that difficult to see why dropshipping is a business model that carries a very high risk for sales tax errors.

The biggest question here is when is it required for you to collect sales taxes? Here's a quick overview of the information you need to know about collecting and paying sales taxes in a dropshipping business:

- ✓ You have to collect sales from the customer if you have nexus in the state where the sale occurred. (Please refer to our definition for "nexus" above.) You need to collect sales tax unless the transaction is considered as tax-exempt.
- ✓ If you and your supplier don't have nexus in the state where the transaction occurred, then you are not obligated to collect sales tax. It is the customer who is obligated to remit tax unless the sale is deemed to be exempt from tax.
- ✓ If you don't have nexus in the state where the sale happened but your supplier does, then it's possible that your supplier is the one responsible for collecting sales tax. However, this is not an absolute rule considering the fact that many states have different takes on the matter. For example, states like Hawaii, Florida, Connecticut, and California hold the supplier responsible for collecting sales tax in this scenario. But many other states don't hold the same position. With that said, it's important that you check the tax laws in your state. Not all states consider drop shipping as a nexus-creating activity.

I know, it can be very confusing. So I highly recommend that you consult with a tax expert and explain your business operations so that he can advise you on whether you are required to collect sales taxes or not. Get the advice of someone who knows the business and tax laws in your own state. In a nutshell, you are going to collect sales tax if:

- ✓ The state you operate from requires you to collect sales tax and
- ✓ The customer who bought the product is located in your state.

Step 7: Make Sure That Everything Is Ready to Go

You are now at the final stages of launching your dropshipping business. All you need to do now is review everything to make sure that they are in place and are ready to go. What some online entrepreneurs do is perform a beta test of their business. That is they launch a test version of their dropshipping website. This is a good way to determine if the features and functions of your website are functioning properly. Get a friend or someone you know to order from your website and see what happens.

You should create a checklist of your website's features and functions so that you can check them one by one if they are working properly. Is the buy button clickable? Is the checkout section working smoothly? Are the payment options in place? Are the product photos displaying properly? These are just some of the questions you need to ask yourself when reviewing your dropshipping website. You have to take note of the amount of time it takes for your supplier to ship the product to the customer. If you promised delivery within three days on your website but the product arrived after more than five days, then there's a problem. You need to talk with your supplier and review your shipping details.

Before launching the business, verify and confirm with your suppliers if they have the inventories ready. It would be a shame if you launch your business but then it turns out that the supplier doesn't have enough inventory or doesn't have any inventory at all. The amount of inventory you order from your supplier should be based on your sales projections. In fact, you should order a little bit more than your sales projections to account for potential surges in sales. For example, let's say that you project to sell 1000 products in your first week. To prepare for the possibility that you might get sales that are beyond this projection, you can instruct your supplier to have an inventory of 1200 to 1500 products.

Step 8: Create a Comprehensive Marketing Plan

This is the final step before you launch your dropshipping business. Marketing is everything when it comes to running an online business. You have to learn how to put your products in front of your target customers. In ecommerce, a high-quality product amounts to nothing if nobody knows about it. What you need to do is write a comprehensive marketing plan which details how you are going to promote your business and your products. It will serve as your guide once you launch your business. This is very important especially if your business is in a really competitive niche.

Writing a marketing plan is not that difficult. If you are clueless as to how you should start, you can try searching for marketing plan templates online. There are dozens of these templates out there that you can download. Some were even specifically written for dropshipping businesses. A marketing plan is basically a blueprint for you and your marketing team. With that said, make sure that everything inside the marketing plan is realistic and actionable. Don't make lofty goals if it's going to be nearly impossible to achieve them. A marketing plan can be a few pages short or dozens of pages long. It all depends on the size and nature of your business.

In writing the marketing plan, don't forget to address the following strategies in online marketing:
- Search engine optimization or SEO
- Social media marketing (Facebook, Twitter, Instagram, WhatsApp, Snapchat, Pinterest, Reddit)
- Content marketing (article marketing, guest blogging, freelance writing, press releases)
- Advertising (direct advertising, advertising programs, Adsense)
- Video marketing (YouTube, Vimeo)
- Blogging,
- Solo Ads (i.e. renting email lists),
- Banner ads (placed on websites where your target customers congregate) etc.

These are the most common and most effective strategies in promoting products online. I suggest that you implement most if not all of them initially to figure out which option works best for you and then work with them in order to maximize your market reach. The more you put yourself out there, the more attention and hype you build towards your business. There is no such thing as over-marketing. Make it your goal to connect with your target customers in as many platforms as possible. Yes, it's going to be very time-consuming, not to mention expensive, but it's going to be worth it if you play your cards right. Marketing is something you should be doing every single day if you want your dropshipping business to be as successful as you have envisioned.

There's one last advice I'm going to offer you with regards to creating a marketing plan. And that is to make your marketing plan flexible and adaptable to changes. When you finally launch your business and you kick off your marketing campaign, you are going to realize sooner or later that some marketing strategies aren't suitable for your business. For example, you realize that your customers aren't keen on connecting with you on social media. Or you realize that not many people read blogs about the products you are selling. Your marketing plan should be adaptable in the sense that you can revise it as you go depending on the effectiveness of the methods you are using.

Step 9: Launch the Business

This is it! This is the moment you have been waiting for. It's time to launch your business and make it official. This is the easiest step in the process of starting a dropshipping business provided that you've completed all of the earlier steps. What's great about launching an online business is that you don't have to spend a ton of money or create fake fanfare to do it. In fact, it's just like any of the days leading up to the launching. You just log into the proper accounts connected to your business and make the business live. You don't have to worry about stuff like ribbon cuttings, inviting guest, etc.

You have to be prepared for the contingencies associated with an online business launch. This is why you need to be very vigilant during the first several days. Anything can go wrong with your website. It can crash due to an overwhelming amount of traffic. It can become inaccessible for hours at a time. Customers may find some of the features and functions not working properly. Customers may not be able to complete their orders. These are just a few of the potential problems that can occur in the early days of your operations. Don't worry, problems like these are quite common for new online entrepreneurs. As I said earlier, you have to be prepared for them. Instruct your technical team and customer support to be extra alert.

Chapter Summary

As you can see, starting a dropshipping business is not a walk in the park. Granted it can be easy once you've established a rhythm and you know what you're doing. However, at the beginning it can be a challenge – especially if you're not well prepared. It requires focus and patience from you. The step-by-step guide I have provided you in this chapter are but a basic framework of the process. Under each step are more steps that you need to complete. As you go through each step, you will encounter issues that may have not been discussed in this chapter. That's okay. No book can ever completely anticipate what you are going to face when you start your dropshipping business. This is why I've mentioned several times in this book that you need to take things slowly. Don't rush because you might make mistakes that you can't undo. Going through this book will help you understand the potential pitfalls and help you correctly anticipate them. You will be proactive instead of reactive.

Did You Know

90% of customers buying decisions are influenced by online reviews. Do you have the right e-commerce data analytics that consolidates and presents all your online reviews for you to take action on?

Chapter 5

How The Supply Chain and Fulfillment Process Works

A good understanding of how the supply chain and fulfillment process works is very important if you are planning to run a dropshipping business. After all, you have to learn how a plane works before you will be able to fly it. That being said, how the supply chain and fulfillment process works is not that hard to understand. There's a slight variation in the process if you are in the dropshipping industry because of the higher number of key players involved. In this chapter, we are going to discuss these key players and their roles in the supply chain and fulfillment process. We'll also discuss them in the context of a dropshipping business model.

But before anything else, let's define what a "supply chain" is. This is but a fancy term used to describe the path which a product takes from conception, to manufacturing, and then into the hands of the intended customer. There are several key players involved in this supply chain and they are as follows:

Manufacturers

This is where the supply chain starts. Manufacturers or producers make the products but in most cases, they are not the ones who sell the items to consumers. Instead, what they do is sell their goods to either wholesalers or retailers. Needless to say, if you are a reseller, cutting out the middleman and buying directly from the manufacturer is the cheapest way to get the products and you get to keep more of the profit margin. However, it's not that simple because most manufacturers require minimum purchases. For example, you need 100 units of the products but the manufacturer requires a minimum purchase of 500 units. As a reseller, you also need to stock the products and then ship them if you are selling these to consumers. Because of these reasons, many entrepreneurs prefer purchasing their products from wholesalers.

Wholesalers

Wholesalers do not produce the goods themselves. What they do is purchase the products in bulk from the manufacturers then sell them to retailers for resale to consumers. Wholesalers earn money by putting a markup on the bulk orders they purchase from manufacturers. For example, let's say Brock is a wholesaler and Cain is a manufacturer. Brock makes a bulk order of 1000 product units from Cain for $1 each. Brock then resells the products to retailers with a markup of 10 cents per unit. If Brock is able to sell the whole bulk to retailers, then he has gross profits amounting to $100 (1000 units multiplied by 0.10).

Wholesalers usually have lower minimum purchase requirements compared to manufacturers. This is understandable given the fact that they don't make the goods themselves. Because they are not into production, wholesalers often purchase products from dozens or hundreds of manufacturers and stock the goods in their own warehouses. Furthermore, wholesalers tend to operate within specific niches and industries. That is they sell a wide range of products but such products belong to the same niche. For example, a wholesaler stocks a wide range of products in the footwear industry (i.e. shoes, sandals, socks) from dozens of manufacturers. Generally, wholesalers don't sell directly to the public. They only sell to retailers.

Retailers

As a dropshipper, this is where you belong. If you purchase products from manufacturers or wholesalers then resell these to the public at a markup, then you are the very definition of a retailer. However, there's a slight variation in the process because you are not the one shipping the products. That responsibility lies in the hands of your supplier. Here's what's interesting if you look at these three players in the context of the dropshipping model. All three of them can be dropshippers. A manufacturer can have a dropshipping operation in-house, a wholesaler can be a dropshipper, and a retailer can be a dropshipper.

Consumers

Customers who order and pay for goods complete the supply chain and fulfillment process. Once the customer receives the product he ordered, it means it has been fulfilled and the process is complete.

The Dropshipping Process in Action

To best understand how the dropshipping process works, I'm going to provide you with an example. We are going to look into the steps necessary to complete a dropshipped order. Let's say that you own a dropshipping business called Smith Company. You sell customized shirts that you order from a wholesaler called Bravo Company. Here's how the process works:

Step 1: Customer orders a shirt from Smith Company.

- A customer named Jerry comes across the website of Smith Company, browses through the products listed, and decides to place an order for a nice shirt. Once the order goes through, Jerry will receive an email confirming his purchase. Jerry's payment will also be captured by the website's checkout system and deposited in Smith Company's bank account.

Step 2: Smith Company sends the order to Bravo Company, the wholesaler and supplier.

- With an automated system, Smith Company's website will simply send the customer order or email the order confirmation to Bravo Company. A sales representative at Bravo Company reviews the order, checks if Smith Company is on their file of retailers, then starts processing the order. With the cost of goods, shipping fees, and processing fees taken into account, Bravo Company then bills Smith Company for the order.

Step 3: Bravo Company ships the product to Jerry, the customer.

- Assuming that Bravo Company has the ordered product in stock and that they were able to bill Smith Company's account, they then put the shirt in a box and ship it directly to Jerry's address. Although the boxed shirt is coming from Bravo Company, the return address is still that of Smith Company. The invoice and packing slip will also contain the details of Smith Company, not that of Bravo Company. After finalizing the shipment, Bravo Company then sends an invoice as well as a tracking number to Smith Company.

Step 4: Smith Company informs Jerry that the shirt he ordered has been shipped and is on its way.

- After receiving the invoice and tracking number from Bravo Company, Smith Company then forwards the tracking number to Jerry. Jerry will use the tracking number as verification when the boxed shirt is delivered to his residence or office. Once Jerry receives the item, then the order has been fulfilled. Smith Company's profit from the process is the difference between the price it charged Jerry and the price it paid Bravo Company to ship the product. For instance, let's say Smith Company sold the shirt to Jerry for $20 and it paid Bravo Company $15 to handle and ship the item. That means Smith Company earned a gross profit of $5 from the sale.

Chapter Summary

The dropshipping model seems easy enough from the surface but it can be very complicated once you are in the thick of the business. Our illustration and example above is just the tip of the iceberg. There are so many other things happening in between the four steps. Furthermore, there are also a lot of errors that can happen in between the steps. Packages can get lost or damaged in transit. Since the packages have a return address containing the details of Smith Company, it's Smith Company who will receive the complaints and requests for returns and replacements. Smith Company ships the damaged or defective products back to Bravo Company and make another request for replacements. In short, there are many parties involved so it's often harder to manage a dropshipping business compared to a standard ecommerce business. A good way to minimize the return rate is to be strategic with your product selections i.e. deal with simple products that are not easily breakable. For example, dropshipping a tennis ball or T-shirt is far less challenging than dropshipping ceramic plates. Of course, first and foremost, make sure there's strong demand for the product and its not too competitive.

Did You Know

33% of UK online sales occur after 6pm. Are you targeting correctly?

Chapter 6

Evaluating Your Sales Channels

One of the biggest benefits of a dropshipping business is that you have access to several sales channels. After deciding which products to sell, securing your suppliers, and establishing your business legally, the next step is to decide how you are going to put your products in front of your target customers. These are called sales channels. The good news is that you have several channels to choose from. You can also try to use more than one sales channels at a time. As long as you have the time and the resources to use several channels, by all means go for it. It's advisable that you slowly go through each of these channels, look into their pros and cons, before deciding which of them you are going to use.

I) Dropshipping on eBay

eBay is an institution in itself, which is why a lot of dropshippers make use of the platform. The company has been around for more than two decades, which means they have proven themselves to be sustainable since they were able to last that long. And there is the fact that eBay is without a doubt the world's largest auction site as far as physical goods are concerned.

The Pros of Selling on eBay

1. It's easy to get started. With the platform, you can simply create an account and start listing your products. You can be in business in under an hour.
2. Access to a really large audience. eBay has millions of active buyers from all over the world. If you list your products properly, it has the potential of being seen by millions of potential customers.
3. It requires less marketing. That is if you compare it with other lesser known online auction platforms. Let's call a spade a spade. In listing a product on eBay, you are piggybacking on the site's enormous popularity. You don't have to worry that much about paying for traffic, search engine optimization (SEO), or marketing in general. This means that eBay will save you a lot of time. Let's face it, marketing is one of the biggest challenges associated with starting a dropshipping business.

The Cons of Selling on eBay

1. You have to pay for listing fees. There are two main types of fees that you have to pay when you list and sell a product on eBay. The first one is the insertion fee. When you list a product for sale, eBay will charge you an insertion fee per listing and per category. This means that if you list a single product to two categories, you are going to pay for the insertion fee twice. The second fee is the final value fee (sometimes referred to as the success fee). The final value fee can be up to 10% or even higher of the sales price of the product you listed.

2. It's very difficult to customize your product listings. This is a huge disadvantage especially if you want to differentiate your products on the platform. Every listing you make should follow eBay's template. This makes it really hard to create a more professional-looking listing that adds value to your products.

3. You need to be constantly monitoring, tracking, and re-listing your products on eBay. Always keep in mind that eBay has an auction-style platform. If the auction period runs out, the item has to be relisted. Just imagine how much work this will be if you have numerous product listings. Of course, there are some tools that you can use to automate the process or outsource it to virtual assistants.

II) Dropshipping on Amazon

Amazon is the largest online marketplace out there so it makes complete sense to consider it for your dropshipping business. However, before you start using Amazon as your sales channel, make sure that you've read the company's policies on dropshipping. You can read the policies when you log into your Amazon Seller account. For example, Amazon requires you to identify yourself as the seller in all the packing slips and other information associated with your products.

The Pros of Selling on Amazon

1. You deal with much lower overhead. You can forget about things like stocking, shipping, storing, and ordering. You can just focus your time on passing the orders you receive to your supplier.
2. You have immediate access to a huge market. Millions of people shop on Amazon every single day. This means your product listings have the potential of being seen by a lot of people provided that you optimized your listings.
3. You will save a lot of money and resources on shipping because you don't have to do it.
4. You don't have to worry about a limited product inventory because no one is stopping you from listing dozens of products on Amazon. As long as you have your suppliers and manufacturers in place, everything should go fine.
5. You have access to a lot of features and functions provided by Amazon's selling platform. These include tracking systems that enable you to collect and analyse data about your product listings and their corresponding sales figures.
6. Amazon allows you to dropship larger items. Again, you are not handling and shipping the products yourself so you have nothing to be worried about. You just have to make sure that your suppliers keep their end of the bargain.

The Cons of Selling on Amazon

1. You are under the mercy of Amazon. They can shut down your account for the slightest infraction. There's really no flexibility for you to do things on your own. In a sense, you are making money not just for yourself but for Amazon as well. This means that the fruits of your labor are divided between you and the retail giant.
2. You don't have access to customer data. You have access to stats about the sales but nothing about the customers themselves. This is unlike running your own dropshipping website wherein you can gather data about your customers.

3. It's hard to find suppliers who will agree to dropship for you through Amazon. Most suppliers prefer working directly with dropshippers because if Amazon is involved, that's another party that takes a cut in the overall profits.

4. Your hard work can disappear overnight. If your listings or your account gets compromised, you have to go through the appeal process which can take days and even weeks. Good if you get your account back but what if Amazon decides to ban it for good?

III) Dropshipping on Shopify

Shopify has become synonymous with dropshipping because the company has been specifically designed to cater to dropshippers. Shopify is now the largest dropshipping platform today. Shopify has done the hard work for you so that you don't have to build your dropshipping business from scratch. The company provides you with the tools and resources you need to run and manage your dropshipping business. For that reason, anyone can start a business using Shopify.

The Pros of Selling on Shopify

1. The platform is friendly to newbies who have zero experience in dropshipping. Shopify even has a lot of articles, guides, and tutorials on how to use the platform.

2. Built-in speed and security for hosting. In online commerce, security is crucial because there is always the risk that a hacker will hack through your website and steal anything he likes. Fortunately, Shopify has a lot of measures installed to avoid this from happening.

3. You get all the necessary features to run a dropshipping business. Whether you want to integrate a payment method or you simply want to customize the look of your store, Shopify has the tools and resources you need to make it happen.

4. Efficient customer support. This is one of the great things about Shopify. You can seek support any time of the day or night. You can reach customer service through phone, email, and online live chat.

5. You have access to a large app store. There are dozens of apps which you can use to extend the functionality of your store. Most of these apps are subscription-based but there are some which are free to use.

6. You can choose from hundreds of free and paid themes for your ecommerce store. These are themes that were made by a team of in-house and freelance designers.

The Cons of Selling on Shopify

1. Shopify charges a transaction fee for every sale, and this is on top of the monthly fee you have to pay the company for using its dropshipping platform.

2. Your monthly costs may add up if you are using multiple apps in your store. Keep in mind that most of the apps in the Shopify App Store are not free. If several of the apps you use are subscription-based, you will be paying a lot of monthly fees on top of your Shopify subscription and transaction fees.

3. Shopify has a lock-in feature which means that if you ever decide to cancel your account, your store and all your data will be permanently deleted. In short, transitioning to a new store is not going to be smooth.

IV) Alternative Sales Channels

Amazon, eBay, and Shopify are by far the most common platforms for building a dropshipping business. But you still have other options in the event that you don't want to use any of the three. One, you can always build your own online store if you have the technical and programming skills to do it. The main drawback of this method is that you have to build everything from scratch. Building your own store however offers several advantages like more control over the business, less third-party fees, and flexibility for growth.

If you don't want to build your online store from scratch either, you can explore other sales channels such as the following: Facebook Shop, Wanelo, Lazada, Pinterest, etc.

Chapter Summary

You have several options as far as your sales channels are concerned. In short, there is no shortage of platforms where you can sell your dropshipped products. Be careful about the sales channels that you use. Make sure that the channels are a good fit for the types of products you are selling. Keep in mind that just because a product sells well on Amazon doesn't necessarily mean it will also sell well on eBay or Shopify. No one is stopping you from using all the sales channels discussed in this chapter.

However, based on experience, it's best to focus your attention on a single channel. This way, you can direct all your efforts and resources into the business. The problem with using several channels at once is that it divides your time and attention. But if you have the time, the resources, as well as extra manpower to use all sales channels, then by all means, go for it.

Did You Know

It is preferred that you show the shipping costs at the very beginning or display it with the price of the product. 34% of the customers have been known to abandon their shopping carts if the shipping costs are shown late in checkout.

Chapter 7

Niche Research and Product Selection

Niche research and product selection are among the most important steps in building a successful dropshipping business. There are no other ways around them. You have to do them if you want to increase your chances for achieving sustained profitability. I'm telling you right now that niche research takes time and effort. It can take you days or even weeks to zero in on products that you think will be embraced by customers. Niche research is about gathering data and gauging demand for your product ideas. In other words, it's a strategy for determining if it's worth it to pursue a product or not.

What is a Niche?

In the simplest of terms, a niche is a specific category or field in an industry. This is in business and marketing terms. For example, let's talk about the broad outdoor equipment industry. Under this industry are dozens of niches. The trail running community is a niche. The mountain climbing community is a niche. The cliff jumping community is a niche. The mountain biking community is yet another niche. And so on and so forth. Even these niches can be further broken down into even smaller niches. For example, the trail running community niche can be broken down into the marathoner's niche and the ultra marathoner's niche.

Breaking down an industry into niches makes it a lot easier for aspiring entrepreneurs to find potential markets they can tap into. It allows you to look for niches that have less competition but have considerable demand. These are the two factors that you must always consider during niche research. One, the competition within the niche shouldn't be too tough in the sense that you can enter it and carve your own business in it. And two, there should be considerable demand for the products you want to offer in that niche. These two factors come hand in hand. Because what's the point of entering an uncompetitive niche if there's minimal demand for products. And what's the point of trying to fulfill a demand that's already being fulfilled by thousands of established entrepreneurs – profit margins will erode due to too much competition.

How to do Niche Research

Always remember that you have two main goals when performing niche research. One, you want to gauge demand for your product ideas. And two, you want to know the level of competition for those product ideas. You will be performing most of your research using various tools like keyword research tools and search volume trackers. Don't worry because most of these tools and resources are readily available and you can use most of them for free. Before you begin with your research, it's important that you already have an industry that you want to target. For example, you want to target the sports gear industry or the weight loss industry. I hope that you are getting my point here. The general industry serves as your starting point.

Create a Quick List of Your Product Ideas

The first thing you must do is write down a quick list of the products that you have in mind. Get a piece of paper and quickly jot down the ideas. This list will be your reference point when you start doing your research. Write down the words, phrases, and terms that come to your mind when you think about your potential products. Allow me to briefly illustrate what this list should look like. Let's say that you want to build a dropshipping business around the hiking niche. Furthermore, let's say that you want to sell hiking footwear on your dropshipping website. Brainstorming for product ideas, your initial list should look very similar to the following list:

- Hiking shoes
- Hiking sandals
- Mountain climbing shoes
- Hiking footwear
- Climbing sandals
- Durable climbing shoes
- Hiking slippers
- Tough hiking shoes
- Mountaineering shoes
- Mountaineering footwear
- Mountaineering sandals

This is just for illustration purposes. Your list can either be shorter or longer than the one above. It all depends on the products you have in mind and the niche that you want to target. My main point here is that you need to create a list of all your potential products. These should be the types of products that you plan on selling through your dropshipping website. Creating this list should take just a few minutes of your time. Some dropshippers would even divide their lists into product categories and create lists within a list. Keep a copy of this list with you as you start with your niche research.

Google Is Your Best Friend

Google controls at least 60% of all online searches so it makes sense that the search giant has the most accurate search data and statistics. Needless to say, if you want to learn about a product's popularity online, Google is where you should go for information. Google has tools that you can use for your research. The two most important ones are **Google Trends** and the **Google Keyword Tool**. Don't worry, both of these tools are free to use. You don't have to pay a dime to gain access to their features and functions. For the Keyword Tool, all you need is a Google account. If you already have a Gmail account, you can start using the Keyword Tool by simply logging into your account.

For the Google Trends tool, you don't even need a Google account to access and use it. For best results, I suggest that you use the Chrome browser when you do your research on Google Trends. Certain features of the tool tend to not work properly when you use other browsers like Mozilla Firefox. Google Trends is a very powerful research tool in the sense that you can determine search volume over time, top and rising search terms, seasonality of search terms, and even the geographical concentrations of searches. You can identify which countries are searching the most for particular products. In the following sections, I'm going to show you how to use the two tools.

How to Use Google Trends for Niche Research

Here's a quick definition of Google Trends from Wikipedia: "It is a public web facility of Google based on Google Search that shows how often a particular search term is entered relative to the total search volume across different regions in the world, and in various languages." It's basically an analytics database of all searches on Google from 2004 to the present. Needless to say, Google Trends is a goldmine for data about ecommerce niches. It contains an immense amount of search data that you can collect and analyse to determine if there's interest or demand for the products that you have in mind.

Let's take a look at the tool's specific features:

✓ **Interest and Search Volume Over Time** – This graphs searches based on the queries they received over time. You can quickly customize a time frame ranging from years to minutes. The graph will show you if the search volume for a particular search query is increasing or decreasing over time. It provides you with an idea if the trends will be in your favor or not. Let's say that you are planning to dropship trail running shoes. Google Trends will provide you with data if searches for the phrase "trail running shoes" is increasing or decreasing over time. If the trend shows that the number of people interested in trail running shoes is growing, then it's probably a good niche and that it's worth looking into. You can compare search data based on time periods. For example, you can compare search data this year to last year's search data. Or you can compare search data this month to last month's search data.

✓ **Interest by Region** – This feature enables you to pinpoint the geographical regions wherein your search term is most popular. It compares the origins of the searches. The interest data also reflects the popularity of the term in a certain region and on a certain time period. For example, you want to know more about the interest for "trail running shoes" during the first quarter of 2018. That's for the months of January, February, and March. What you do is customize the parameters in Google Trends so that it will reflect interest about "trail running shoes" during these months. The data will then show you the regions where queries for "trail running shoes" are most popular.

However, you should take note that the geographic regions are organized based on search proportions. Needless to say, some smaller countries might score much higher compared to larger countries. Interest for searches are scored by Google Trends from 0 to 100. You can determine search interest not just by country. You can further break down the interest data by states or provinces. For example, if you are doing research in the United States, you can access interest data by state.

✓ **Related Topics** – What this feature does is provide a quick list of other topics that the user also searched. Users searching for your term are also searching for these terms and topics. In our example, if you input "trail running shoes" into Google Trends, the related topics that you receive include the following topics: vapour, venture 6, sports shoes, tights, cross training, track spikes, back country running, vibram, under armour. This means that whoever is searching about trail running shoes are also interested in these general topics. How does this benefit you in your research for a niche? Well, it provides you with a ton of ideas about other products that your target market might be interested in. From our example, we can see that people searching for trail running shoes are also interested in running shorts and running spikes. These are products that you might also want to feature in your dropshipping store.

✓ **Related Queries** – A lot of people often confuse this with the Related Topics feature. The two are very different from each other. In Related Topics, you get a list of topics that the user also searched for. This means that these are general topics. In Related Queries, you are presented with a list of terms that the user also searched for. This means that people searching for your main term are also searching for these queries. In other words, these are specific queries. In our example on trail running shoes, the user also searched for the following queries: best trail running shoes 2018, black and yellow running shoes, fila trail running shoes, brooks Cascadia, zero drop running shoes, best waterproof trail running shoes, salomon speedcross 4, best trail running shoes women, and trail running shoes for hiking. These are very specific queries that the user is also searching for. Again, how will this information help you with your niche research? My answer is the same. The information helps you with more ideas about which products to promote and sell. It also provides you with ideas about other niches that you might want to further explore.

✓ **Top vs. Rising Queries** – When you look at the list of queries and topics under the Related Topics and Related Queries features, you can toggle the terms between Top and Rising. In Related Topics, the Top designation refers to the most popular topics. The Rising designation refers to topics with the largest increase in search frequency since the previous time period. In Related Queries, the Top designation refers to the most popular search queries. The Rising designation refers to search queries with the largest increase in search frequency since the previous time period. The data you gather from these features paint a picture of what's currently popular and what topics and terms have the potential to become popular.

✓ **Breakout Search Queries** – This is a feature which identifies whether a topic or a query is receiving a breakout number of searches. A topic or query is tagged as a "breakout" if there is a tremendous increase in interest and search volume for it. For example, if the search volume for "zero drop running shoes" last week was in the mere hundreds but during the current week the search volume ballooned to searches in the thousands. It will most likely be tagged as a "breakout" topic or query. However, you should be careful about breakout topics and queries because these are usually seasonal in nature. This is especially true for products that are seasonal. For example, Christmas sweaters are often tagged as breakout topics and queries weeks before Christmas day. For sure, it would be a good idea to start dropshipping Christmas sweaters but the interest will quickly die out within a month or so. If you want to build a sustainable dropshipping business that is profitable all year round, you should target products that are not seasonal in nature.

Making Sense of Google Trends as a Niche Research Tool

When you go to the Google Trends main page, just type in the term you want to do some research on. In our example, just key in the phrase "trail running shoes" into the search bar. You will be presented with an interface containing the features we just discussed above. You then customize your search based on several parameters. These parameters are as follows:

1) **Country** – Choose the specific country where you want to pull the search data from. If you want data and information from all countries, then choose the "Worldwide" option.

2) **Time Period** – You can select from any of the following options.
   - ✓ Past hour
   - ✓ Past 4 hours
   - ✓ Past day
   - ✓ Past 7 days
   - ✓ Past 30 days
   - ✓ Past 90 days
   - ✓ Past 5 years
   - ✓ 2004 to present
   - ✓ Custom time range

3) **Categories** – You can select from any of the following options. If you want to gather data from all of these categories, then you should choose the "All Categories" option.
   - ✓ All categories
   - ✓ Arts and entertainment
   - ✓ Autos and vehicles
   - ✓ Beauty and fitness
   - ✓ Books and literature
   - ✓ Business and industrial
   - ✓ Computers and electronics
   - ✓ Finance
   - ✓ Food and drink
   - ✓ Games
   - ✓ Health
   - ✓ Hobbies and leisure
   - ✓ Home and garden
   - ✓ Internet and telecom
   - ✓ Jobs and education
   - ✓ Law and government
   - ✓ News
   - ✓ Online communities
   - ✓ People and society
   - ✓ Pets and animals
   - ✓ Real estate
   - ✓ Reference
   - ✓ Science
   - ✓ Shopping
   - ✓ Sports
   - ✓ Travel

If you choose the right parameters, then you should be provided with accurate information and data. I highly recommend that you keep a notebook with you where you can jot down important information you gather from the data presented to you. Jot down the related topics and related queries that you might want to check on later. If you are not the pen-and-paper type, you can always download the search data provided to you by Google Trends. You can download data from the following features: Interest by Region, Related Topics, and Related Queries.

How to Download the Graphs and Data from Google Trends

On the top portion of each feature are buttons signifying actions you can take. Find the one that looks like an arrow pointing downwards. This is the universal symbol for "download". If you hover over it, it says "CSV". Just click on the button to commence downloading. Downloading will take just a few seconds. To open the file, just go to your desktop's "Downloads" folder. You can also embed the graphs from Google Trends. Just click on the

Embed button and you will be provided with HTML code which you can just copy and paste into any page that supports HTML.

In a nutshell, Google Trends has almost everything you need to look for a profitable niche for your dropshipping business idea. For most experienced dropshippers, Google Trends is all they need to find the next product they are going to sell. But if you are just a beginner, the data and information you collected from Google Trends may not be enough. That brings us to the Google Keyword Tool. If you are a complete newbie, I suggest that you make use of both tools in researching for your niche products.

How to Use the Google Keyword Tool for Niche Research

The Google Keyword Tool is the most popular keyword tool out there. There's no doubt about that. Almost all online marketers use the tool in one way or another. It's accurate, easy to use, and most important of all, it's completely free. To access the tool, all you need is a Google account. If you are a Gmail user, you can use the same login details to sign in into the keyword tool.

The tool has more than a dozen features and functions at your disposal. You might be confused as to why you should use the keyword tool when you already know which products to sell based on the research you've done in Google Trends. Here's what you need to understand between the two tools. Google Trends provide you with a general idea of the popularity of certain terms. The Google Keyword Tool provides you with the numbers and other specific information about the terms. The Keyword Tool allows you to determine the approximate number of searches that a term gets every week, every month, or every year.

Google has recently changed the interface for its keyword tool. It is now called the Keyword Planner and you can access it through their Google Ads program. When you click on the Keyword Planner tab, you will be directed to a window that makes you choose from two options depending on what you wish to do with the planner. The two options are as follows:

1. **Find new keywords** – This enables you to find keyword ideas that might be able to help you reach people who are interested in the products that you plan on dropshipping.

2. **Get search volume and forecasts** – With this option, you will be able to access data on search volume and other important historical metrics that are relevant to your keywords. You can also get forecasts about how your keywords might perform in the next months or years.

If it's your first time to use the Keyword Planner and you are not sure which option you should go with, I highly recommend that you read Google's comprehensive primer about the tool. When you open the Keyword Planner window, scroll down to the bottom of the page and look for the tab that says "How to Use Keyword Planner". Click on the tab and read the guide. This will provide you with the basic information you need about using the Keyword Planner. The guide is always there so you can read it whenever you want.

Find New Keywords

For beginners, this is what you should use first. All you have to do is enter the keywords you want to do research on. The next window will show a huge list of related keyword ideas, their average monthly searches, and the level of competition. There are other data present but you should focus on these three factors (keyword ideas, average monthly searches, and level of competition).

For example, if you type in "trail running shoes" in the search bar, you will receive 828 keyword ideas. That's a lot. For each keyword idea, there's corresponding data on its average monthly searches and competition level. For the keyword idea "Nike running shoes", the average monthly searches for it range from 100,000 to 1 million. The level of competition for the keyword is tagged as "high". Levels of competition in the Keyword Planner are either low, medium, or high.

Here's what you should do. Create a list of all the keyword ideas that you believe are most relevant to the product you have in mind. You should also get the data on average monthly searches and competition for each keyword. Your goal is to find keywords that are getting a good amount of searches but whose level of competition is within the low to medium range. These are the best types of keywords because they are getting a lot of searches but there are not that many websites providing content about them. Go over these keywords one at a time to remove the ones that aren't a fit for your dropshipping business idea.

Go over the keywords until you are left with 10 to 20 main keywords. The final list can even be less than 10 keywords especially if you are targeting a very small and very specific niche. Create a copy of these final keywords and keep them in your files. You can do individual analysis of each main keyword using the Keyword Planner but this is optional. It's up to you if you aren't satisfied with the list you already have.

So what are you going to do with the list of keywords you have? You are going to use it as your basis in coming up with the products that you are going to sell in your dropshipping website. The keywords will also help you in creating content for search engine optimization (SEO) purposes. It's also worth mentioning here that you can add filters when using the Keyword Planner. You have the option to exclude keywords in the results. Just click on the "Add Filter" button then type in the words and keywords you want to exclude in your research.

Get Search Volume and Forecasts

This option is specifically geared towards users who want to purchase ads from Google's advertising program. With that said, there really isn't much that you can glean from this feature if your main intention is to look for profitable keyword ideas and niches. Majority of the data and information you get about the search volume and forecasts are related to costs per click (CPC) and potential ad impressions. For example, if you want to get an ad for your website targeting the keyword "trail running shoes", the Keyword Planner forecasts that you will have to spend around $37 to get about 30,000 clicks on your advertisement.

What I am trying to say here is that the keyword ideas and competition data you need for niche research are available using the Keyword Planner's "Find New Keywords" feature. But if you want to dig deeper, you may use the "Get Search Volume and Forecasts" feature. The data here is very valuable if you have plans of buying advertisements for your dropshipping business down the line. You can get estimated costs and conversion metrics that will help you decide if purchasing ads is a good investment or not.

In a way, you can also use this feature of the Keyword Planner to gauge competition. Usually, if purchasing an ad for a keyword is expensive, it means that the competition is high for that keyword. Many entrepreneurs and online marketers are bidding for that keyword which subsequently increases the price of advertising for that keyword. Needless to say, you will get an idea about the level of competition for your targeted keywords based on the price of ads associated with them. The higher the price is for an ad featuring a keyword, the more competitive that keyword is. This is something you should always remember especially if you have plans of being aggressive with your ad buys.

Things to Look Out for When Selecting Products

Now that you have a good list of keywords related to the niche you want to enter, the next step is to zero in on the products that you are going to sell on your dropshipping website. There are several factors that you must consider, the most important of which are as follows:

1. **Price** – When dropshipping products, your prices should be competitive. It shouldn't be too high or too low. If it's too high, people will say it's overpriced. If it's too low, people will assume that your product is of low quality thus the low price. Most of the time, your customers are people who are too lazy to go out and buy the product themselves from department stores or groceries. So it's okay to dropship products at a slightly higher price compared to department store prices. Most consumers will understand the difference in the price.

When you look at the price of a product, you have to consider the markup associated with the dropshipping model. For example, if a pair of shoes you are planning to sell costs $20 on a retailer's ecommerce store, you have to assume that if you are going to dropship the same product, it will have to cost a little bit more. The markup should not be too much in the sense that the gap between your price and the other retailer's price is too much for the customer to justify.

2. **Marketing potential** – The product should be an item that can be marketed online on most promotional platforms. You should be able to promote it via social media, blogs, forums, direct advertising, content marketing, advertising programs like Adsense, podcasts, etc. Your target customers are online and the only way to reach them is through online marketing channels. For this to work, the product has to be marketable on such a platform.

3. **Lots of related accessories** – As a dropshipper, you have the option of selling accessories that are related to your main product. Accessories are a great source of additional sales and income. In fact, some dropshippers make more money from their accessories than from their main products. The term "accessory" is a rather broad term so allow me to explain it further in the context of the dropshipping business model. Let us go back to our example of dropshipping trail running shoes. Accessories that you can sell which are relevant to your main product may include the following:

- Trail running socks

- Shoe gaiters
- Shoe blinkers
- Shoe glue
- Anti-blister socks
- Five finger socks

Adding accessories to your ecommerce store is a great idea. They are usually a lot less expensive so they get bought much quicker. And not to mention the fact that they are easier to pack and ship. You can also try to sell accessories in bundles or packages. Use these packages to entice your target customers to purchase your main products.

4. **Low Return Rate** – It's far more strategic to deal with products that are simple in nature in order to minimize the chance of something going wrong e.g. one would expect to see a higher return rate when dropshipping a fragile ceramic plate which is more likely to break on transit, especially if it's packaged properly. Furthermore, electronic appliances are likely to malfunction which might lead customers to return them. However, dealing with simple products like a shoe, T-shirt, tennis ball, phone leather/rubber case etc. isn't quite as risky. As a result, it's easier to meet customer expectations and you're less likely to get unsatisfied customers asking for a refund.

5. **Hard to find locally** – Look for products that are rarely sold in department stores and grocery stores in your area. This is a good strategy especially if you are planning to dropship products to a specific location. For example, if trail running shoes are difficult to find in your town or city, then it would be a good idea to set up a dropshipping business selling trail running shoes and targeting customers in your town or city.

A Quick Recap of Measuring Competition

As I have mentioned several times already, you need to gauge the competition for a product before you decide to add the item to your dropshipping business. The general consensus is that if the competition is very tough, you should abandon the idea and brainstorm for others. This is true in many levels but there is an exception. Don't abandon the idea entirely. The fact that the competition for the product is very tough means that there's a lot of money to be made with the product. What you should do is further break down the product idea into niches and find the ones with less competition. This way, you are within a competitive niche but you are targeting a product with less competition niche-wise. Doing so basically allows you to take advantage of the demand while avoiding too much competition.

Another powerful way of gauging competition is by examining the number of organically listed sites on the first page of Google. Type in your main keyword and analyse the results. If several pages of the results contain the exact keyword, then it's a very competitive niche – these many people wouldn't be running ads if there weren't money to be made. Look at the top results and think if you can compete with them. Do you think you can optimize your dropshipping website and make it rank high in the results page? Or are the top results too established that it would be nearly impossible to reach or even topple them? You have to be realistic with your analysis especially if there are a lot of big brands in the top search results. For example, you are overconfident if you think that you can compete with the likes of Nike or Adidas when it comes to selling running shoes online. They have a lot of marketing power and a sizeable budget. You have to avoid competing against the big dogs by finding your own niche.

Find a Niche Where You Can Add Value to the Product

One way of getting ahead of the competition is to add value to the products you are dropshipping. This is especially true if you are selling a generic product (one that is also being sold by countless other dropshippers). Differentiate your business by creating a unique value proposition. The next obvious question is how do you do this? One of the best ways to add value to a competitive product is to create a loyalty program for your customers. This is a great strategy if the product you are dropshipping has a high turnover rate. What you do is reward your most loyal customers in the form of discounts and promos.

Another great way of adding value to a product is to offer discounts for bulk purchases. A good example of this is a buy one take one sales model. It provides customers with a nice incentive that is too hard to refuse. Your customers will be getting more of your products at less costs. For this sales model to work, you also need to negotiate with your supplier or manufacturer for lesser costs when it comes to bulk orders. You can also arrange to bundle complementary products your customers will like to buy together e.g. a tennis ball and a racket, shoe and socks of matching brands, phones and phone cases etc.

Another method of adding value to your product is to customize its design and packaging. Beautiful packaging creates additional perceived value in the eyes of your customers. When a customer looks at your product, the very first thing they see and feel is the quality of the packaging. Having a good product design could make the whole difference between a buyer and a non-buyer. Making the product packaging as attractive as possible helps in making the customer decide to purchase the item.

Chapter Summary

Finding a profitable niche and selecting your products is a long process so you should take your time with your research. Don't rush things. You have to make sure that the data, statistics, and other information that you gather about your niche are as accurate as possible. Starting your business with bad data can be disastrous for your business. Using bad data can cause a lot of early problems like overestimating your market, picking the wrong supplier, and miscalculating the costs of running the business.

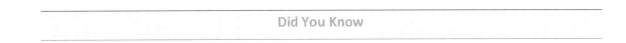

Did You Know

According to a business insider study, 23% of online shoppers fall between the ages of 35 and 44, while only 18% of the US population is that age. What are you doing to effectively target this demographic?

Chapter 8

Finding and Working With Suppliers and Manufacturers

Your dropshipping business will only be as good as the supplier and manufacturer you work with. If you have a bad supplier, it will reflect on the reputation of your business. If your supplier is always late in shipping products to your customers, it's you who is going to take the blame and criticisms. Think of your suppliers as the other half of your business operations. If they don't do their jobs properly, that means half of your business is hurting your operations. The bottom line here is that you should be serious in finding good and reliable suppliers. In this chapter, I am going to show you how you can improve your chances of snagging the right suppliers for your business.

There are so many factors that you must consider when looking for dropshipping suppliers. You need to make sure that the ones you get are reliable and trustworthy. Your ultimate goal is to find the right product from the right supplier. The good news is that there are dozens of online marketplaces out there that make this a lot easier for you. These are often referred to as wholesale and dropship directories. Some are free. Some charge a fee which could be a recurring monthly fee or a one-time fixed fee. We're going to look into some of the most popular of these wholesale and dropship directories in this chapter.

How do you find dropshipping companies and wholesalers?

The first thing you should do is subscribe to a dropshipping directory. As I stated above, there are dozens of these directories but a lot of them are low-quality and they provide little value. See to it that you only subscribe to legitimate directories. These are directories that look into the backgrounds of the companies that apply for listings. An example of a good dropshipping directory is World Wide Brands. I say they are good because they pre-screen the thousands of dropshipping companies that want to be listed in their directory.

Do extensive research about a dropshipping company before entering into a deal with them. Look into the products that they are dropshipping. Are these of good quality? Are there very little customer complaints about the products? Look for reviews about the supplier. Most dropshipping directories have review features wherein entrepreneurs can leave comments and reviews about the suppliers listed in the directory. You should be able to gauge the reliability and trustworthiness of a supplier by reading a lot of these reviews.

What are the requirements to work with a dropshipping supplier?

If your dropshipping business operates within the United States, most legitimate suppliers will require you to present them with an EIN (employer identification number). You will only get an EIN if you register your business so this is the first thing you should do. Other than this, the requirements vary depending on the supplier or wholesaler you are dealing with.

How to find legitimate wholesale suppliers:

1. Thoroughly check the supplier's profile. This is the very first thing you should do before you even think of entering into a deal with a prospective supplier. If you found the supplier through a dropshipping directory, don't forget to look at the supplier's in-site ratings and reviews.

2. Request for product samples. A legitimate supplier should be more than willing to provide you with samples especially if you have shown an intention of buying from them in bulk. Always request for samples if you have doubts about the quality of the products in question.

3. Attend trade shows especially those in your chosen niche or industry. This is one of the most effective ways on building and growing your business. What's great about trade shows is that you will be talking and dealing with suppliers in person unlike online wherein everyone is cloaked in anonymity.

4. Subscribe to your industry's newsletters and trade publications. There's usually a trade magazine or newsletter associated with an industry so find this trade magazine and see what you can find inside its pages. There are usually lists of suppliers, manufacturers, and traders complete with their information and contact details.

5. Join industry groups, forums, and other professional networks in your niche and industry. Networking is very important especially if your dropshipping business belongs to a very competitive niche. The connections you make will always come in handy down the road. You can get referrals or recommendations for reputable suppliers from your connections in the industry.

How to spot fake dropshipping wholesalers and suppliers:

1. They have vague contact details.

The only reason a supplier has incomplete and vague contact details is that they're covering something up. Legitimate suppliers provide several and complete contact details that may include a physical address, phone numbers, email addresses, and other basic details.

2. They refuse to provide samples.

During the negotiation process, you have every right to request for samples from the supplier. If the supplier refuses even if you are going to pay for the samples, then something is definitely wrong. A supplier who is hesitant to send samples is a huge red flag. Requesting for samples is not just a strategy to check the quality of the products, it's also a good way of verifying if the supplier is legitimate or not.

3. They sell to the public.

Be very cautious with any supplier who sells directly to the public. They are contradicting the core principle of being a dropshipping supplier when they themselves are retailing their products. Them being sellers make them direct competitors of the same entrepreneurs they are supplying.

4. They claim to provide you with very high margins.

The general rule is that if a supplier's offer is too good to be true, then it's probably not true. It's no secret that margins in the dropshipping industry are often extremely low. If someone offers you a very high margin, then something is fishy.

5. They ask for monthly membership fees.

This is not right, plain and simple. This is usually a fraudulent tactic used by scammers to deceive unsuspecting victims. There's no reason why a supplier should be charging you a monthly fee.

6. They refuse to sign contracts.

The only reason why a supplier wouldn't sign a contract is that he doesn't want to enter into a legally binding agreement. He should be more than willing to sign a contract if he's really interested in doing business with you.

Here are your options in paying for the goods you dropship from your suppliers:

1. **Credit card** – If you are just starting out, this is usually the mode of payment that most suppliers want. It's fast and convenient. It's also fairly secure. Using your credit card to order goods also allow you to rack up reward points or frequent flier miles.

2. **PayPal, Payoneer, or other online payments system** – Many suppliers prefer PayPal and other online payment systems because the transactions are often lightning-quick. The main drawback of using PayPal is that it's usually difficult to resolve an issue should something go wrong during a transaction.

3. **Net Terms on Invoice by Check or Bank Draw** – This is a very common practice in the dropshipping industry. Basically, the supplier will provide you with a certain number of days upon which you should pay for the products you ordered. For example, let's say that you ordered goods with "net 20" terms. This means that you have 20 days to settle the purchase with your supplier either by check or bank draw.

Here are dropshipping directories where you can find suppliers and wholesalers:

➢ Wholesale Central - http://www.wholesalecentral.com/
➢ Salehoo - https://www.salehoo.com/suppliers/new
➢ Doba - https://www.doba.com/
➢ Worldwide Brands - https://www.worldwidebrands.com/
➢ Megagoods - https://www.megagoods.com/
➢ Albany Distributing - https://www.albanydistributing.com/
➢ Alibaba - https://www.alibaba.com/
➢ Oberlo - https://www.oberlo.com/
➢ AliDropship - https://alidropship.com/
➢ Dropified - https://www.dropified.com/

➢ Dropship Direct - https://dropshipdirect.com/
➢ Sunrise Wholesale - https://www.sunrisewholesalemerchandise.com/

Chapter Summary

Finding a good and reliable supplier or wholesaler is a crucial step in starting and growing your dropshipping business. Don't rush this step because it can come back and completely ruin your business. Never underestimate the negative effect of a bad supplier on your business. I'm not just talking about low quality products here. Low quality products from a supplier is one thing. Unreliable service from an unreliable supplier is another thing. With that said, you should only deal with a supplier who offers you two things:

1. High-quality products and
2. High quality service

If you get these two from a supplier, you are in good hands.

Did You Know

The top 10 retail eCommerce countries based on current size and future potential are, in order: USA, China, UK, Japan, Germany, France, South Korea, Russia, Belgium and Australia (Source: AT Kearney)

Chapter 9

Managing Inventory and Multiple Suppliers

In a dropshipping business, you are not going to hold inventory but this doesn't mean there will be zero inventory management required from you. You still need inventory management skills. You have to be constantly communicating with your suppliers to make sure that orders are being fulfilled and sent on time to customers. This is sometimes referred to as indirect inventory management. In this chapter, we are going to take a quick look at how you can efficiently manage inventory and multiple suppliers.

Best Practices for Inventory Management in a Dropshipping Business

Pick products that are easier to manage.

The bigger and more fragile a product is, the more difficult it will be for you and your supplier to manage your inventories. This is why most dropshippers prefer items that are small and less likely to get damaged during transit. Have you ever wondered why so many online entrepreneurs dropship clothing? It's because clothing inventories are one of the easiest to manage. And there's the fact that clothing don't get easily damaged during shipping. In a nutshell, if you want to avoid inventory headaches, you should stick with products that are easy to store, stock, and ship.

Use multiple suppliers.

I think I've touched on this topic in an earlier chapter. Dealing with a single supplier can be disastrous to your business operations. What if that supplier suddenly runs out of stock? Or what if your only supplier keeps on delaying the shipment of product to customers? In any case, it doesn't look good for your business. The best way to fix this problem is to enter into a deal with multiple suppliers. If supplier A runs out of stock, there's supplier B or supplier C on stand by to fulfill the incoming customer orders.

Regularly check on your suppliers regarding stock availability.

In a lot of cases, inventory problems are often due to miscommunication or lack thereof. It's not always the fault of the supplier. With that said, you should make it a point to contact your suppliers every now and then to talk about product inventories. This is especially true if you are selling products that move quickly and have fast turnaround times. These are the types of products that often run out of stock.

Avoid overselling.

Overselling refers to the bad habit of accepting orders from customers even though you are not sure if your suppliers have enough inventories in stock to fulfill the orders. The general rule is that you shouldn't sell more than what your suppliers can fulfill. Overselling will hurt your business more than you think especially if it happens too often. Online consumers are a fickle bunch. Not delivering what you promised can completely turn them off. In short, overselling will lose you a lot of customers so don't do it.

Recognize that all suppliers are not alike.

If you have entered into deals with several suppliers, the quality of their services often vary. You should prioritize those who you deem to be the most reliable and most trustworthy. In the dropshipping business, nurturing relationships with your best suppliers is one of the keys to achieving success. Always think of your suppliers as long-term business partners.

Automation and technology.

You can't separate the dropshipping business model with technology tools and automation systems. These are deeply embedded together. For you to efficiently manage inventory and multiple suppliers, you have to make use of automation programs and other technological tools. You can't do everything manually and on your own. Always be on the lookout for new automation software and other digital tools that you can potentially implement on your dropshipping business.

How to Manage Multiple Dropship Suppliers

If you plan on working with multiple suppliers, you should be aware of the risks and added responsibilities that come along with it. The first rule is that you should only work with suppliers you can trust. Please refer to the chapter in this book which pertains to finding good suppliers. You have all the information you need in that chapter to find trustworthy suppliers. Now, let's say that you have entered into deals with multiple suppliers. How do you manage your responsibilities towards each supplier?

Your best bet is to make use of software that allows you to connect and communicate with several suppliers with ease. There are tons of these software out there. Find the one that's most appropriate for your business. Using automation software in managing multiple suppliers is standard practice in the dropshipping industry. It allows you to have orders fulfilled by more than one suppliers even if the orders are coming from a single customer. Trying to fulfill these orders manually will be next to impossible. With that said, my advice to you is to invest in an efficient automation software that bridges the gaps between your business and the multiple suppliers who fulfill orders from your customers.

How to Deal with Out of Stock Orders When They Occur

No matter how hard you try to ensure that your suppliers can always fulfill orders, there will be those times wherein they just can't. What do you do if this happens? The first thing you should do is contact the customer and inform him directly that the product he ordered is out of stock. If you are confident that your supplier can restock their inventory within a certain period, you can tell the customer that the product he wants will be available soon. Provide him a timeframe of when the product will be available for purchase.

If you are not sure if your supplier will be able to restock their inventory, you can try to offer the customer a similar product or even a better product. It's possible that the customer hasn't seen such a product in your listings. Inform the customer of similar products you have that have the similar features and functions of the original product he wanted. In short, don't be afraid to suggest alternatives.

Another good way to deal with out of stock orders is to outsource the orders from another supplier. In this scenario, you should find a supplier who can quickly fulfill the orders. This is not too difficult to do if you have a lot of contacts for suppliers in your niche.

Chapter Summary

For sure, managing inventory and multiple suppliers is not going to be an easy task. In fact, the complications in this sector of the business is one of the biggest reasons why a lot of new dropshippers give up. But with the right mindset and with the proper tools, you will see this as an opportunity, deal with the challenges and problems and grab more market share for yourself. It's going to be difficult at first but you will soon get used to the grind. As you gain more experience, you will be able to deal with the issues faster and with less hassle.

Did You Know

There is a huge opportunity for eCommerce growth in India – in 2014, there were 243 million internet users (19% of the population) but this is forecast to grow to 730 million users by 2020 (Sources: PwC & Nasscom and Akamai)

Chapter 10

Dealing with Security and Fraud Issues

You are running an ecommerce store which means you will always be susceptible to security and fraud issues. As your business grows and increases its profits, you will become more of a target for hackers and thieves. In this chapter, we are going to look into the best procedures on how you can protect yourself from these security and fraud issues. We are also going to talk about the solutions you can implement if your business gets actually compromised by a security and fraud problem.

How to Deal with Fraudulent Orders

A fraudulent order can be one of two things. One, it can be an unauthorized transaction by the customer. For example, a person uses another person's credit card without permission to purchase a product. Two, it could be a transaction coming from a legit source, but it was intended to defraud you. For example, a person orders a product from you, but claims that the product didn't arrive, or he claims that he didn't make the order to force you to give a refund. These fraudulent orders can result in chargebacks, which will cause you to lose a lot of money.

Here are some practical ways on how you can prevent fraudulent orders:

1. Install a built-in anti-fraud system on your dropshipping website. Again, there are a lot of software programs out there that were specifically designed to deal with fraud in businesses that follow the dropshipping model. You have many programs to choose from. You should also ask your supplier to do the same to ensure that both ends of the transactions are safe and secure.

2. Verify IP address. See to it that the IP address where the order is coming from is legit and not shady. There are also tools and software programs that allow you to automatically detect and flag down suspicious IP addresses.

3. Call the phone number associated with the order. If you will be making a big order, which means there are hundreds or even thousands of dollars involved, you should go out of your way to call the phone number and verify everything to make sure that you are fulfilling a legitimate order.

4. Search email address. Check the email address used by the customer to order from your website. Does it look suspicious? Search the email address and see if you can dig up more information about the owner of the address. Sometimes, scammers would use bots to create fake email addresses that they then use to try and defraud ecommerce sites.

5. Check if the billing and shipping addresses match. It's often rare for a customer to use a billing address that's different from the shipping address. With that said, if the two addresses don't match, then you should treat it as a red flag. It's possible that it's an honest mistake but it's more likely that the order was fraudulent.

6. Be cautious of multiple orders with different billing addresses. If a customer places multiple orders with you but all the billing addresses are different from each other, something is definitely not right. You should check and verify with the person placing the orders. Request for an explanation why the orders have different billing addresses.

7. Review high value orders. If a customer orders thousands of dollars' worth of products from you despite the fact that you only sell products with low selling prices, something is definitely off. If a customer wants to purchase in bulk, he should be dealing with a wholesaler and not with a retailer like you. With that said, you should always review high value orders that go your way.

8. Install fraud prevention apps. There are a few dozen apps out there that can help you protect your ecommerce store from fraud and other forms of online attacks. Some of these apps have been specifically designed and developed for dropshipping businesses.

Ensuring That the Credit Card Numbers of Your Customers Are Safe and Secure

If your customers are paying you through their credit cards, it's your responsibility to ensure that their card information are always secure. Data breach can affect any online platform. Even the largest online companies are not immune to these malicious attacks. To safeguard the credit card data and other sensitive information of your customers, there are certain protocols you need to follow.

First, you should only make use of approved and tested equipment and software. The hardware and software you use should be compliant with the Payment Card Industry Data Security Standard (PCI). This applies to companies of any size that accept credit card payments from customers. If you plan on accepting card payment, then you need to host your data securely with a PCI-compliant hosting provider.

Second, don't store electronic track data or the customer's card security number in any form. This is the data contained at the black magnetic strip behind most credit cards. Track data are supposed to help merchants verify if a customer trying to purchase using the card actually has the card in his or her hands. The data also contains information that are not displayed on the surface of the card. Keep all these information secure by not copying and storing them in any form.

Third, see to it that when you store credit card account numbers, these are completely encrypted. If you are also storing the numbers in paper form, make sure that these are secured as well. Proper electronic storage of credit card numbers require a robust encryption algorithm. Even if your computer gets stolen or if someone gains access to your website, they can't just copy the credit card account numbers because these are encrypted.

Chapter Summary

Dealing with credit card security and fraud problems is serious business. Even before you launch your business, you have to review its fraud and security risks. Many hackers and credit card info thieves often target newly launched ecommerce websites because the owners are usually busy on running the business. I suggest that you get the help of a security expert to review your ecommerce website and all the software you use to make sure that every security flaw and loophole is fixed.

Did You Know

Smartphones have overtaken laptops as UK internet users' number one device, emphasising the need to have an eCommerce website that is mobile friendly to maximise sales opportunities (Source: Ofcom)

Chapter 11

Understanding and Minimizing Chargebacks

Also often referred to as a reversal, a chargeback is a return of funds to the account of a customer. In dropshipping, the chargeback can be applied on a purchase made through a credit card or through an online payment platform like PayPal. A chargeback occurs when a customer disputes a purchase made using his or her credit card. The customer either claims that the purchase was fraudulent or the purchase was made without his knowledge or permission. During a chargeback, the credit card company reverses the transaction so that the customer is reimbursed of his money.

Needless to say, as a dropshipper, dealing with chargebacks can be a huge problem. Not only will chargebacks reduce your income, it might also cause credit card companies to penalize you if the chargebacks happen too often. When the credit card company reverses the transaction, you will usually receive an explanation for the chargeback. The reason could be any of the following: fraud, technical error, clerical error, or the customer claimed to have received a product that's inferior to what he paid for.

To reduce the number of chargebacks you deal with, here are some practical tips to help you out:

1. Get proof of shipment or delivery from delivery companies. If a customer claims non-receipt, you can always show the proof of shipment to make the point that the product made it to its destination.

2. Get in touch with the customer claiming a chargeback and verify his purchase details. Sometimes, customers forget that they've made a purchase or there's a chance that they weren't able to recognize the name of the business that appeared on their credit card statement. Have the customer recheck his transactions.

3. As much as possible, avoid manual sales processing. This is why you should make use of reliable software that automates the ordering and payment process. If you take orders manually, there's always the possibility that you make a clerical error like charging the wrong amount or charging the customer more than once.

4. Make it very easy for customers to get in touch with you. Sometimes, customers are forced to ask for a chargeback if they find it very difficult to contact and talk with you. Encourage your customers to contact you first before they start requesting for a chargeback.

5. Be responsive to customer queries. If a customer asks about a recent purchase, answer immediately. Always make it a point to respond quickly and professionally to all reasonable inquiries by your buyers.

6. Provide a crystal-clear product return policy. Make sure that your policies on refunds and returns are clear and easy to understand. If a customer doesn't know how to proceed with a possible product return because your policies are vague, he would just ask for a chargeback because it's easier to do.

7. Suggest a dispute resolution. If a customer requests for a chargeback, try resolving the issue first. Most customers are more than willing to hear suggestions on how the problem can be resolved.

Chapter Summary

As a dropshipper, you will always be dealing with chargebacks. Whether customers are paying for their purchases via credit cards or via PayPal, anyone can file for a chargeback. It's also worth mentioning here that in most cases, credit card companies and PayPal favor customers by default unless you can provide undeniable proof that the problem causing the chargeback was not your fault. You can lessen your chargeback problems by following the practical tips I've discussed above.

Did You Know

Clothes and sports goods are the most popular categories from which people buy online from in the UK
(Source: Statista)

Chapter 12

Dealing With Product Returns and Shipping Issues

Product returns and shipping issues are a huge source of headaches in dropshipping. This is why it's very important that you come up with a comprehensive return policy. Such a policy should cover all instances of returns due to damaged goods, destroyed goods in transit, defective goods, and goods returned for the simple reason that the customer wasn't satisfied with it. Setting up a return policy in a dropshipping business is further complicated by the fact that you aren't the one shipping the products. But this shouldn't intimidate you. Dealing with product returns doesn't have to be that difficult. In this chapter, I'm going to show you how you can make it easier for you.

When Does a Return Happen?

A product return happens when a customer who previously bought an item from you wants to return the product and requests for a refund or a replacement. There are various reasons why a customer would return a product. These include the following: incorrect product, incorrect size, product no longer needed, product does not match the description, product did not meet customer's expectations, and deliberate fraud. With regards to how to deal with deliberate fraud, please refer to Chapter 10 and Chapter 11.

If a buyer wants to return a product, the process looks like this:
1. A customer gets in touch with you and asks for a return
2. You contact your supplier who fulfilled the order and ask for an RMA (return merchandise authorization)
3. The customer ships back the product to your supplier. The RMA number should be highlighted on the shipping address.
4. After receiving the product, your supplier refunds you the cost of the product.
5. After getting your refund, you in turn send a refund to the customer for the amount he paid for the returned product.

However, the process is not always this simple. Complications can arise due to defective products and restocking fees. A restocking fee is basically a surcharge for the products returned by your customers. It's best that when you write your return policy, don't make your customers pay for the restocking fees. You should handle the restocking fees yourself.

When it comes to defective items returned by customers, it's bad business practice to have the customer pay for the fees associated with shipping the product back to the supplier. Again, you should handle the fees. It's part of the costs of running an online dropshipping business. When writing your return policy, make sure that you make it clear that you will be handling the postage and shipping fees for products that are returned due to defects. It's simply not right to make a customer suffer and then let him incur further expenses when shipping the defective product back to your supplier. Taking care of this also gives the customer confidence and will increase the chance of him/her buying from you.

Dealing with Shipping Issues

When pricing the products you list on your dropshipping website, you should take into account your shipping costs. Calculating these can be challenging especially if you are working with several suppliers who are in different locations. It can be difficult to accurately calculate the shipping rates for different orders. When calculating the rates, you can use the following methods:

1. **Real-Time Rates** – You calculate the shipping rates by taking into account the destination of the shipment and the collective weight of all the products purchased. This method provides you with an actual real-time price quote. It's an accurate method but it becomes problematic if customer orders are being fulfilled by several suppliers from different locations.

2. **Per-Type Rates** – With this method, you assign flat shipping rates to products based on their types or categories. Let's say you are selling two types of a product (Type A and Type B). Type A products will be shipped for a flat rate of $15 while Type B products will ship for a flat rate of $30. Needless to say, this is a much simpler method but the shipping rates aren't as accurate compared to real-time rates.

3. **Flat-Rate Shipping** – This is the simplest method for the simple reason that you charge a single flat rate for all your products regardless of their type or category. It's the simplest but it's also the least accurate. Never use this method if you are selling a lot of products whose prices vary widely.

International Shipments

If you plan on selling your products to an international market, there are several factors you must take into account when it comes to shipping costs. One, shipping rates aren't always similar for different countries. Some charge much more and some charge much less. Two, most suppliers will request for an additional fee from you for processing international orders. This is understandable because processing international orders requires more work. Three, shipping heavy and large products internationally can be very costly. My advice is that you should avoid selling heavy and bulky products internationally. And last but not the least, you should take into account the fact that it's often difficult to resolve shipping problems associated with international orders. You will not only be dealing with shipping issues in one country, you are dealing with shipping issues concerning two countries.

Chapter Summary

Before you launch your dropshipping business, make sure that you have a complete and clear return policy in order. The policy should discuss in detail how customers can return products and how they can request for refunds. Don't make the mistake of writing a vague return policy because this will only confuse your customers. When writing the policy, you should also take into account the types of products you are selling and the countries you are shipping them to.

Likewise, you should also try to understand all the issues associated with shipping your products. What are the costs of shipping your products? How should you compute these shipping costs? Based on your computations, is it worth it shipping your products internationally? These are just some of the important questions you should ask yourself with regards to the shipping aspect of your ecommerce business. Again, if you are not yet sure on how to proceed, I highly recommend that you consult with someone who has the proper knowledge and experience about dropshipping returns and shipping issues.

Did You Know

Because of forced account registration, online users abandon their shopping carts 26% of the time. Shopping cart abandonment accounts for $18 billion in lost revenue each year!

Chapter 13

10 Beginner Mistakes and How to Avoid Them

Learn from the mistakes of those who went ahead of you. This will be the mantra for this chapter. If you are inexperienced, it's expected that you are going to make mistakes along the way. That is normal and it happens to everyone. In this chapter, we are going to look at the most common mistakes that beginners make when they start and build a dropshipping business for the first time. Being aware of these common mistakes would help you in avoiding them.

1. Selling a lot of products right off the bat.

Dropshipping a single product in itself is very hard. What more if you are selling several products. I am not saying that selling a lot of products is bad. I'm saying that you shouldn't do it if you are just starting out. You're not building a general store wherein you need to sell a lot of products. It's very difficult to carve your own market in the industry if you are selling too many products. Selling niche products is still your best chance of attracting a good number of recurring customers online because you'll be able to fully understand the customer requirements in that niche i.e. your customer avatar

2. Not checking the background and experience of a supplier or manufacturer.

Newbie dropshippers often focus on cheap products and low shipping costs that they fail to verify if the supplier is reliable or not. I say it again, your business is just as good as your supplier. If you have a bad supplier, it follows that your business is going to be bad. This is why you should only deal with suppliers and manufacturers whose reputation can be verified online via reviews and referrals. Never enter into a deal with a supplier whose background and experience you know nothing about.

3. Not requesting for samples of the products to be dropshipped.

It may be hard to believe but a lot of new ecommerce entrepreneurs make this completely avoidable mistake. Not requesting for samples of the product is a recipe for disaster. Getting samples is the only way for you to know if the products are up to your standards. You have to check if the products look and function the way the supplier advertised them. If a supplier refuses to send you samples, then something is amiss. If the supplier truly wants to do business with you, he should be more than willing to send you product samples. Sending you the samples shouldn't be a problem because in most cases, you are going to pay for the samples yourself.

4. Not getting your finances in order.

Many newbies often make the rookie mistake of building a business financially blind. That is they are clueless with regards to how much they need to get started and where they are going to get the funds. They start ordering products without assessing what their profit margins (i.e. net profit as a percentage of revenue) will be. They start dealing with suppliers without determining if their prices are too high or too low. The best way to get your finances in order is to get the services of an accountant, a business consultant, or any related professional who can help you get a clear understanding of your expenses, costs, and projected earnings.

5. Relying too much on vendors.

Putting too much trust in a vendor is seldom a good strategy. This is something you should be wary of especially if you are dropshipping products from a one or two vendors. You have to ask the question: what if the vendor suddenly bails out on you? Your business will done because there's no source for products. You need to start all over again from scratch. To avoid this problem, what you should do is deal only with vendors who have verifiable track records. For insurance purposes, you should draw out a contract which you and the vendor agree to. Last but not the least, try dealing with several vendors, not just one vendor.

6. Expecting to make instant money.

Many people have the wrong assumption that dropshipping is a get-rich-quick operation. Nope, it's not. Although there are those who get lucky and make a ton of cash from the get-go but for most starters, it's a long road towards profits and success. Don't be greedy. Don't believe in the lofty claims of those who are saying that you can be rich overnight with dropshipping. To reach that point, you have to work hard and work smart. Start the business with realistic goals and expectations.

7. Selling trademarked products.

You cannot sell products that are registered copyrights or registered trademarks of another company. You can only sell them if you have asked permission from them and they obliged. In most cases, you are required to get a license before you are able to sell them. You should also be careful about the suppliers and manufacturers where you are sourcing your products. See to it that they are not using trademark-protected elements like logos, images, and designs. To avoid getting entangled in trademark and copyright issues, you should focus on selling white-label products. What's great about white-label products is that you can customize their logos and designs to make them your own. You can run a quick trademark search at the United States Patent and Trademark Office website.

8. Giving up too soon.

This is one of the biggest reasons why most people who try dropshipping never reach their full potential. How can they reach their goals when they gave up at the first sign of trouble? As I kept saying in earlier chapters, you are going to face a lot of problems and challenges along the way especially in the early stages of your business. These failures, big and small, can be very discouraging. But you should not let them break you down and cause you to give up. Just keep going. Learn from your mistakes and make sure that you don't make them again.

9. Unreliable customer support.

A lot of newbie dropshippers often take customer support for granted. They sometimes assume that this part of the business is handled by the shipping party. Often unprepared, they are clueless as to what to do when they are inundated by complaints and shipping problems. Customers, especially online shoppers, get easily pissed off by bad and unreliable customer service. Bad customer service will prevent you from growing your business. In short, you need to invest in a reliable customer service system.

10. Picking the wrong niche.

Beginners often stumble when it comes to choosing the right niche for their dropshipping business. They often go chasing lucrative but very competitive niches. Another common mistake by beginners is that they get into a niche where they have very little knowledge about. This is problematic for two main reasons. One, it will be very difficult for you to answer questions and inquiries by customers. And two, your competitors are more knowledgeable about the products than you and this will reflect in how they present their unique value proposition. So who will the customers most likely to support? You who know very little about the products? Or your competitors who present their products in a way that appeals to the customer in addition to having all the answers to every customer inquiry?

Chapter Summary

The bottom line here is that it's okay to make mistakes and make the wrong decisions early on in the business. It would be unrealistic to expect the business to be sailing smoothly without encountering any problems. What you can do is either try to avoid making these mistakes or prepare for them. The common mistakes we have discussed in this chapter should be more than enough to help you prepare and anticipate. Go over the list a few more times before you start working on your dropshipping business. Understanding these mistakes can save you a lot of money, time, and resources down the road.

Did You Know

A single second delay in your website loading time can result in a 7% loss in conversion, and 40% of web users will abandon a website if it takes longer than 3 seconds to load.

Chapter 14

How To Scale Your Dropshipping Business

Scaling a business is never easy. People often make the assumption that scaling a business is just a matter of adding products to your inventory or doubling your operations. In reality, it's not as simple as that. Selling five products instead of two products doesn't automatically scale the business. There are so many other factors that determine if the business is being scaled or otherwise. In this chapter, we are going to discuss some of the best strategies on how to actually grow and scale your business.

Here are 7 powerful strategies you can use to scale up your business:

1. Add value to your products.

What is meant by adding value to your products? It means improving the product so that a customer will purchase it from you instead of purchasing it from a competitor. Needless to say, adding value to a product is very important if you are promoting products that are very similar to what other entrepreneurs are selling. You need to add value to your products to make them unique in the eyes of consumers. But how exactly do you accomplish this? Well, you have a lot of options.

There are several ways to add value to your products. One, you can customize their designs and packaging so they look more enticing to customers. Two, you can offer accessories on top of your main products. Three, you can create a loyalty program wherein customers get significant discounts the more they buy from you. You may not know it but offering a lower price is actually a form of adding value to your products. Four, you can also offer discounts for bulk purchases. For example, if a customer buys ten units, he will get one unit free. That one free unit is considered as added value by the customer.

Last but not the least, just make your products better than everybody else's. The better you make your products, the more valuable they are in the eyes of your target customers. Better products also translates into more sales. More sales means your business is being scaled to higher heights.

2. Focus a lot of your attention on marketing and search engine optimization (SEO).

In many ways, scaling a business is synonymous to ramping up your marketing campaigns. That means if you want to scale your dropshipping business, you have to double or triple your marketing efforts. The harder you promote a product, the more customers you attract and the more sales you make. That's scaling in its purest form. Now, there are many strategies on how to promote a product online but you should focus most of your attention on just a few ones. These strategies are as follows:

✓ **Search engine optimization** - Organic traffic or traffic coming from search engines is the best type of online traffic. These are people who are specifically looking for your product. This means that they are more than likely to purchase the product from you. Organic traffic is much easier to convert into paying customers compared to other types of traffic because they know what they want and they know your product will help them satisfy their need. Now, the only way for you to get organic traffic is through search engine optimization or SEO. You have to optimize your dropshipping website with the proper keyword combinations for it to be able to attract traffic from Google.

✓ **Social media marketing** – Social media traffic is starting to catch up with the level of traffic that Google has. In fact, next to Google, the most visited websites in the world are social media sites (i.e. Facebook, Twitter, Instagram, and YouTube). With that said, it would be a huge mistake if you aren't active in promoting your products and dropshipping business on social media platforms. Most social sites are free to use so there's absolutely no reason why you shouldn't leverage them to your advantage.

✓ **Content marketing** – This is a rather broad term but it's basically about creating online content that's designed to promote and drive traffic to your dropshipping website. Forms of content marketing include blogging, guest writing, article marketing, sponsoring posts, and press releases. For example, you write an article and distribute it to bloggers if they are interested in publishing it. It's up to you if you decide to pay them or not. They publish the article on their blogs. The article would contain a mention of your business and a link to your website. This is content marketing in its purest form.

✓ **Advertising** – To make money, you have to spend money. This is especially true today wherein the competition among online entrepreneurs is getting tougher by the day. Sometimes, the only way to get ahead of your competitors is to be aggressive with your advertising campaigns. Fortunately, you have many options when it comes to advertising online. You can make use of advertising programs like Google Adsense or you can directly advertise in websites and blogs you specifically choose. You should also consider purchasing ads in popular social media sites.

3. Leveraging Facebook ads to drive traffic to your dropshipping website.

Facebook is the perfect platform to promote your dropshipping business. The social networking site has more than a billion active users and it's growing by the thousands every single day. This is a huge market you can tap into. The best way to promote your business on Facebook is to take advantage of its advertising program. It's very cheap, it's very easy to use, and most importantly, it gets good results.

Getting Started with Facebook Ads

➢ All you need to get started is a Facebook account and a Facebook page for your business.
➢ You have several options on how to promote something on Facebook. You can purchase an ad for the page itself, an ad for a specific post in your page, or an ad that promotes a link which directs to your main dropshipping website.
➢ The first time you purchase an ad, you will be required to add a payment method to your account. You can use a credit card, a bank account, or PayPal. Facebook will charge you through any of these payment methods every time an ad campaign of yours is completed.

Advantages of Using Facebook Ads for Your Dropshipping Business

- It's very cheap. You can purchase an ad and have it run for a whole day and pay just a few dollars for it. You can attract thousands of eyeballs from that one ad alone depending on how effective your targeting is. A well crafted customer avatar makes a huge difference.

- You can pause and cancel an ad any time you like. If you realize that the ad isn't getting the number of clicks you expected, you can always pause it so that you can optimize it for a better performance. Alternatively, you can cancel the ad altogether. You will only pay for the period during which the ad has been live.

- You only pay for the ads after the campaign. For example, you purchased an ad for one week and you set a budget of $200. You will only be billed at the end of one week.

- Facebook ads allow you to narrow down your target audience. You can customize an ad by geographical location, age range, gender, and interests. You literally specify the types of Facebook users who will be able to see your ads. This is perfect if your dropshipping business caters to a small and specific niche.

- Facebook provides you with data and statistics about the performances of your ads. You can determine how many clicks, views, likes, and shares your ads are getting. In short, you can better analyse if your target customers are engaging with your ads or not.

Disadvantages of Using Facebook Ads for Your Dropshipping Business

- Sometimes, you get very low engagement because most people use Facebook to be entertained and not to look for products. Ads on the site are often treated as nuisance by a lot of users.

- It costs money. Although advertising on Facebook is cheap, it can still be an issue especially if you have a very tight budget.

Its fair to say the advantages significantly outnumber the disadvantages. Facebook is a tool that you should be using to advertise and scale your business. The social site's advertising program has quite a number of flaws but these are trivial compared to the immense benefits you can get from taking advantage of the program. If you're interested in learning, step-by-step, how to fully take advantage of the Facebook advertising platform to scale your business, I invite you to take a look at my book – Facebook Advertising: Learn How to Make $10,000+ Each Month with Facebook Marketing.

4. Specialize or niche down your products.

This refers to the strategy of increasing your products by further dividing your niche into categories. In short, you niche down your products. For example, let's say that you are selling running shoes on your dropshipping website. You can niche them down by creating categories like trail running shoes and road running shoes. Trail running shoes are designed for rugged, rough, and uneven trails while road running shoes are designed for even pavements and roads. You are niching down while increasing the number of products you are selling. You can further divide the categories based on metrics like brand or even the materials used to manufacture them.

5. Automate your store.

In automating your dropshipping business, you are not only making it easier for your customers and your team, you are also freeing up a lot of time and resources which you can then further invest in growing the business. In automating the business, you are hitting two birds with one stone. Automation also allows you to add more products to your listings without increasing the burden of running the business.

6. Private label or retail arbitrage.

How retail arbitrage works is quite simple. You look for products in an online marketplace like Amazon or eBay or AliExpress then list these in your own online store. If a customer purchases a product from your website, you order the product from the online marketplace where you found it. The original source of the product processes and fulfills the order. You earn from the difference between your selling price and the original source's price. You can scale your dropshipping business by engaging in this sales model.

On the other hand, private labeling refers to the business practice of rebranding products by another company and selling these as if they are your own. For example, let's say you enter into a deal with a private label company to produce a line of beauty products for you. These are usually generic beauty products. You customize them and make them your own by putting your own designs, logos, and choice of packaging on them. You can make a deal so that the supplier also handles shipping of the products to your customers. You receive the orders from customers then forward these to your supplier.

7. Offer outstanding service.

How you deal with your customers plays a very important role in the growth of your business. Scaling your business will be very difficult if your core customers are not satisfied with your services. Good service nurtures loyalty among your customers. Good service is a driver of growth. Let me put it this way. A customer buys a product from you and because you delivered a high-quality product on time and at the right price, that customer will likely buy from you again or even spread the good word about your business to their friends and family via word of mouth. And just like that you've potentially doubled or tripled your business because of that one customer. Just imagine if most of your new customers turn into repeat customers. You will be scaling your business in no time.

Chapter Summary

As you can see, scaling a dropshipping business takes a lot of work and time. There's a long road ahead of you so you need to work harder, and most importantly, smarter. When setting your scaling goals, make them long-term and set clear actions steps you can take to achieve them. This way you won't overwhelm yourself. With that said, don't be too hard on yourself. That's one of the keys in ensuring that you always have the right mindset and that you are always on the right track. If you implement all the scaling strategies I have discussed above, you will be well on your way to achieving sustained success. At the end of the day, that's what matters. As long as you are doing things right, growth will come sooner or later.

Did You Know

Amazon is king of the ecommerce jungle. Speaking of not having a close second. Amazon brought in $79.2 billion in sales in 2015. The next closest online retailer is wal-mart.com which brought in $13.4 billion. Following suit are Apple with $12 billion and staples.com with $10 billion. It doesn't seem like a fair contest, does it?

Chapter 15

15 Practical Tips and Lessons From Successful Dropshippers

This chapter is what I call the Inspiration Chapter. It's always a good idea to watch what successful dropshippers are doing and listen to what they have to say. If you want to make money from dropshipping, then you should learn from those who have already done it. I wrote this chapter to provide you with inspiration and the added drive to be successful in this industry. So let's dig in:

1. Don't be greedy.

Greediness is a nasty attribute that has no place in the dropshipping business. If your plan is to make as much money as you can in the shortest time possible, then you are in the wrong business. It's more likely that your business will crash and burn, and leave you with irredeemable costs. Dropshipping is not a get-rich-quick scheme. Most of the successful dropshippers you see out there didn't get to where they are by being greedy and aggressive. They built their dropshipping businesses through hard work and smart decisions. These are the same things you need to start and build your own successful dropshipping business.

2. Focus on evergreen products.

What is an evergreen product? In the simplest of terms, an evergreen product is a product that is still in demand regardless of the time of year. It's the very opposite of a seasonal product. T-shirts are evergreen products. Christmas sweaters are seasonal products. Jackets are evergreen products. Halloween costumes are seasonal products. I am not in any way saying that you should completely ignore seasonal products. You can still build a successful dropshipping business selling seasonal products, but if you want to create a business that's sustainable and profitable *all year round*, then your focus should be on evergreen products.

3. Find a niche that's connected to something you are passionate about.

In our example, if you love and enjoy trail running, then it makes complete sense to start a dropshipping business that sells all sorts of products related to trail running. These may include trail running shoes, accessories, hiking sandals, running shorts, etc. The biggest benefit of building a business around a hobby or interest is that there's little chances of you burning yourself out. Why should you burn yourself out when you enjoy what you are doing most of the time? The more you love the niche, the more you will enjoy running the business. Work becomes play. That's something that a lot of aspiring entrepreneurs dream about.

4. Constantly find ways on how to automate aspects of your business.

There are so many tools and resources out there that enable you to automate your dropshipping business. Many of these tools are even free to use. Automation is very important especially if you can't focus your whole attention on running the business. Automation also helps in growing and scaling your business quickly. Some of the things you can automate include marketing tasks, advertising tasks, emails, ad retargeting, and even customer service. Simplifying and automating the tasks associated with managing a dropshipping business have never been easier. You just have to find the right tools, plugins, and add-ons.

5. Invest in a good website design and theme.

Here's something you should know about online consumers. They often judge ecommerce stores based on their designs. If your dropshipping store has a bad design, people will likely think that you have bad products as well. Badly designed websites are less trustworthy in the eyes of online consumers. With that said, you should invest in a good website designer who can create for you a simple but professional-looking ecommerce store. It's not that difficult to find an experienced developer these days considering the proliferation of freelancers. It's best that you hire a developer who mostly works in building dropshipping-related websites. Freelancers can be found on sites like Upwork and Fiverr.

6. Offer Exceptional Customer Service

Customers may not always remember the product they bought from your website but they will always remember how you treated them. Customer service is very important in the dropshipping business considering the fact that you are not handling the products yourself. Somebody else is shipping the products to your customers so there's a higher risk of product returns and complaints. If your business receives a lot of orders in a day, I highly recommend that you provide customer service on a 24/7 basis. Hire two customer service representatives. One will work in the morning and one will work at night. Offering exceptional customer service is one of the most effective ways in building loyalty among your customers.

7. Request for Product Samples Before You Start Shipping Them to Customers

Don't rely on the words of your supplier or manufacturer. The general rule is that before you even list a product on your ecommerce store, make sure that you have thoroughly checked a sample of the product. There's no other way around this. You have to check the product first before you start selling it. Instruct your supplier to send you a batch of the products so that you can check several of the items. Don't assume that the products look exactly how they were advertised.

Requesting for product samples offers several benefits. These include the following:

- It offers you the chance to experience what it is like to buy a product from you. This allows you to identify issues with the process and come up with possible solutions.
- You can use the sample products for online advertisements, review videos, and other promotional materials.
- Being able to touch and look at the physical product helps you in coming up with a better and more detailed product description.
- The samples help you in getting better quality photos of your products.

8. Only work with a supplier who has extensive experience in the business.

When browsing through a dropshipping directory, you are going to come across thousands of dropshippers. Most of them have very little experience in the business. It would be a mistake if you are going to anchor your business on an inexperienced supplier. It's easy to spot inexperienced suppliers in a dropshipping directory. One, they usually have zero or very few reviews and comments. And two, their prices and costs tend to be much lower than average. Suppliers with extensive experience in the industry are often much more expensive but you are better off dealing with them. At least you are assured of the quality of their products and services. Dealing with inexperienced suppliers is just too risky especially if it's your first time to start and build an ecommerce store.

9. Look for light and durable products instead of heavy and fragile products.

When it comes to deciding which products to sell through dropshipping, it's very tempting to decide on items that have a lot of suppliers around. But before you start thinking of selling products like home theatre systems, porcelain vases, and other profitable but fragile products, remind yourself of how risky these products are. Selling fragile products is a recipe for disaster. Before you know it, you are dealing with countless product returns and chargebacks. Logistics is among your most important concerns when shipping products. It is always better to consider light and durable products instead of heavy and fragile items. They are easier and much cheaper to ship.

10. Sell Products That You Know

It's always a safe choice to promote and sell products that you are knowledgeable about. Having the right knowledge about the products you are selling means you will be able to take out the guesswork out of your choice of products. Your knowledge and expertise about the items you are selling will show in the level of customer service you can provide, in your confidence in the deals you offer, and in the way you present your products in your ecommerce website. Another important benefit of selling products that you know is that it will significantly improve your ratings as a seller. Seller ratings are a major driving force in dropshipping. It helps in improving the confidence that customers have towards you and your products.

11. Consider paying extra for tracking numbers and shipping insurance.

In dropshipping, there is always the risk that a customer's package gets damaged or lost. It would be very difficult to try and retrieve the lost products if you don't have a shipping insurance or if you don't have a system for tracking numbers. There are two major problems you can face if you don't have tracking numbers and shipping insurance. One, you can lose a lot of money from lost packages. And two, you will get a lot of negative and unflattering reviews and feedback from your customers. With that said, I suggest that you consider paying extra cash for tracking numbers and shipping insurance.

12. Be ready for product returns, back orders, and lost packages.

These are the biggest problems in a business with a dropshipping model. Never forget the fact that you do not have direct control over the handling and shipping of your products to the end customers. You have to plan properly and prepare for these contingencies. Your best strategy is to discuss policies about these returns and back orders with your suppliers. It should be clear who is going to handle these problems. Discuss the responsibilities and obligations of all parties involved (you as the business owner and the supplier as your dropshipper). This ensures that all parties exert their best efforts in avoiding product returns, back orders, and lost packages.

13. Use a reliable order management and dropshipping system.

There should be a reliable and secure connection between your business and your supplier. Getting the system to work properly can be difficult especially if you are dealing with more than one suppliers. Working with more than one suppliers means you have to set up more than one system connections. It's also worth mentioning here that some suppliers also deal with several ecommerce website owners. This means that they are also managing several accounts and this can further complicate the process. There are many platforms that you can use to make this simpler. Again, you should take your time in weighing your options. Some of the more well-known order management systems today include Orderhive, Ordoro, and Sellbrite.

14. A high quality presentation of your products should be among your top priorities.

Here is something you should understand about online shoppers. They often judge products based on how these look on their browsers and devices. If the photo of a product you have listed in your ecommerce website is blurry and amateurish, it would be very hard for a customer to take it seriously. Needless to say, you should invest in a good camera that allows you to take clear, crisp and professional-looking photos of your products. Also learn image-manipulation skills so that you can further improve the presentation of your products. If you don't have time for all these, try hiring a professional product photographer or a graphics designer. Presentation plays a very important role in ecommerce. If people visit your website and they see bad product photos, they'll likely click to leave.

15. Try building a brand around your dropshipping business.

Branding is very important in online sales. Consumers tend to support businesses that they can easily recall or relate with. Branding is not just about putting your products in as many platforms as possible. It's also about maintaining a set of products that have the same feel, look, and quality. Your business should have a strong voice. The brand you are going to create around your business should be catered towards your target market. For example, if you are targeting teens and young adults, the look, feel, and language you use in your website should be relatable to teens and young adults.

Chapter Summary

In the dropshipping industry, watching and learning is one of the best ways to steer your business to success. Watch what successful dropshippers are doing and try to model them. Look at the most successful entrepreneurs in your niche and watch closely what they are doing. How are they presenting their products online? How are they marketing their products? What kinds of software are they using? Where are they getting their suppliers? How are they running their customer support systems? How are they dealing with product returns? All these questions have been answered in this chapter. Try rereading the chapter to fully understand the great importance of every single tip and advice discussed herein.

Did You Know

Asia is the largest online purchasing group. As large and staggering as US online sales are, Asia claims close to 37% of online sales volume. To be clear, this includes China, South Korea and Japan. On a related note, the UK can claim close to 27% of web-based revenue.

Chapter 16

How to Promote Your Dropshipping Business

I don't have to tell you that the competition online is as tough as it gets. This is especially true if you decide to enter a popular market where there are literally thousands of online stores selling the same products. The thing about online competition is that it's going to get even tougher in the coming months and years as more entrepreneurs try their luck with ecommerce. This is something you should be aware of by now. With that said, you have to do everything to get ahead of the competition. Aside from offering high-quality products at very affordable prices, another proven method of getting ahead of the competition is to market your business like crazy.

Marketing is the key to being successful online especially in the dropshipping business. You have to devote a lot of your time and resources in telling people about your products and how good these products are. You should take a page from Coca-Cola's marketing strategy. Do you know why Coca-Cola is the biggest soda seller for decades? It's because they have mastered the art of marketing their products to every single platform available. Everywhere you look, there's a Coca-Cola logo or advertisement. It has come to the point wherein if you think about soda, Coca-Cola always comes to mind.

Applying the same marketing concept, you should try to promote your products and business in as many platforms as possible. Put your products out there where more people will get to see them. Since you are running an online dropshipping business, nearly all of your marketing efforts will be concentrated online. What's great about online marketing is that you are on an even field with the big companies. You may not have the same marketing budget as them but you have the chance of reaching millions of potential customers with the right marketing strategy.

Alright, without further ado, let's now take a look at some of the most effective marketing strategies that you can use to promote your business and products online. These are very practical strategies that can be easily implemented so there's absolutely no reason why you shouldn't apply them. You don't have to do all of them especially if you are too busy doing other things. But you should at least try them whenever you get the chance.

1. Content Marketing

How content marketing works is pretty simple and straightforward. You create content which can be in the form of articles, images, infographics, videos, or a combination of all of these types of digital content. You then distribute this content to as many platforms as you can. For example, you can write a long and detailed article then send it to media outlets, press release portals, blogs, websites, and forums. Those who want to publish the article can publish it. So how does this benefit you and your business? It's simple. The content you distribute mentions you and your business or it contains a link that redirects to your own website.

In a way, content marketing accomplishes two important things. One, it helps in spreading the word about you, your business, your brand, and your products. Imagine if a major news outlet like the New York Times publishes your article. This is a major boost to your business and brand. The second important thing that content marketing accomplishes is traffic generation. Content marketing is very good in driving web traffic to your website. And we're not just talking about ordinary traffic here. We are talking about traffic that's genuinely interested in what you are offering.

How good is content marketing in generating traffic to your website? Again, imagine if an article you wrote gets published in the New York Times. This is a major media outlet that generates millions of hits a day. That single article can drive hundreds of thousands of new visitors to your website if it gets traction on the New York Times website. The traffic can be in the millions if the article goes viral. Of course, this is just an example and the chance of getting published in the New York Times is small at best but you get the idea. Content marketing is a very powerful traffic generation strategy. Even if you are targeting smaller platforms like blogs and forums, the new traffic you get is just as valuable.

2. Social Media Marketing

If you are not using social media to market your business and products, then you are missing out on a lot of sales and opportunities. Ignoring the power of social media is akin to shooting yourself in the foot. You may be ignoring the social platforms but you are hurting yourself and your business in the process. If you are not already leveraging social media, now is the time to get on the bandwagon. Social media is the future of online marketing. This is not an exaggeration.

Just come to think of it. The largest and most influential online companies today are social media sites. There's Facebook, YouTube, Instagram, Twitter, WhatsApp, and Snapchat, just to name a few. These are the most visited websites on the internet today. The only online platform that beats them when it comes to organic traffic is Google, which is a search engine. But if you look at the data and trends, more and more people are moving away from search engines and towards social media sites. They get their news and entertainment from social sites. They get news updates from Facebook. They entertain themselves on YouTube or Instagram. The direction of the trends are pretty simple. More people are getting involved in social media. And it would be tragic to your business if you don't take advantage of this phenomenon.

Social media marketing is not that difficult to do. Of course, your marketing strategy should be tailored depending on the social media site that you are using. Marketing on Facebook is very different from marketing on YouTube. There are tons of tools and resources online that will teach you exactly how you can promote products on specific social media sites. You should take advantage of these resources whenever you can.

3. Search Engine Optimization (SEO)

I'm sure that you have heard of search engine optimization one too many times. You're probably sick and tired of hearing about it. But that doesn't take away the fact that SEO is one of the most powerful ways on how to market something online. The goal of optimization is very simple. And that is to improve the rankings of your website on Google's search results. If you run a dropshipping business that sells customized soccer balls, then you would like your website to appear at the top of the search results when someone types the phrase "customized soccer balls".

To be able to conduct SEO properly, you need to understand how Google ranks websites in the search results. There are several factors that the search engine takes into account when deciding how a website ranks. These factors include the quality of the content of the website, the age of the website, the number of links that point to the website, the social media chatter around the website, and the relevance of the website's content to the searcher's query. Needless to say, if you want to optimize your website, you need to address most if not all of these factors.

To start with the optimization process, you need to find out about the words, terms, and phrases that people use to look for your products. These are commonly referred to as keywords. In your perspective as a dropshipper, there are two main types of keywords. There are the keywords that people are currently using to arrive at your website. And then there are the keywords that you want people to use to arrive at your website. There's a big difference between the two. The first one consists of keywords that you are already ranking for. The second consists of keywords that you want to rank for.

Keyword research is the best way to look for the keywords that are most relevant to your business and products. There are several keyword research tools that you can use but I highly recommend that you use Google's own keyword tool. It's free and it offers the most accurate data on keywords. All you need is a Gmail account to access the tool. With the tool, you can determine how many people are searching for specific keywords on a monthly basis. This allows you to decide whether it's worth it to target a keyword or not.

After doing your keyword research, you should have in your hands a comprehensive list of words, terms, and phrases that people would use to search for your products. The next step is to create content that integrates these words and phrases. However, you need to be careful when writing keyword-optimized content. Don't overdo it or your website will be tagged for keyword stuffing. This refers to the unethical practice of putting too many keywords in an article in an attempt to game Google's algorithm. This strategy is against Google's quality requirements. If you are caught doing it, Google can penalize you by demoting your website in the search rankings. If you break the rule one too many times, Google might go as far as banning your site altogether. Needless to say, keyword stuffing is something you should never even think of doing.

4. Direct Advertising

The term direct advertising is a loose term but it allow me to offer a basic definition and interpretation in the context of the dropshipping business model. As the term implies, what you do is directly get in touch with the owners of websites, blogs, or social media pages where you want to advertise your website. For example, let's say that you run a dropshipping business selling soccer shoes. What you need to do is approach webmasters and owners of websites, blogs, and social sites that are relevant to the sport of soccer. The readers of these websites are soccer fans so it makes sense that you are going to purchase direct advertising from them.

One of the biggest benefits of direct advertising is that you can negotiate for the prices you want. This is different compared to other online advertising programs wherein you don't have control over the advertising prices. You are directly dealing with the website owners. This gives you more room in the negotiation table.

To be successful in direct advertising, you have to learn the tricks of the sales pitch. The sales pitch is your ticket to getting a good deal with a website owner or manager. In writing the sales pitch, you have to convince the website owner that your business is a good fit for the website. That you are offering products which the readers of the website will likely be interested in. You have to explain that not only are you paying the website owner for the advertising space, you are also offering value to the website's readers. With a good sales pitch, it shouldn't be that hard to find websites that will enter into an advertising deal with you.

To help you get the most out of your direct advertising efforts, here are some practical tips you can follow:

- Make your sales pitch as simple as possible. This is especially true if you are targeting a fairly popular blog or website. If you are sending the message via email, make it just a few paragraphs. Simply tell the website owner what your website is all about and why you would like to rent advertising space from him. Make sure to add some information as to why your business would be a good fit for the website's readers. Don't beat around the bush. Just go straight to the point.

- Be very clear about the types and sizes of ads that you want to display on the website. You should understand that ads are priced based on their sizes and where they are displayed on the website. The bigger the ad, the more expensive it becomes. If a website owner is interested in taking you in as an advertiser, that's when you start talking about ad sizes and ad locations.

- Make use of attention-grabbing headlines. This is one of the most effective strategies in online marketing. You have to create headlines that immediately grab the attention of readers. Again, you have to make it short and simple because most of the time you are working with very limited space. There's just not much that you can fit in a 300x300 advertisement, for example.

- Make use of call-to-action buttons. What are call-to-action buttons? These are the digital signifiers that instruct people to do something or follow up on something. For example, you come across an advertisement in a website that says "Click here", "Call now!" or "Subscribe now!". These are call-to-action buttons. They are effective in the sense that people tend to do things when they are reminded to do them. An advertisement that contains a "Buy now" call-to-action button performs better and generates more sales compared to an advertisement that contains no call-to-action buttons.

- Use a combination of textual, image-based, and video-based advertisements. It would be a mistake to focus on a single type of advertisement. It's not that difficult to create image-based and video-based ads these days. There are so many online tools and resources that you can use to create these types of ads. Textual advertisements are perfect for content-heavy websites. Image-based and video-based advertisements, on the other hand, tend to perform better when shown in image and video sites.

- Follow up on your sales pitches. Just because a person you messaged earlier doesn't respond to your proposal doesn't necessarily mean that he's not interested in your advertising offer. It always makes sense to send a follow-up email or message. Ask if he has read your earlier message and if he would still be interested in your proposal. When it comes to business proposals, it pays to be relentless with your pitches. Don't give up if you really want to rent advertising space on a website that's relevant to your dropshipping business.

- Track the performances of your ads. This is something that a lot of dropshippers often ignore and take for granted. Tracking and monitoring the results from your various ads allow you to determine which ads are working and which ads are a waste of money. Monitoring ad performance also provides you insights on how to improve your advertisements.

- Try A/B testing for your advertisements. This is a great way to determine what types of ads work and what doesn't work. This testing method involves creating two types of ads with intentional differences e.g. two ads with the exact same message but a different headline – used to test which headline is most effective. You then run the ads for a specific period of time. During the test run, you should track the ads and gather information with regards to clicks, views, conversion rates, etc. At the end of the testing period, you compare the statistics for both types of ads.

5. Start a Newsletter

Almost everyone these days have an email address. You need an email address to sign up with anything online. You need it to sign up with Facebook. You need it to be able to upload videos on YouTube. You need it to be able to send or receive money through PayPal. You need it in order to digitally transact with government agencies. And so on and so forth. Why am I saying this? Because I want you to know of the ubiquity of email messaging and realize how huge a market it is when it comes to online promotion. I want you to realize how effective a newsletter will be in reaching out to both your established and potential customers.

But what exactly is a newsletter? In the simplest of terms, it's a content-delivery model that involves sending content to subscribers through email. I'm sure that you have come across blogs or websites wherein you are asked to subscribe by entering your email address into a form. That is a perfect example of a newsletter. Most blogs and websites these days utilize a newsletter to stay in touch with current readers as well as to recruit new subscribers. You can use the same model to grow the customer base for your dropshipping business. This is especially true if your dropshipping business revolves around an interesting niche that often gets news and media coverage. Starting a newsletter allows you to update your customers and subscribers about these latest developments.

Starting a newsletter is not that difficult. If you are a skilled programmer, you can choose to build it from scratch. If you are not a programmer, don't worry because there are tools out there that can help you create a newsletter with ease. There are companies like Aweber and MailChimp that enable you to create and build a newsletter in just a few minutes. Integrating tools and programs like Aweber into your blog and website is also hassle-free. In most cases, it is just a matter of copying and pasting code.

Here are a few tips on how you can get the most out of your newsletter:

A. Provide valuable and informative content, not just sales pitches.

Receiving sales messages over and over again can be annoying as hell. We all know that and we have all experienced that. I understand that you are running a dropshipping business and that you want to sell to the people who have subscribed to your newsletter. But everything doesn't have to be about sales and money. There should be a balance between sales pitches and informative content in your newsletter. Always keep in mind that your subscribers can easily unsubscribe with just a click of the mouse button. To make sure that they don't do such a thing, you should send them informative content every now and then.

B. Don't overdo it.

For example, sending a message every day is overdoing it. You are not running a news business wherein you need to inform people about events every single day. Only send a message through your newsletter if it's important or if it's content that you think your subscribers will find informative or helpful. Put yourself in the shoes of your subscribers and ask yourself the question: "Is this something that can help me?" If the answer is yes, click on the "Send" button. If the answer is no, don't send it. Your subscribers are probably subscribed to countless other newsletters. You will only be clogging their inboxes if you send messages too often.

C. Be direct in your messaging.

As a lot of marketers often like to say, keep it simple, stupid (KISS). The attention span of online readers are so low that if you don't grab their attention within the first few seconds, you will lose them. They will click on the delete button and move on to the next message. Online users usually don't have the time to read through blocks of text. Looking at a long email message can be too intimidating to a lot of people. In short, getting the attention of your subscribers requires brevity. Don't write a two-paragraph message if you can get your point across in just a single paragraph. Don't write two sentences if you can make your point in just one sentence.

D. Use your newsletter as the announcement platform for discounts, promos, coupons, and other sales-related offers.

This strategy provides an incentive for people to remain subscribed to your newsletter. If they unsubscribe, then they will miss out on your future promos and rewards programs. In fact, if you have high quality products, your subscribers will be looking forward to receiving updates about promos and discounts.

E. Instruct your subscribers to add your newsletter address to their contacts list.

In a lot of cases, your messages especially if you are sending them through an automated platform like Aweber will be tagged as spam or unimportant by email providers. If your messages go straight to the spam folder, then less people will read them. This is why it's important that you inform them to add your address to their contacts list. This way, your messages won't get buried in the spam folder.

F. Make it as easy as possible for people to subscribe to your newsletter.

Make the subscription form very prominent on your website or blog. It should be one of the first things that visitors see when they land on your website. The best way to do this is to create a pop-up window which appears the moment your website finishes loading on a visitor's browser. Use a direct call-to-action in telling people to subscribe to your newsletter. Furthermore, you should ask for minimal details when asking people to subscribe. Just asking for people to input their email address is enough. If you start asking about their age, or their location, etc., these can turn them off and they end up not completing the subscription process.

G. Promote your newsletter in other online platforms you are using like social media sites.

If you have a sizable following on Facebook, it would make complete sense to tell them about your newsletter. Inform them that they will be receiving important updates about your business and products on their email inboxes. If they find you interesting, they will be more than willing to subscribe to your newsletter.

6. Email Marketing

This is very similar to starting a newsletter. Sending content to your customers via a newsletter is the most common form of email marketing. It would be redundant if I discuss this matter all over again. However, there are certain points that I would like to discuss with regards to email marketing that I haven't already discussed in the newsletter section. You see, email marketing is an industry in itself and newsletter marketing falls under it. Email marketing encompasses all marketing strategies that involve email.

Email marketing is a very powerful promotional technique. The trick lies on how good you are in building your email list. As the term implies, an email list is a list of contacts that you think will be interested in buying your products. There are various ways on how to build your email list. Starting a newsletter is one of these ways. Buying email lists from other people is also a good strategy. However, you have to be careful when purchasing email lists because scams are rampant here. You should only buy email lists from reputable sources.

Another great email marketing strategy is collaboration. What you do is collaborate with another online entrepreneur. There are various types of deals that you can enter into. You can rent the other entrepreneur's email list. You can cross-promote each other's businesses. That is you promote the entrepreneur's products in your own email list. He should do the same with his email list. This is a great way to reach out to new and potential customers. Not only do you see an increase in sales, you will also see an increase in the number of people subscribing to your email list.

7. Create a Lead Page

A lead page is basically a standalone website that serves as an entry point for another website. Before anything else, the term "lead page" is a broad term. It is most commonly used to describe a website that collects email addresses and other contact information of visitors. However, that is not the definition we are going to use in the context of dropshipping. In our case, a lead page is a website that you use to drive more traffic to your main dropshipping website. This means that the lead page is a marketing tool, nothing more and nothing less. You use it to attract traffic then redirect the traffic to your main dropshipping business website.

Your main goal in creating a lead page is to convince people why they should buy your products. In other words, it's a glorified sales pitch. You follow three simple steps when developing the content for the lead page. The first step is to remind visitors of the problems or issues they are having relevant to your products. For example, if you are selling weight loss products, you are going to talk about why being overweight is bad and how it can lead to a lot of diseases.

The second step in developing the content for your lead page is to offer a solution to the problems the visitors are dealing with. In our example, you are going to offer your weight loss products as the solution. This is where you go in-depth about the merits and benefits of your products. You put everything in there. This step is crucial because this is where visitors will make the decision of whether they are going to buy your product or not. You have to be convincing with your pitch.

The third and last step in developing content for your lead page is to write the call-to-action. You reminded visitors about their weight problems, you told them about your awesome weight loss products, now it's time to tell them to buy these products. This is where you redirect people to your main website where they can order and pay for the products. Just a simple linked button that says "Buy Here Now!" will do. Since the visitor is ready to buy, you just have to redirect him or her to the sales page.

To get the most out of lead pages, you should consider creating several of them. This strategy is effective if you are selling different products in your dropshipping website. Creating one lead page for each product category is something you should consider doing. Sure, it's going to take a lot of your time but it's worth it.

8. Collaborate with Online Influencers

Have you ever come across the term "influencer marketing"? If you haven't already, allow me to define it for you. It's basically an online marketing strategy that involves paying internet influencers to promote your product. An online influencer is anyone who has a sizable following or reputation on the internet. An online influencer could be anyone. It could be a make-up artist with thousands of subscribers on YouTube. It could be a video gamer with millions of followers on Twitch. It could be a fashion enthusiast with thousands of followers on Instagram. It could be a blogger whose blog attracts millions of hits a day.

In short, influencer marketing is the online version of celebrity endorsements. You simply pay online celebrities to endorse and help promote your products. For example, let's say that you run a dropshipping business that sells a line of makeup kits. You go to YouTube and look for channels that focus on makeup tutorials. You find the most popular ones and get in touch with the owners of the channels. Send them proposals informing them that you are going to pay them if they can use your products for their next makeup tutorials. Not all of them are going to respond but there are those who will be interested. You negotiate the deal and that's it. You send the products, the influencer uses these in their videos, and you pay them for their efforts. That's basically how influencer marketing works.

Influencer marketing is a great way to build your business and brand. Sure, it will cost you money but it's completely worth it if you deal with the right team of influencers. And it's the best strategy to reach your target customers. In our example, influencers in the makeup industry command the respect and attention of thousands of people who are genuinely interested in makeup products. If you own a business that sells makeup products, dealing with these influencers provides you with a direct line to your target customers.

9. Start a Blog

I'm sure that you have heard this before. And I'm going to say it again. If you want to market products online, you need to start a blog. Don't listen to people who downplay the importance of a blog. They will tell you that it's a waste of time. Well, I'm telling you that they are completely wrong. Blogging is a very powerful strategy if you play your cards right. Since you are going to blog in connection to your dropshipping business, there are two ways you can approach it. You can either host the blog within your business website or you can create a separate website using a different domain.

Personally, I would recommend the latter option for several reasons. First of all, if you are going to host the blog within your main website, it will often be very difficult to find. It can create clutter or even confusion. The reason I want you to create the blog as a completely separate entity is that it will be easier to manage. A separate website also offers flexibility and more control over the types of content that you publish. You can install plugins, widgets, and all sorts of tools without compromising your main business website.

As far as the content of the blog is concerned, you should solely focus on creating content that's related to your business and products. It's your own way of providing additional content for your customers. For example, you have a product that is too sophisticated that customers often don't know how to use it properly. Well, you can use your blog to write in-depth tutorials or guides on how such a product is used. You can write anything on your blog but always make sure that it's relevant to your business. If you sell beauty and health products then your blog should be about beauty and health as well. That's the content that your customers need so that's the type of content you are going to provide them.

10. Collaborate With Other Dropshippers

Collaborating with other dropshippers is all about cross-promotion. You collaborate with the hope that you get to promote each other's products. Hell, you can even collaborate with your competitors. Here's what you need to do. Look for dropshippers that are in the same niche as you. They should be selling products that are relevant to your own products. Write them a proposal letter informing them if they would be interested in collaborating with you. You tell them about your products and how these could be a good fit for their existing customers. The catch is that you will also promote their products to your own customers. It's a win-win situation for both parties so most entrepreneurs will find it hard to ignore the proposal.

So basically, you promote their products and in return they promote your products. How you promote each other's products depends on your negotiations. For example, you can promote each other's products on your respective websites. You can tap into each other's email lists or newsletters. You can offer discounts through a referral system. In short, there are various collaboration tactics you can choose from.

When collaborating with other dropshippers, make sure that you always deliver your end of the bargain. This creates trust and lasting business relationships that may benefit you in the long run. In the dropshipping industry, creating and nurturing connections is very important. A former collaborator might refer you to a supplier or manufacturer who can produce your products at much cheaper costs. Or you might get tips on how to drive your production costs down so that you can increase your profit margins. These are just a few of the benefits you can get by nurturing connections with other dropshippers.

Chapter Summary

I'm not going to lie. Promoting and marketing your dropshipping business is going to take a lot of your time, money, and resources. It comes with the territory. However, I have to remind you that although these are costs, they are also investments. The time, money, and resources you spend on your dropshipping business are investments that will return to you as rewards down the road. This is the kind of mentality you should cultivate. If you treat costs as irredeemable expenses, then you are doing it wrong.

Conclusion

Before anything else, I would like to congratulate you for reading this book up to this point. That only shows that you are truly serious in pursuing opportunities that will earn you sustainable passive income. Being serious about it is a good start. It also prepares you in developing the right mindset. As I've mentioned in the beginning of this book, having the right mindset is *crucial* to your success. Most of the people who fail in this journey do so because they didn't have the right mental approach. They were lazy. They got discouraged too easily. They didn't have patience. If you truly read this book and follow it up by implementing the tips and strategies discussed within, I am confident that you are going to reach your passive income goals.

Before anything else, I would like to congratulate you for getting this far. The fact that you made it to this page means that you are truly serious in starting and building a successful dropshipping business. You have put your mind into it and you are ready to go for it. Here's the good news. If you've read and understood every chapter in this book, then you have all the knowledge you need to be successful in the dropshipping industry. That is not an exaggeration. You just have to implement everything that you've read here and you will be on your way towards success.

Of course, there is no *guarantee* that you are going to be successful. I'm lying to you if I'm going to claim that you are going to achieve success 100%. That's not what I'm telling you in this book. My main intention in writing this book was to provide you with the knowledge you need to dramatically increase your odds of achieving success in the industry. What you do with this knowledge is up to you. Think of this book as a guide, a mentor, or let's just say a reference book. It helps you get things done. It helps you nurture the right business mindset. It helps you decide on which directions to take. It helps you weigh your options. I wrote the book to guide you towards success not to hand over to you on a silver platter.

As I've said numerous times in this book, running a dropshipping business seems simple but in reality, it can be challenging. There are so many gears going on at the same time and you have to manage every single one of these gears. I'm not saying this to discourage you. I'm saying it to make sure that you know what to expect. I need you to be realistic about your goals and be practical about your plans in achieving them. Going in with the wrong assumptions and unrealistic expectations will most likely set you up to a disastrous start. Getting started the right way requires that you know what to expect and that you are aware of the risks.

Another very important point I need to remind you about is that it takes time to build a successful dropshipping business. Don't buy into the myth that dropshipping is your ticket to fast cash and instant riches. There is no such thing. You could get lucky and earn a lot early but that's very unlikely. Your best chance in becoming successful is to work harder and smarter and focus on building the business with a long-term plan. Don't fall into the trap of rushing things. Rushing doesn't fast-track you to success. In fact, it usually sets you up for failure.

Now, before you go out there and start building your dropshipping business, I have one last piece of advice to give you. DON'T GIVE UP AT THE FIRST SIGN OF FAILURE. In most cases, the difference between failed dropshippers and successful dropshippers is that the latter persevered while the former gave up at the first sign of trouble. Most dropshippers make almost zero profits on their first weeks or months. They lose money. Their websites get inundated with error after error. Their suppliers bail out on them.

There's a good chance that these will happen to you. But you shouldn't let these deter your ultimate goal of building a successful and profitable online business. Learn from these mistakes and failures and just keep moving on. There's a positive side to these mistakes and failures. They'll teach you not to make the same mistakes again. As you learn more lessons and gain tons of experience, you'll get better in running the business. It gets better and better from this point on.

That's it. If you've read the entirety of this book, you're ready to play the dropshipping game. Good luck with your journey and I can't wait to hear about your success story down the road. To success, cheers!

Facebook Advertising

Learn How To Make

$10,000+ Each Month With

Facebook Marketing

By

Michael Ezeanaka

www.MichaelEzeanaka.com

Introduction II

Social media, no doubt, changed the business landscape. People now leverage social media sites like Facebook, Instagram etc. to sell and promote their products and services. Marketing is no longer confined to face-to-face conversations.

Advertising on Facebook and other social media platforms has become the most practical (and arguably cost effective) way of promoting one's brand. Even big companies have recognized the importance of having an online presence.

In this book, you'll discover:

- What the Facebook Advertising platform has to offer your business and why you need to get on board today (Chapter 1)
- A concise overview of more than 10 incredible Facebook features including one that allow you to interact with potential customers without sending them a private message or email alert! (Chapter 2)
- How to open a secure Business Page using two-layer permission model that allows you to securely maintain and manage your Pages, Ad Accounts and Catalogs. (**Chapter 3**)
- How to leverage the Facebook Ads Manager to create highly optimized and profitable Facebook Ads (Chapter 4)
- How to monitor specific actions potential customers take while on your website and, more importantly, how to use the Facebook Pixel to retarget those same people on Facebook (Chapter 5)
- How to create a highly effective customer avatar that will boost your conversion rates while keeping ad costs extremely low (Chapter 6)
- The A-to-Z of a Facebook Ad Campaign including how to choose the right objective for your ad, add payment methods, set suitable budgets etc. (Chapter 7)
- How to set up a highly converting sales funnel, incorporate the sales funnels with Facebook, create a lead magnet and build your email list (Chapter 8)

And much, much more!

More importantly, a case study is presented at the very end of this book. This case study will bring together all the concepts discussed and show you exactly how you can leverage the skills and knowledge you'll gain from this book to **make $10,000+ each month with Facebook Advertising**.

It is my sincere hope that what you'll discover in this book will equip you with the skills and knowledge you need to take your business or brand to the next level.

Finally, the screenshots used in this book have been made as large as possible to enhance readability. However, if you find any of it not to be large enough, don't worry. I have created an image booklet that contains an enlarged version of *all the images* used in this book. Click here to download the booklet

Without further ado, let's get started!

Chapter 1

Social Media Marketing

Communication is a basic human need. It is just as important to individuals in their personal lives as it is to marketers and entrepreneurs in their businesses. Because of social media, constant interaction has become a major way of life. Social media has indeed simplified communication and with it, opportunities have been created for marketers to reach their target audiences.

Among all the social media platforms, there seems to be one clear winner not just in terms of the number of active users but more importantly, the excellent tools and options it is able to provide for businesses.

Is Facebook advertising worth jumping into? Let's find out as we explore some of the most known benefits and possible drawbacks of using this social media platform for your advertising requirements.

Advantages of Using Facebook as a Marketing Platform

Reach a wide audience

Facebook undoubtedly has the greatest number of active users among all social media platforms. It is unbeatable when it comes to sheer size and number. And, more importantly, these are active users, ready to engage and interact using the platform.

Excellent targeting options

Facebook makes a lot of targeting tools available that allow marketers to reach the right audience. For a marketer, this reduces your chance of wasting a lot of money reaching the wrong people.

Low cost

With Facebook, you can advertise for as little as $5 or even $1 a day. And because of the targeting options, you have a better chance of getting the most value per dollar spent.

Customer loyalty

Facebook allows marketers not only to reach more people and increase awareness. It also provides them an avenue to keep their existing customers engaged in order to build loyalty and long-term profitable relationships.

Flexibility

There are plenty of ad formats available from single image ads to video ads. Advertisers can also use a carousel of images or tell stories about their brand. The possibilities are virtually endless with all the tools at your disposal.

Easy to Use

For the most part, it does not take a rocket scientist to figure out Facebook advertising. Admittedly, it does take some getting used to initially but Facebook provides all the necessary tools and information to assist marketers in navigating the features.

Innovation

The number one reason why this platform has stood the test of time and keeps getting stronger is innovation. The Facebook team constantly comes up with new ways to improve user experience. They also continuously develop new tools that make advertising on Facebook intuitive, easier and much more attractive.

Possible Issues with Facebook Advertising

Lesser organic views

Facebook has changed the algorithm so that brand message visibility is limited. This means that among a fan base, only 8% may be able to view your posts. While this is disappointing for marketers, it's actually a good decision that can be very beneficial in the long run.

What Facebook is trying to do is maintain the *social* aspect of the platform. This is what makes people keep on using Facebook to document their everyday lives, interact with friends near or far, get information from their feeds, etc.

Cost is an issue

Although the minimum cost of Facebook advertising isn't significant, cost can still be an issue for advertisers with a very limited budget. The good news is there are other ways to reach campaign objectives with free tools. Although it will take much more time and more effort, it is worth considering and integrating with paid promotions in order to achieve the best possible return on your investment.

Requires commitment

As with other social media marketing tools, Facebook advertising requires commitment and a lot of effort. Although Facebook provides the platform and the tools to allow you to market and promote effectively, how you leverage these resources at your disposal is entirely up to you. You have to put in effort to learn. This book will help you achieve that objective.

29 Incredible Reasons to Use Facebook Advertising

As you probably already know, Facebook is an incredible social media platform. At the same time, it has paved the way to the success of many business startups. The wide variety of tools made available to marketers and business owners make it possible to reach new customers, engage them to build and maintain a lasting relationship. The best part (and a lot of people aren't aware of this) is a lot of these tools are free.

Ranging from the custom audiences to lookalike audiences, the Facebook marketing tools offer plenty of features and options to connect with a vast network of audiences. Here is a list of Facebook tools and features for businesses.

1. Facebook Page

Packed with features such as Messenger chat and appointment scheduling, Pages is a great way for businesses to connect with potential customers. It can be used for showcasing products and services. Customers can also rate and add reviews about the business. The call-to-action buttons are great for inciting a positive response.

2. Page Insights

This analytics tool is valuable for businesses that signed up with Pages. It tracks and analyzes responses from customers including number of likes. Business owners and marketers can also see exactly where those likes are coming from. Data like content reach, daily post breakdown and visitor demographic profile among others are monitored. It can also tell you which particular sections of your Page people are actually responding to.

3. Pages Manager App

This app allows you to manage and monitor activity on multiple Pages via mobile. You can post updates instantly, as well as, respond to messages and comments. Through this app, latest updates on Page Insights are also much more accessible. The app is available on iOS and Android.

4. Messenger

This is a free app for texting and video calling. It also allows users to send payments. The platform has undergone many iterations and improvements that have proved useful for businesses. Among those updates include Messenger Links to Pages and Messenger codes that can be used for scanning. It also lets businesses create customized notes sent automatically to users who try to connect with them.

5. Canvas

Quality content is important in engaging customers. Canvas makes this possible. Through this free tool, still images can be combined with videos to create interactive content. In addition, Call to action buttons can also be incorporated. Multimedia ads produced with this tool can be opened to full screen when users click on the ads.

6. Power Editor

This is an excellent tool that advertisers can use for controlling ads, campaigns and ad sets. Multiple ads can be edited through the Power Editor and this can be used across campaigns.

7. Ad Creation Tool

This tool can be used for something more than producing ads. It also lets advertisers control which audiences to show the ads according to age, location, interests and other factors. A Facebook ad for instance, can be used to provide store directions. It can also direct a user to download an app, check out videos, add items to cart or any other action on the advertiser's website.

8. Ads Manager

Creating ads is just the first part. Ads Manager allows you not only to manage ads but also to measure its effectiveness. You can check on the performance of each ad or monitor ad sets (i.e. multiple ads grouped together). You also get access to campaign tools like campaign media, audience insights and custom audiences. For large campaigns, you can use the Power Editor.

9. Page Post Engagement Ads

If you want to make sure that more people see, like, comment and share the content on your Page, this is the right tool to achieve those goals. You can create an ad, pick your objective to "boost your posts" and then choose Page Post Engagement. Select the Page and choose which post you want to boost. This Facebook tool also allows you to include website address and send it to people. You can even use a conversion pixel that will allow you to monitor the results.

10. Page Like Ads

This is an incredible tool you can use to boost awareness of your Page. To use it, create the ad, choose **Page Likes** from the ad tool, select the Page you want to promote and begin building awareness of that particular page.

11. Clicks to Website Ads

Driving traffic is one of the most important aspects of marketing. You can use this tool to send more people to your business website through an ad. Upon creating the ad, choose Clicks to Website and add the website address where you want to send traffic. It could be your website homepage, your online store, or a product page.

12. App Installs and App Engagement Ads

If you have an app, this is one of the best ways to promote it. You can use it to drive awareness and encourage people to install your app. Create an ad specifically for your app and through the App Engagement tool, you can link the ad to specific areas of the app from the registration page itself to the online store where visitors can get more information about the app and make a purchase. As the ad makes an appearance on News Feeds of your target audience, you provide them with an easy avenue leading to the app you're promoting.

13. Event Response Ads

Facebook changes the way you promote ads. Instead of creating an invite to your event as an ad, you can use this tool to get users to add your event directly to their Facebook calendar. Once added, they can receive reminders pertaining to your event. You can then monitor the number of people who have responded to the event.

14. Offer Claim Ads

Creating an offer or a promotion through special deals or discounts is a great way to get people's attention. You can do this more effectively with Offer Claim tool. With this feature, you can set the duration of the offer, choose the audience and select the number of people who can make a claim to the offer. To use this feature, create your promo ad and set your campaign objective as "get people to claim your offer" and then select Offer Claims.

15. Video Views

Video ads can be more engaging for the viewers. The challenge is to create memorable ones. This tool proves helpful in this matter. First, create your video ad and set your campaign objective to "get video views." Upload the video and carefully select an eye-catching thumbnail. This is the first thing people see even before they get to view the ads. It's an important part of creating an excellent teaser.

16. Local Awareness Ads

For a more targeted post, this tool allows you to select your locality as well as set the age and gender of the target customers you would like to reach. All that's left to do to start sending these potential customers to your business is to add the Get Directions button.

17. Slideshow Ads

This is a feature that allows you to easily produce video ads and edit them. Because slideshows are generally lighter using less data, they can load faster which makes them more accessible to users. It is an important consideration when users are mobile and connected with low bandwidth.

18. Carousel Ads

Creating a story around multiple products can even be more effective. The Carousel makes this possible. It also allows you to showcase multiple products using one ad. You can take advantage of this feature by introducing the products at various angles and providing important details. To use this tool, choose multiple images in one ad when prompted to select how you prefer your ad to appear.

19. Dynamic Ads

People who have visited your website or Page, checked out your posts, dropped by your Instagram have already shown interest. Dynamic Ads tool allows you to retarget them by presenting these users with relevant products.

There are some prerequisites to start using this feature and they are as follows:

- A product catalog,
- A Business Manager account, and
- Facebook Pixel.

Once you launch Dynamic Ads, you can promote your business on Instagram and Facebook, as well as, use Audience Network to showcase your products exactly where potential customers are spending most of their time.

20. Lead Ads

Facebook has made it easier for users to sign up and get information from various businesses in the form of quotes, special offers and newsletters. This is what Lead Ads are all about. Through this feature, you can build contact forms within your ads with pre-populated contact info including email addresses. This will allow you to follow up on leads more efficiently.

21. Canvas Ads

The Canvas app lets you create multimedia adds combining still images with videos and finishing it up with a call-to-action button. It is a more interactive way of showcasing your products. With it, users can run through carousel of images, view them from various angles and zoom in on them to access the details.

22. Instagram Ads

Instagram has more than 500 million active users. It's a little on the short side compared to the number of Facebook users but a combination of these two in your marketing plan can prove to be highly effective. If you use Instagram, you can manage them using the Power Editor and Ads Manager of Facebook.

23. Business Manager

Security and control are among the things that business owners are concerned about. With Business Manager, you can easily manage your Facebook assets from your Pages to your ad accounts. It puts all these things together (in one place) and the best part is, it doesn't cost anything to set up!

24. Facebook Pixel

One of the most exciting features of Facebook advertising is the Pixel. It is essentially a piece of code embedded on your website which will allow you to build your audience for all your ad campaigns, measure and optimize them. Basically, when a user pays your website a visit, clicks on something or take any kind of action, Pixel records and reports this to you.

In addition, the pixel will try to find and match the action to a Facebook user. In this case, you will not only know that someone went to your website, you will also find out if the user took such action as a response to your Facebook ad. You can then choose to retarget this user using Custom Audience.

25. Hashtags

Phrases and topics can become clickable links on posts either on your Page or timeline. Hashtags make this possible. It will then allow users to locate posts according to your topics of interest.

26. Custom Audiences

Custom Audience can be created to run ads specifically targeted to users you know of. You can start doing this by uploading contacts from a data file or email list. You can either copy and paste them or import those contacts straight from MailChimp, Aweber etc. Assign a name and set a description for your Custom Audience. To run ads for them, choose the Audience field and select the name you created for the Custom Audience.

27. Lookalike Audiences

If you want to grow your customer base, you can use this tool to find more Facebook users that match the traits of your current customers using pieces of information like age, job role, location, gender and interests. To use this feature, proceed to the Ads Manager and choose Audiences. Click on the Create Audience button and select Lookalike Audience. From the Source field, choose the Page, Custom Audience you want to manage and the conversion-tracking pixel.

28. Audience Network

This is a good tool for monetizing mobile apps and websites. It's basically a network of publisher-owned apps and sites where you can show your ads. People spend a lot of their time on Facebook and Instagram. But they are also spending time on other apps and sites.

Audience Network helps advertisers reach more of the people they care about in the other places where they're spending their time. With Audience Network, you can choose from various formats including banner, standard interstitial and custom native units for video and display. Furthermore, Audience Network ads use the same targeting, auction, delivery and measurement systems as Facebook ads.

29. Facebook Blueprint

Facebook offers a variety of avenue for you to promote your business and reach customers. You can learn more about what tools you can use and how to boost your results further by using the Facebook Blueprint. From this, you can select courses and customize your training according to your business objectives.

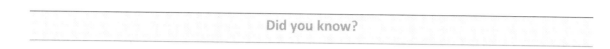

Did you know?

Video will be more important for social media content marketing than ever. According to Smart Insights, 90 percent of all content shared by users on social media in 2017 was video!

Chapter 1 Quiz
Please refer to the Answer Booklet for the solution to this quiz

1. Which analytics tool monitors visitor demographic profile, daily post breakdowns and content reach?

   A) Canvas
   B) Page Insights
   C) Ads Manager
   D) Pixel

2. Which Facebook feature allows you to widen your reach by matching the traits of your current customers or visitors?

   A) Custom Audiences
   B) Lookalike Audiences
   C) Audience Network
   D) Interest Lists

3. Which tool helps ensure that you're delivering the right message to the appropriate audience?

   A) Pixel
   B) Ads Manager
   C) Ad Relevance
   D) Facebook History

4. Facebook offers a variety of avenue for you to promote your business and reach customers. However, you can learn more about what tools you can use and how to boost your results further by using this Facebook feature?

   A) Facebook Blueprint
   B) Facebook Help
   C) Facebook Guide
   D) Facebook Tutorial

5. What are the available formats you can use with Audience Network?

   A) Banner
   B) Standard Interstitial
   C) Custom native units for video and display
   D) Click links

6. Which tool can help you create a quality image for your profile photo and cover photo

    A) Facebook Pixel

    B) Canvas

    C) Hashtags

    D) Canva

7. With this tool, you can manage and monitor activity on multiple Pages on mobile. You can also post updates instantly and respond to messages and comments immediately.

    A) Multi-Page app

    B) Pages Control app

    C) Pages Manager app

    D) Pages Monitoring app

8. This is an excellent tool that advertisers can use for controlling ads, campaigns and ad sets. Multiple ads can be edited through this tool, which can be used across campaigns.

    A) Canvas

    B) Edit Tools

    C) Power Tools

    D) Power Editor

9. This tool allows you not only to manage ads but also to measure its effectiveness. You can check on the performance of each ad or monitor ad sets.

    A) Power Editor

    B) Ad Creation Tool

    C) Ads Manager

    D) Business Page

10. You can use this tool to send people to your business website through an ad. Upon creating the ad, choose this feature and add the website address where you want to send traffic.

    A) Reach

    B) Traffic

    C) Page Like Ads

    D) Clicks to Website Ads

Chapter 2

Facebook Advertising

There are standard Facebook features that most advertisers rely on. Although the tools mentioned in the previous chapter can do wonders for your business goals, there are actually other features that most take for granted. Are you merely scratching the surface with the tactic you're currently using? You probably are if you're not using the tools you're about to see.

You may not have heard about some of them or you're familiar with them but just don't see their great potential yet. Before we go into detail, here's a quick overview.

- For content curation, use Save for Later and Interest Lists features.
- For page management, use Tagging, Pinning, Post Attribution and Filtering.
- For ads management, use Ad Notification, Email Manager and Ad Relevance.
- For competitive advantage, use your competition's top posts and Facebook history.

No, lets talk more about these features.

1. Save for Later

This Save feature can be used for saving music, TV, movies, places and links. There are too many link posts that appear on your news feed on a daily basis. It's quite difficult to keep up with them.

How does this feature help your business? For one, the saved content can help you come up with more relevant content for your target audience. You may find some interesting ones that you can either reuse or rehash. Two, it can also get you more Likes. To save a link, choose a post and go to the arrow at the top right corner. Click on the arrow and select "Save for Later."

2. Interest Lists

This is a feature that will help you be in full control by staying organized. Keeping up with updates, news and info can be challenging if you're working on multiple projects. Interest Lists make it simpler to cope. With this feature, you don't have to go through the task of finding the best Pages whenever you need to. You get them in one place, your Interest Lists. You can create your list according to the following.

- By Interests such as books, movies, sports, outdoors, etc.
- By Medium, i.e., citizen journalism or traditional journalism
- By Industry like consumer goods, aerospace, advertising, etc.
- By City/ State/ Country/ Region

3. Tagging

Tagging is not just for photos among friends, you can also tag users on your Page. It's a great way of interacting with potential customers. You can use the tagging feature instead of sending a private message or an email to alert them. You can also tag an influencer when you share their content. Tagging also works for notifying winners when you're running a promotion.

To tag personal profiles of customers on your Facebook Page, follow the steps below:

- Create a post on your Page.
- View the post and look for the downward-facing arrow at the top right corner.
- Click the arrow and choose Edit Post from the dropdown menu.
- In the textbox, type @ followed by the user's name. Facebook will automatically offer suggestions. If you find the user's name from the list of suggestions, click it. If the user's profile doesn't appear, try typing in the full name.
- Click on Done Editing. This will automatically send a notification to the user.

4. Pinning

To boost visibility, you can pin some posts and keep them at the top portion of your timeline. If you want to drive attention to a particular post, pinning it to the top will ensure better visibility. Follow these steps to start using the pinning feature.

- Go to the post and click on the downward-facing arrow from the top right corner.
- Choose Pin to Top from the dropdown menu.

5. Manage your Fan List.

After Facebook updated user interface for Pages, you can still access and manage your fan list. This will allow you to eliminate fake accounts and pay more attention to the genuine active ones. Follow these steps to access your fan list and weed out the fakes.

- Access your Page Settings.
- Choose Banned Users from the left sidebar.
- Select Banned from the menu.
- Click People Who Like This from the dropdown.

6. Post Attribution

To maintain transparency and credibility, make sure you post on your page with the correct identity. You can do this using the Post Attribution settings. For instance, when you use mobile, set the Post Attribution to your Personal Profile. And when you're on your desktop, set Post Attribution to your Page. To make these changes, follow the steps below:

- Access Post Attribution by going to the Page Settings.

- From the left sidebar, choose Post Attribution and click your preferred identity.

7. Filtering

Manage your post through the filtering feature. It will help you save valuable time. For instance, if you want to access your previous posts, it can take a lot of time to go through your Page. However, if you filter them by type, you will find it easier to find anything you have posted before. To do this, click on the Activity Log found on the left sidebar and select the post type. Page Posts can be filtered using the following categories.

- Offers
- Events
- Notes
- Questions
- Posts by others
- Your posts
- Comments
- Posts marked as spam
- Video posts
- Image Post

8. Ad Notification and Email Manager

Getting a barrage of emails from Facebook for every approved ad, rejected ad, scheduled ad report and the like can be quite a work to go through. But do you know that you can reduce the clutter in your inbox? You can do this by following these steps.

- Proceed to the Ads Manager and choose Settings from the left sidebar to access Ad account settings.
- Go to the Emails Notification section and scroll down.
- Only select the notifications you want to receive.

Find what is necessary for you. For instance, you may still want to be notified about rejected ads so you can quickly address the issue.

9. Ad Relevance

As the name implies, this ad analytic tool measures your ad's relevance and awards a score (from 1 to 10) – the higher the score, the more relevant your ad is. It helps ensure that you're delivering the right message to the appropriate audience. This will let you know if you're ads are under-performing, so you can make the necessary improvements to meet your Return on Investment (ROI) goals.

The relevance score allows you to make a pilot test for your new ads even before you set your budget. If the pilot ad receives 500 impressions, your relevance score is measured and reported to you. Relevance scores also reduce your cost of getting through to your target audience especially in the long run.

To check if you can access the tool, you can follow these steps.

- Proceed to the Ads Manager.
- From the left sidebar, choose Campaigns.
- Click on the name of your campaign and proceed to the ad set.
- Check the fifth column from the right side.

10. Check out top posts from your competitors.

This isn't exactly a tool, but Facebook allows you to get a glimpse of your competition. You can do this within Facebook Insights. Follow these steps.

- Click on Posts tab.
- Choose Top Posts from Pages You Watch.

11. Access Facebook History

Keeping track of your Page's history allows you to review all the posts, videos and images you have shared. By doing so, you also access chat conversations and messages. It will also allow you to review all of your clicked ads, access facial recognition data and check out past information you have shared in your About section.

After downloading your Facebook history, you will get to re-access all the information Facebook has saved for you. Essentially, it will further extend options for your demographic target. After all, there's more to people than just their age and gender.

To download your Facebook history, follow these steps.

- Go to Settings.
- Choose **Download a copy** and **Download Facebook History**.
- You will then get an email that will let you know when you can download your archive.

When used effectively, these Facebook tools can get you more Likes, save time and significantly improve your ROI. There are however, a couple of things you should take note of. Your ads will have to go through the Facebook Ad Review Process. That said, you have to make sure you follow their advertising policies. This is what we will look further into the next section.

Creating a Facebook Page

You've caught a glimpse of the most powerful Facebook features you can use to boost your business. Among the biggest and most essential ones is a business page. Now we look at the benefits of having one.

Why do you need a Facebook Page?

In today's world, a Facebook page is essential for organizations and businesses looking to grow their online presence and reach. Below you will find the top reasons why you need one too.

Connect with your target customers.

A Facebook Page is one of the best ways to connect with your audience. It's like having a focus group that you don't necessarily have to pay for. Your audience will be expecting useful information and that's what you have to deliver. At the same time, you also get to collect useful information from your audience like their needs, pain points, expectations etc.

With the help of Facebook Insights, you get to *mine* more usable data about how they use your page and interact with your content. By interaction, feedback, and comments, they can tell you exactly what they want. You provide them an avenue to directly engage with your brand.

Through Facebook Page, you can humanize your business.

Genuine social connections are what social media is all about. With a Facebook Page, you give your business a name, a face, and a personality that people will be able to relate to. You get to represent your business but also initiate non-business interaction.

You can build a community.

In a Page, existing customers and potential customers can give reviews, testimonials and feedback. You allow them to share their opinions and voice any concerns they may have. And you can immediately address them. Building a community around your brand through a Facebook Page isn't rocket science. You can do it in many ways including the following.

- Post relevant, useful, and interesting links to articles, videos etc.
- Initiate conversations by asking your fans for comments, opinions etc
- Encourage them to participate through promotions, giveaways and contests
- Set a section for them to leave feedback and reviews
- Provide incentive for staying active on your Page (i.e. most active member award, recognition, gift cards etc.)

It's a great way to attract new customers and build a relationship with them. If you are successful in bringing them together, you can count on a loyal following that you can keep on growing and nurturing.

You can also use your Facebook Page for Search Engine Optimization or SEO.

Creating a page isn't just a venue for you to drive traffic to your blog and website. SEO is a longer-term advertising strategy that you can maximize through your Page. Your links, posts and activities published on the Page are all indexed in search engines like Google. It can contribute to your SEO efforts and attract more traffic to your business. To achieve your SEO goals, make sure to fill your Page with rich and relevant content. These things will help improve your search engine rankings.

Make your business accessible to customers and clients every single day.

Most people log in to Facebook every day and plug in to their favorite Pages. This means it is crucial for you to regularly update your status, share videos and links as well as other pieces of valuable information. It will strengthen your connection with your customers.

To date, Facebook has over 2.2 billion active users and the number is steadily growing. There are also an increasing number of users that use Facebook to search for brands, products and services. Your presence in the platform makes it easier for them to find you. When they find you and connect with you, they are more likely to stick with you. When you manage to keep them interested and satisfied, they'd be more than happy to remain loyal and even share their connections with you.

Your competition has one.

Why should you create a Facebook Page to represent your business? Why not when your competition has one? Absence in social media leads you to miss out on opportunities. If your competitors have one and you don't, then they have a significant edge over you.

A Facebook Page is one of the most powerful and effective ways to broaden your reach. It is also a cost efficient way to increase awareness of your business. Most importantly, it allows you to build a genuine connection with your current customers, your potential customers and your fans.

How to Create a Facebook Page for Your Business?

This Page will be attached to your Facebook personal profile. It is a separate entity, it works with an independent presence and can be used effectively to promote your brand, business or any cause. There are many features available to a Page that are not accessible to personal profiles. Among them are post scheduling, advertising and analytics. To get started, here's how to create your business Page.

1. Go to your personal profile.

To begin, you have to log in to your personal Facebook profile. Once you're logged in, proceed by clicking on the **Create** button, which you will find next to your name and the **Home** button. In the window that appears, choose **Page**.

2. Enter your business information.

After clicking on Page, you will be prompted to choose between **Business or Brand** and a **Community or Public Figure**. Choose *Get Started* under Business or Brand.

You will then have to fill in the following information.

- Page Name
- Category
- Address (Street Address, City, State and Zip Code)
- Phone Number

You will be given a choice not to show the address. If you choose to tick the box, Facebook will only show that your business is within the city, state region.

3. Upload a profile picture and cover photo.

The next step is to add a profile picture that represents your business well.

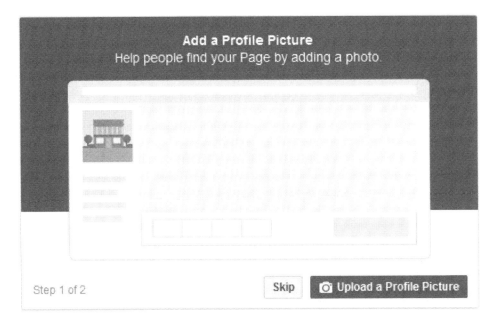

An attractive image can draw attention to your page. Consider using a product photo. For instance, if you're running a restaurant, adding a delicious looking dish from your menu may be a good idea. If you're promoting a beauty salon, try using a fabulous hairstyle. Another idea is to use your business logo or any image that customers can easily associate with the business like a storefront or street sign.

The same applies for the cover photo. It has to represent the business but also be of great quality, as well as, visually appealing. To look the best, it has to be 828 by 315 pixels. Canva is one of the resources you can use for this. It allows you to create a quality image with the right dimensions. When choosing the image either for your profile picture or the cover photo, you should keep the following rules in mind.

- Pick something visually appealing.
- It should represent your business.
- It must be a high-resolution image. A profile photo should be at least 170 by 170 pixels. A cover photo should be at least 828 by 315 pixels.

Don't skimp on the images. If you have the budget, hire a photographer for product shots. You can outsource the job on websites like Fiverr or Upwork.

4. Complete your business details.

When you're done with all the steps above, Facebook will offer you tips on how to maximize the potential of newly created business page. While a visually appealing profile picture and cover photo can paint a thousand words, it is still essential that you complete the details and provide as much information as possible in order to bring life to your page.

Short Description - Tell your target audience what you are all about. This is your opportunity to humanize your brand or business. Write a quality description with smart use of keywords relevant to your industry/niche.

Keep it short and concise. As much as possible, do not exceed one to two sentences. You can describe your page's or business' focus.

Business Hours - Let your potential customers know your store opening hours.

Username – Your chosen username will be attached to your Facebook URL (facebook.com/username). Because of this, you should choose an easy and memorable one. This will help people find your page effortlessly.

Website Link – If you have one, do not forget to add your website URL. Get attention from potential customers through Facebook and drive them to your website.

Create a Group – This is definitely something you should consider. Create a section for your audience to connect with each other. It will give them a chance to talk about your business, your products and services. We will talk about this further in the next section.

5. Add call to action buttons.

If you look at the upper right hand corner of the Page, you will find the option to Add a Button. Take advantage of the traffic you're getting to prompt visitors into taking action and get the results you hope to achieve e.g. visit your website, visit your online e-commerce store etc.

Book Service - There are two options for buttons here. *Book Now* is ideal for traveling agencies, hotel or B&B's. The second button is *Start Order* which is appropriate for businesses in the food industry or any business offering products.

Get In Touch - The following five button options will direct them to various points of contact you make available.

> **Call Now** - Let people call you without memorizing a number.

> **Sign Up** or **Contact Us** - These buttons will direct users to your website and a form for their details. It's best for subscription capture and lead generation.

> **Send Message** - This allows users to send you a private message through your page.

> **Send Email** - For lengthy messages, customers can use this button to use email from the Page itself.

Learn More - Use this button to provide more information about an offer, a product or service or anything about your brand or business. There's also an option to Watch Video for people who want to see a full video post on Facebook itself or viewed from your website.

Make a Purchase or Donation - You can use this button to take them to your product page. Link it to your website. One click can take them where they need to be and purchase products or avail themselves of your services.

Download App or Game - This is best used if you're promoting or using an app to improve user experience. The Play Game button can also make your Page more interactive.

You have several options. Feel free to explore them all before you decide which is best for your business.

6. Adjust privacy and security settings.

Whether or not you're getting help in managing your business page, it's incredibly important to ensure the security of your Page. We'll look into the different settings you can customize.

General Settings

This is where you control your page. You can access the General Settings page by clicking on *Settings* located at the top right corner above the Page cover picture and next to *Help*. It should contain the below information:

Shortcuts	Page is pinned to shortcut	Edit
Page Visibility	Page Published	Edit
Visitor Posts	Anyone can publish to the page	Edit
News Feed Audience and Visibility for Posts	The ability to narrow the potential audience for News Feed and limit visibility on your	Edit

	posts is turned off	
Messages	People can contact my Page privately	Edit
Tagging People	Only people who help manage my page can tab photos posted on it	Edit
Others Tagging this Page	People and other Pages can tag my Page	Edit

There are a couple of essential things you must do on this page and they include the following.

Shortcuts

This is about saving time by pinning your page to shortcuts section. One click from your personal profile will take you directly to the business page.

Visitor Posts

In this section, you can allow your visitors to post, add photos or publish videos to the page. At the same time, you can review the content first to make sure no inappropriate content goes through. To do this, tick the box for reviewing the posts made by others. This will give you a chance to either approve or disapprove posts before they get published.

Messages

You have to make sure that visitors are allowed to send you messages through Messenger. In fact, you should encourage them to. You can get started by checking the box for Messages.

Others Tagging This Page

Allowing individuals and businesses to share and tag the page can further expand your audience. Tick the box to allow it.

Age Restriction

If you're selling or promoting age-sensitive products like tobacco and alcohol, it is necessary to prevent minors from accessing your page.

Page Moderation and Profanity Filter

If it's important for you to keep things clean, it would be wise to edit these settings. Blocking comments containing words you may consider offensive or inappropriate will help you control published content. Do this by adding words on the prohibited section.

Similar Page Suggestions

By ticking this box, you allow the system to include your page in results of relevant searches. For instance, if you have a pet grooming business and a user searches for pet products, your page will appear as a relevant search.

Page Updates

Whenever you change or update any information from your page like a phone number or description, the system can send out notifications. It's also possible to stop Facebook from publishing those updates.

Post in Multiple Languages

If you're catering to non-English speaking audiences, you can make your page multi-lingual. This will make your page and posts appear to visitors in their local language.

Comment Ranking

Comments can be ranked so that the most recent ones or the most relevant ones appear at the top. Use this setting to indicate your preference according to what will be more beneficial to your business or brand.

Content Distribution

Your page's followers can download published videos. You can allow it or restrict it by editing this section.

Messaging Settings

When traffic volume on your page increases, it can become more challenging to manage. This is the best time to start thinking about automation.

A Response Assistant is useful in delivering automated responses to queries or any messages you receive through your page at least until you are able to respond to them. You can even customize the response to mention the name of the user who sent the message. With auto-response, you can let the sender know that the message has been received and you'll be responding yourself soon.

Page Settings

Even though Facebook Pages come with a set of tabs in default order, you can actually customize it. Pay particular attention to the tabs under the profile photo. Open to edit the settings and customize the order by clicking and dragging the tabs in the sequence you prefer. For instance, if you want to focus your strategy on videos, put that tab first.

Notification Settings

You get notified every time an activity occurs on the page. You can adjust the notification settings so you can receive them as they happen or schedule them every day. Moreover, you can choose the type of activities you want to be notified. For instance, would you like to be informed whenever your followers share your post, when you receive a comment or when someone mentions your page? You can also set to receive information through text or email or both.

Page Role Settings

This is essential if you're working with a team. Each role is assigned access to specific areas of the page. This helps clear up communication channels and delegate responsibilities among your team members.

People and Other Pages Settings

The people and pages that clicked the Like button on your page will appear here. If you ever want to ban anyone, this is where to do that.

Preferred Page Audience Settings

This is where you can specify your target audience so that the right people see your page. You can also edit this setting so they can access your posts.

7. Finalize the details.

Whenever you can, take advantage of opportunities that allow you to bring granular information pertaining to the brand or the business. Here are a few additional things you should not forget when polishing the details on your page.

- Add your other Social Media account information under Contact Info.
- To build a stronger brand and make it more personal, you may also want to consider connecting your team by linking their profiles to each other.
- Add product descriptions.
- You may also add menu.
- If you've won awards, let the public know.

After completing your page profile, save your changes and you're ready to go live and start connecting with your target audience.

Creating a Facebook Group

If you want to grow your brand or business, you would need the support of the online community. An online presence can help you stay in touch with your target audience, collect useful insights, spread the word about your business and build customer loyalty. A Facebook page will help you achieve all these. However, a group creates a more intimate and exclusive setting for your target audience to discuss among themselves and connect with each other.

What can you achieve with a Facebook Group?

- Provide ongoing updates, support and promotion to your audience who are already interested in your business and the products or services that you offer.
- Convert casual visitors to fans and then to paying customers.
- Make sure you keep your current customers happy, maintain their business and encourage loyalty.

- Always stay in touch with your business' or brand's customer base.

How to create a Facebook Group?

While you're on your way to creating your own Facebook Group, do not forget to check out existing ones. There are a couple of industry-focused groups you can learn from. They gather professionals within the industry to exchange experiences, ideas and talk about trend. They can inspire your posts that can ultimately help your business grow.

To start creating your group, follow these steps.

1. Go to your Page.

Log in to your Facebook Page, click the Create tab at the top menu bar and choose Group. This will bring up a new window where you will be asked to enter your Group details.

- Create a name for your Group. As much as possible, keep the name relevant and close to your Page's name.
- Add people to the Group.
- Include a personal note with your invite.
- Set your Group's privacy settings: closed or public.
- Pin your Group to shortcuts for easy access.

Complete the details and make all the necessary changes on your settings, then click Create.

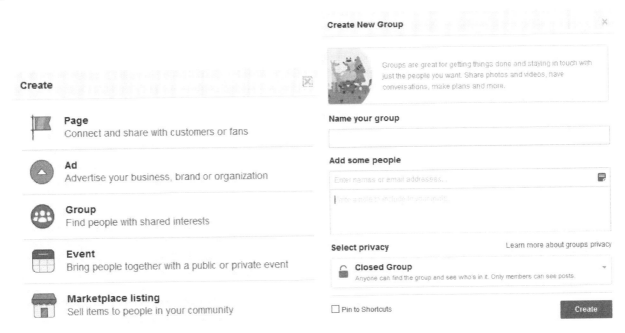

2. Assign roles.

Your Facebook Page can be the automatic admin for the group. However, you may also want to use your personal profile as a backup admin. This will allow you to manage the Group using both your profile and your page. To do this, go to the Member's tab and click the dots that show beside your name. From the dropdown menu, choose Make Admin.

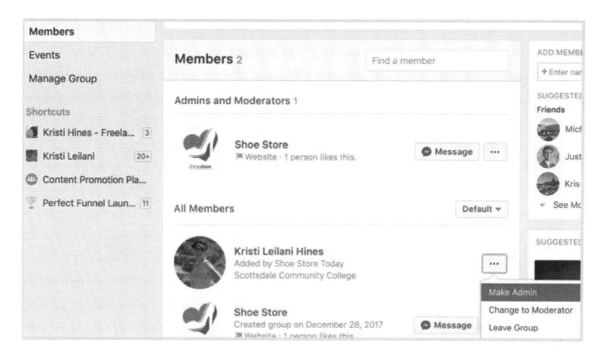

3. Add a cover photo.

Images make everything much more interesting. Personalize your Facebook Group by uploading a cover photo that best represents the group's personality.

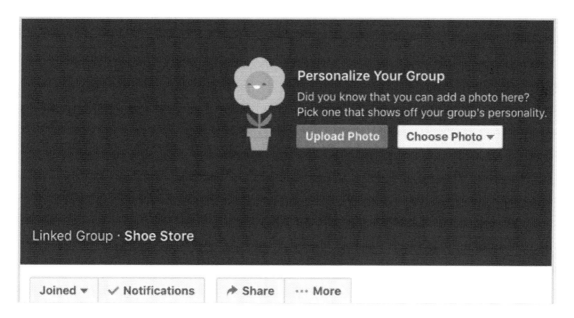

4. Edit your Group Settings.

Complete your Group's profile by adding a category, including a description, some tags, locations, and other important details.

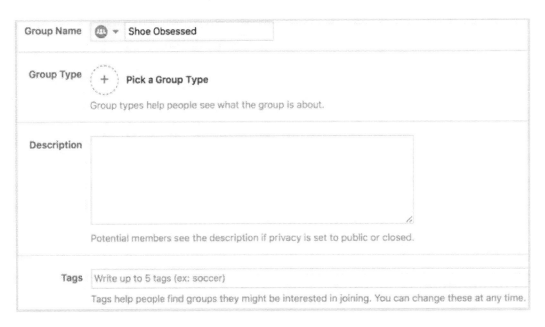

5. Promote your Group.

After making sure that your group profile is open and inviting, you have to start working on promoting it. To grow your community, the following strategies will help.

- Add your group's link in your correspondences with your current customers.
- Create a post about your group in all your social media accounts. Pin the post to the top of your Page so it's the first thing your visitors see. You can also tweet about it to get the word out.
- Consider boosting posts about your group.
- Invite more people who are possibly interested in the group. Make sure you customize the message of the invite.

6. Check out Group Insights.

You can learn much from Group Insights. This can be accessed from your Page. Click on Insights and Groups from the left sidebar. This will show you analytics data about your members, their demographics, comments, posts and reactions. Note however, that Group Insights only become available when you reach over 250 members so keep growing your numbers.

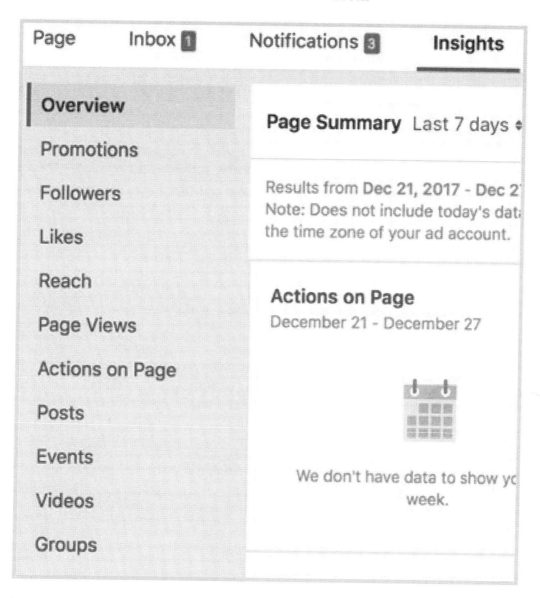

This is not just about collecting members for your group. It is extremely important that you keep them interested, engaged and active. Here are a few things you can do.

Regularly update your posts.

Continue generating new content that your members can discuss among themselves. Keep updating yourself about the hottest topics within your industry. Your members will appreciate your effort to keep them informed. Engage them by posting questions, surveys etc. Encourage them to add comments.

Share other content.

Don't be too self-centered. You will probably find other relevant articles worth sharing. Do not hesitate to do so. Stop selling and promoting all the time. Take a break from the sales pitch and become a genuine source of valuable information.

Explore other Facebook features.

You may also want to consider putting a face on the brand. And one of the best ways you can do this is through Facebook Live. Take the opportunity to showcase your products. You can also do Q&A or simply offer them an exclusive insight to any aspect of your business.

Keep trying different things. Through experience, you will be able to figure out what strategies work best for you. Test the waters and don't hold back. You may even want to use paid ads in order to grow your fan base.

What are Boosted Posts and Why You Should Take Advantage of Them

Facebook boosted post is one of the options you have to increase your organic reach. This feature is available to you as long as you have a business page. Taking advantage of this feature means you can get more people to see your post. However, boosted posts cost money.

If you are to spend money on anything, it is essential that you make sure the tool is worth it. Let's talk about the top benefits of boosting your posts.

A. Reach a wider and more targeted audience.

You may be happy with the number of your page subscribers but its possible you can reach more. With boosted posts, you can reach people outside your subscriber list. You can also choose the parameters and the specific types of people you want to target. For instance, you can choose a specific demographic like a certain age group, ethnicity, education, religion etc.

B. They're quite easy to use.

After clicking Boost Post and once Facebook has reviewed and approved the content, it will go live immediately. You can boost any type of post containing website links, videos, images or even short messages.

C. You have full control.

When you choose to boost a post, you're not locked in. If you're not getting the results you were aiming for, you have the option to stop the boost or boost another in its place.

D. Evaluate the boosted post's performance.

You have analytics tool at your disposal. Facebook Insights offer you a detailed summary of performance. You will be able to assess your boosted post according to the number of clicks and shares it's receiving, the extent of its reach, the quality of comments and reactions. If the boosted post is doing well and meeting your goals, you can apply the same tactic to other posts in your page.

What can you include in a Facebook boosted post?

The type of content you choose to boost is entirely up to you. You can boost a call to action, a promotion or an announcement. However, there are 3 major factors you have to consider when choosing the boosting feature.

1. Who is your audience?

Start with demographics when defining your target audience. How old are they? Where are they located? Are you targeting male or female audience or both? What are their interests?

Creating custom audiences based on your current contacts is also an option. You can create lookalike audiences that are based on the contacts who have already shown interest in your Page and posts.

2. What is your budget?

Your goals will dictate your budget. You have the freedom to spend as little or as much as you can to meet these goals. Your daily budget can be set to as low as $1. When setting low budgets, you need to adjust your expectations. If you do it properly, you can maximize your low budget. In which case, you need to plan accordingly and be as strategic as possible.

3. How long will you run it?

You can set a specific period when to run your boosted posts. You can run it for a day, a week etc. You can also turn it off manually.

How much does a boosted post actually cost?

Let's face it, there's only so much you can do for free. Especially when it comes to social media marketing, promotions cost money. How much should you expect to spend?

Unlike other social media ads, you're free to set your own budget with a boosted post. The bare minimum you can expect to spend is $1 a day. If we base it on the minimum, a boosted post with a $7 ad budget can run for as little as 7 days. Will you be able to get the results you're aiming for with this budget? The harsh truth is the more you pay the more people you can reach. The Facebook team will give you an idea about your estimated reach for any given budget.

Let's say your target audience are people above 18 years-old who are living in the United States. A $2 daily budget will allow you to reach anywhere between 163 to 872 people. If you increase it to about $5, you will probably be able to reach between 432 and 2,070 individuals. If you increase it further to $15, your estimated reach is 1,506 to about 6,834 people. The number is not set in stone. Demographics also affect the numbers.

You are encouraged to experiment with variables in order to get a better idea about your expected cost and the corresponding estimated reach. Once you get this information and the full price estimation, you can then make a final decision about your budget.

Creating a Facebook Boosted Post

Now that you have some basic info about boosted post, let's learn how to make them.

1. Choose which post to boost.

You can boost an existing post or create a new one. If you're in the process of creating a post, look for the Boost Post button found in the lower-right corner like in the image below.

You can also go through all your previous posts and proceed to the Insights tab where you will see all of them. Each of the post will appear with a Boost Post option next to it.

2. Decide on your targeting options.

After selecting a post to boost, you will see a menu of targeting options. The default setting targets the people who are already following your Page. It may also include their friends and followers. You can be a little more specific by setting demographics for your target audience. You can create one or multiple custom audiences to target. To do this, start by clicking the option to **Create New Audience**.

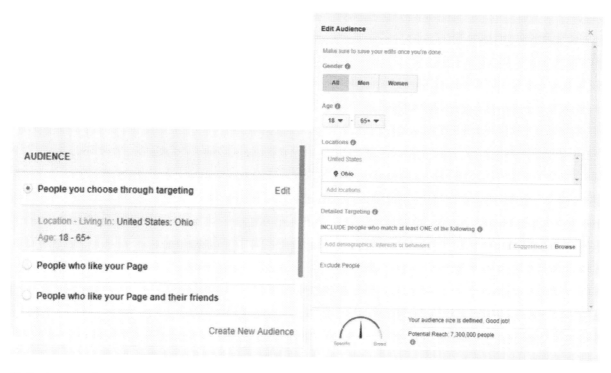

You will find several options that allow you to define your target audience further like setting the age range, adding, or deleting locations or including people interested in topics related to your Page or your posts.

3. Choose your budget.

The next step is to set your campaign budget. With your target audience defined, you will have a realistic estimated reach. You can adjust the reach according to how much money you're willing to spend or base your decision on how far you want to go with reach. As we mentioned before, the lowest you can set is $1 a day. You can choose to spread your budget by choosing the duration as well.

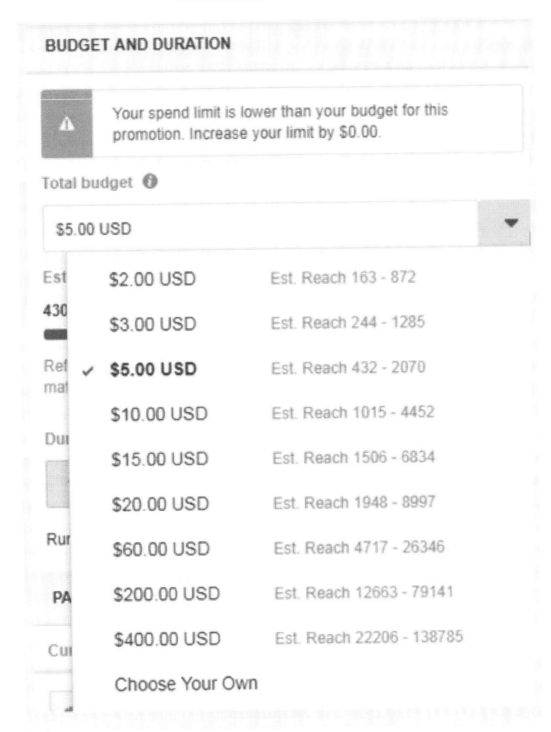

4. Set the duration.

You can choose from the default options: 1 day, 7 days or 14 days. At the bottom, you can also set the date if you have a specific one in mind. You have full control with regards to how long you want your boosted post to run.

5. Preview

After putting in the details of your campaign, it is important that you preview your post. Check the copy to make sure it looks the way you want it to. You're going to be spending money on it so it is important that it's error-free. Review the visual elements and check the links. Make sure they're working. You can still make changes at this point so go through it carefully.

6. Choose your payment option.

When you're satisfied with everything, you will be taken to a page where you select your preferred payment method. Here's how the section looks like.

Your post is ready for a boost! It will go through the review process. Once approved, Facebook will publish it. The process may take some time. You can review the status by checking it out in the Ads Manager. You will find the information in the Delivery column.

Did You Know?

Fifty-eight percent of social media users said they follow brands through social media (MarketingSherpa):

- 95 percent aged 18-34 (Millennials) follow brands through social media
- 92 percent of adults aged 34-44
- More women (61 percent) follow brands on social media than men (55 percent)

Chapter 2 Quiz

Please refer to the Answer Booklet for the solution to this quiz

1. What are 3 major factors you have to consider when choosing the boosting feature?

   A) Audience
   B) Duration
   C) Budget
   D) Social Media Accounts

2. This will show you analytics data about your group members, their demographics, comments, posts, and reactions.

   A) Audience Insights
   B) Members Insights
   C) Group Insights
   D) Group Data

3. Which of the following can help you promote your Group?

   A) Add your group's link in your correspondences with your current customers.
   B) Create a post about your group in all your social media accounts. Pin the post to the top of your Page so it's the first thing your visitors see. You can also tweet about it to get the word out.
   C) Consider boosting posts about your group
   D) Invite more people who are possibly interested in the group. Make sure you customize the message of the invite.

4. What are the benefits of having a Facebook Group?

   A) Provide ongoing updates, support and promotion to your audience who are already interested in your business and the products or services that you offer.
   B) Convert casual visitors to fans and/or paying customers
   C) Make sure you keep your current customers happy, maintain their business and encourage loyalty
   D) Always stay in touch with your business' or brand's customer base

5. You can use this section to either allow or restrict your page's followers to download your published videos.

   A) Content Distribution
   B) Video Distribution
   C) Member Distribution
   D) Exclusive Access

6. Comments can appear with the most recent ones first or the most relevant ones at the top. Use this setting to indicate your preference according to what will be more beneficial to your business or brand.

   A) Post Ranking
   B) Comment Ranking
   C) Post Pinning
   D) Comment Priority

7. By ticking this box, you allow Facebook to include your page in results of relevant searches. For instance, if you have a pet grooming business and a user searches for pet products, your page will appear as a relevant search.

   A) Same Page Result
   B) Similar Page Result
   C) Same Page Suggestions
   D) Similar Page Suggestions

8. If it's important for you to keep things clean, it would be wise to edit these settings. You can block certain comments that include words that you may consider offensive or inappropriate.

   A) Page Moderation
   B) Profanity Filter
   C) Age Restriction
   D) Page Updates

9. If you're selling or promoting age-sensitive products like tobacco and alcohol, it is necessary to prevent minors from accessing your page. Use this setting to restrict minor access to your page and posts.

   A) Page Moderation
   B) Profanity Filter
   C) Age Restriction
   D) Page Updates

10. In this section, you can set and choose to let visitors post, add photos and videos to the page. At the same time, you can review the content first to make sure no inappropriate content goes through.

    A) Guest Post
    B) Visitor Post
    C) Member Post
    D) Messages/Posts

Chapter 3

Facebook Business Manager

Facebook business manager sounds fancy, but do you really need one? First of all, it is a free account. Its main objective is to help businesses, companies, or individuals in managing and organizing their Facebook Pages and other advertising accounts. It's an alternative to tying all of these work stuff to your personal Facebook account.

Remember we talked about using your personal profile log in to create your Facebook business page earlier? That in itself is an okay option. However, if you have several Pages under your name and you simply prefer not to connect your business Pages with all your friends, family, or co-workers on Facebook, you can use this free tool instead. Before we get into detail about creating one, let's take a look at the benefits, drawbacks, and some issues you should know.

Advantages of Having a Facebook Business Manager Account

Business Manager offers a solution to many pain points for businesses. Having one for yourself will allow you to reap the following benefits.

1. It helps prevent the mixing of your personal and professional profile.

A lot of people take advantage of their personal connections to get the word out about their business or brand. However, there are times when this can be an issue. Let's say you posted something on your page which you want to be strictly professional. In this case, you hope that it will be published on behalf of your business persona. However, it also gets displayed in your personal profile where it can be viewed by all your personal contacts.

If you use a Business Manager, on the other hand, you can make sure that a mix up like this never occurs between your personal and professional life. After creating a business manager account, you will see a visible grey at the upper portion of your page. This lets you know that you are currently working, posting, and acting on your professional profile.

2. It makes managing multiple accounts easier.

If you have several user accounts to manage, it is your best interest to create a business manager account. This will allow you to synchronize and manage your multiple accounts from one central place. It is also ideal if you're working with a team. It will allow you to assign different roles and responsibilities to each member. You can assign usage rights on the Page of the account.

3. It makes business interaction more professional.

Because you avoid any chance of mix up, you can maintain a professional image and limit adding accounts to those relevant to your business or brand. Through this, you can add and manage your business assets as well as communicate with other business entities. You can include your ad accounts, apps and product catalog pages and display them according to your target audience. If you're in the advertising business with several clients, you can also add their Facebook pages and have full control over what they can and cannot access.

4. You can access additional functions.

There are simply more tools and functions that become available to you with a business manager account. For instance, if you have an app, you can add it to the developer's section. Your business manager account also includes one-pixel code. This will allow you to customize the settings according to the requirements of each ad accounts. Managing your product catalogs, linking other sources, adding product feeds, adding people and other business tasks become much simpler. Essentially, it makes your job easier.

To sum it up, here are the things you can do with a Facebook Business Manager account.

- Access Pages and ad accounts without sharing everything with your personal connections.
- Limit access to clients' Pages, ad accounts and other Facebook assets.
- Avoid sharing logins and prevents the need to change passwords for security purposes.
- Add or remove agencies and employees to the account with ease.
- Grant varying permission levels according to your business objectives.
- Manage several Pages and multiple ad accounts using a single Business Manager.
- Organize your Pages and accounts by grouping them into projects.
- Allows a more collaborative opportunity among team members.

Overall, it leads to a better and more efficient management of all your Pages and ad accounts.

Disadvantages of a Facebook Business Manager Account

We can't deny the many opportunities a business manager account opens up. However, the platform is not perfect. There are downsides to using one as well. Among them are the following.

1. There is a risk of bugs.

It doesn't happen all the time but it has happened before and you should prepare yourself to the risk of a bug incident happening. In the past, people reported bugs (or malfunction) and in the worst cases, have lost their accounts. There have also been reports and complaints about their admin rights changing without prior information. If this happens to you, you could lose pertinent business information.

It is worth mentioning that most of these incidences occurred at the early phases of introduction i.e. the beta testing phase. Facebook has probably made necessary changes to prevent such cases from happening in the future. Be that as it may, it is still a risk for your business and is something worth considering and preparing for.

2. It takes time to get used to the platform.

Migrating from a personal account to a business manager account is a big change. There is a huge difference in the process which means it will take some time to learn. One of the major differences is that unlike a personal account where you can schedule posts before your preferred launch date, a business manager account does not offer the same option. Things have to be done in real-time which may result in extra manual work for you especially if you're handling multiple clients.

If you're doing social media marketing, chances are you're not only using Facebook. You probably have several social media handles. Managing them all can be quite challenging. On Facebook, you are allowed to publish them on your multiple pages. However, you may not be able to publish them on selective groups.

This may mean you will have to incorporate various tools in your media strategy combining the use of Facebook business manager, page posts and power editor. It's not an impossible feat but it is a complex process that increases the risk of making mistakes.

3. Information is limited.

One of the best reasons why a lot of people have had success with Facebook marketing is that they can laser target consumers from different categories. They can group their target audience according to demographics, educational level, purchasing power, etc. Whether or not the same option is available for Business manager account holders is unclear.

4. It doesn't operate like a personal profile.

If you're used to using your personal profile for your business, you may find moving to a business manager account beneficial but also limiting. There are a lot of tasks and tools that may not be available to marketers such as scheduling posts.

Is a Facebook Business Manager account necessary?

With all these said, it is still important to note that each personal user account is only allowed to link to one advertising account. A business manager account eliminates that problem which is a significant advantage. Not only will you be able to link multiple accounts, you are also able to link to different time zones and corresponding currencies. There is a limit to the number of accounts but with Facebook's permission, the limit may be increased.

If you are handling multiple ad accounts anyway, it may be a better option to set up a business manager account. Having one will allow you to work more efficiently.

What do you need to set up a Business Manager account?

One of the prerequisites of a Business Manager account is a page. The Facebook page should be about the business you are promoting. In addition, you need to link it to your FB account. Facebook uses it as reference for verification purposes and for security reasons.

Two Layer Permission

The Business Manager account does offer more security for businesses. It offers a two-layer permission model which allows you to securely maintain and manage your Pages, ad accounts and catalogs.

The first layer of security allows you to add people to the account either as admins or employees. Team member who are assigned as admins have full control of all the aspects of the account. This means they can modify the business or delete it. They can also remove people who are in the employee list. On the other hand, business employees may be able to view business data settings. However, they are not able to make changes unless they are given the role of Finance Editor.

The second layer of security grants agencies or partners the ability to manage your business assets including business accounts and Pages. The Page and ad account can only be handled by one Business Manager at a time. However, there can be multiple individual accounts and partners who can post, manage, and access ads on its behalf. The shared permission may be changed at any time.

There are various things you can do in a Business Manager account. Such tasks and privileges include the following.

1. Assign roles to people.

Different roles with varying degrees can be assigned to partners, agencies or employees. For security reasons, you are strongly advised to limit access. As much as possible, keep access to a minimum while allowing them to fulfill their roles.

Admins versus Employees

There are two roles available in the account for businesses. These are admins and employees. Let's look at what each can do.

Admins can...

- Add or delete employees or partners
- View the settings and change them
- Manage permissions given to employees
- Add ad accounts, Pages and assets
- Handle ad accounts, Pages and assets assigned to them

Employees can...

- View business settings

- Handle ad accounts, Pages and assets assigned to them by admins
- Can apply changes to business settings ONLY when admins assign them as Finance Editor

Admin versus Advertiser versus Analyst

There are 3 roles to assign for ad accounts. Their roles, responsibilities and access are as follows.

Admin can...

- Manage the settings on ad account
- Add people and delegate ad account roles to them
- Create ads and edit them
- Edit the source of funding
- View the adds
- Access reports

Advertiser can...

- Create ads and edit them
- View the adds
- Access reports

Analyst can...

- View the adds
- Access reports

Admin versus Editor versus Moderator versus Advertiser versus Analyst

There are several roles that are available for Pages.

Admin can...

- Manage and control roles and settings
- Edit Page
- Add apps
- Create and remove posts
- Send messages in behalf of the Page
- Respond to and remove comments
- Delete and ban users from the Page
- Create Page ads
- View Insights

Editor can...

- Edit Page
- Add apps
- Create and remove posts
- Send messages in behalf of the Page
- Respond to and remove comments
- Delete and ban users from the Page
- Create Page ads
- View Insights

Moderator can...

- Send messages in behalf of the Page
- Respond to and remove comments
- Delete and ban users from the Page
- Create Page ads
- View Insights

Advertiser can...

- Create Page ads
- View Insights

Analyst can...

- View Insights

Catalog Admin versus Catalog Advertiser

These are the two roles that can be assigned for catalogs in a Business Manager account. Each role's responsibilities include the following.

Catalog admin can...

- Add people and give them catalog roles
- Share the catalog with agencies and partners
- Choose a product set or catalog to create an ad for
- Preview the ads for a product set
- View and choose catalogs, catalog settings, events in the Catalog Manager section
- View and remove data feeds and product sets in the Catalog Manager section
- Link a pixel or an app to a specific catalog

Catalog advertiser can...

- Choose a product set or catalog to create an ad for
- Preview the ads for a product set

- View data feeds
- View and choose catalogs, catalog settings and events
- View and remove product sets in the Catalog Manager section

Finance Editor versus Finance Analyst

For finance management, these are the two roles available. While a Finance analyst can only view details, the Finance Analyst can both view and edit the following.

- Credit card information
- Contact information and financial details
- Invoices or transaction information
- Invoice Groups
- Details about account spending
- Payment methods

2. Manage people, ad accounts, assets, settings, apps and video.

In a single account, you can organize everything your business requires on Facebook. This is why the Business Manager is referred to as the best management tool on the platform. You can edit, control and manage all these things under the Accounts section of your Business Manager.

People

You can add, remove and assign roles to people using the account. Here are some of the things you can do as far as people are concerned.

- **Add individuals.**

Note that you can definitely add an agency or a partner. But in order to add individuals you can go to the Business settings, choose People and click the option to Add. Use the email address of the people you want to add to the account and choose the role to assign them. They will get an email about the invite. As soon as they accept the invite, you can assign them roles to ad accounts, Pages and other assets or even to the Creative Hub project.

- **Add an agency or a partner.**

You will find the option to add a Partner from the Business Settings. After selecting the business role and access to the Partner, Facebook will automatically generate a link and send it to the partner. This link must be opened within 30 days. Otherwise, it will expire.

- **Accept invitation for Business Manager.**

Facebook sends the invite. When you receive it, you must sign in with your personal account. This is for identity verification. Facebook will match your FB identity with your work email address. To accept or decline the request, you can go to Business Setting and choose Request.

- **Delete people from the account.**

With a business manager account, you can also remove people that you have previously added. This is useful when someone leaves the team whether an admin or an employee, you can immediately take action and remove their access.

- **Assign assets to people.**

To assign people to assets, you can go to Business Settings and click People under the Users section. Choose the person you want to assign to the asset and click on Assign Assets. You can assign them roles in the Catalogs, Ad accounts or Pages.

- **Make changes to people's roles.**

Aside from assigning roles, you also have the freedom to edit those assignments. Select the name of the person and choose Update Person.

- **Remove yourself from the account.**

Not only will you be able to add and remove people or update their roles, you can also remove yourself from the business. To do this, proceed to the Business Settings section and choose Business Info. If you scroll down, you will find My Info and the option to Leave Business.

Ad Accounts

A newly opened business account is allowed to create one ad account. Upon activation of the ad account through active spending, a business will be able to host as many as 5 separate ad accounts. As of yet, this is the limit that Facebook sets. There are three ways to create an ad account under Business Manager.

Once added, the account will be permanently under Business Manager. You won't be able to transfer it to an individual owner. Here's how it's done.

- Proceed to Business Settings.
- Next, choose Accounts and click Ad Accounts.
- Select Add and choose any of the following options: Create a new Ad Account, Add Ad Account or Request Access to an Ad Account.
- Create new ad account when you're starting from scratch.
- Add an ad account when you have an existing ad account and want to move it to Business Manager. To be able to do this, you must meet the following requirements: be the owner of the account and be the admin in Business Manager. As with creating a new ad account, the existing account will permanently belong to Business Manager once moved.

After successfully adding it, all management actions will be made within the Business Manager profile. You will not be able to add an account that is owned by another person or another Business Manager. However, if you need access to work on the account, you can choose the third option.

- Request access to an ad account when the account is not under your name and you are not an admin to the Business Manager. When the request is granted however, the admin can grant you access or permission to do work on the said account.

The current limit is 5 ad accounts for every Business Manager. There is no option yet to delete an existing ad account. Deactivating it is an option. However, you will not be able to add a new one in place of the deactivated account. It will still be counted as one of the 5 ad accounts you're allowed to create.

To add an existing ad account or request access to one belonging to another Business Manager, you can simply enter the account ID. Facebook will generate it for you.

Why can't I add an ad account?

There may be some instances when you are unable to add one. It could happen because of any of the following reasons:

- The ad account may already be under another business listing. It can only be owned by a single Business Manager.
- A personal ad account has already been added to Business Manager.
- Only one ad account from your personal FB account can be moved to Business Manager.
- You have already reached the limit for adding new accounts to the business although it may be possible for you to adjust the limit if your advertising spending is increased.

If you are unable to add an account you still need to work on, keep in mind that you have 2 other options which are to request access to the existing account or create a new one except when the limit has already been reached.

Delete an account audience.

You may not be able to delete the ad account itself. However, you can remove the ad account audience. If you want to do this, follow the below steps.

- Go to Business Settings.
- Choose Audiences.
- Pick the audience you want to edit.
- Go to Actions.
- Click on the Delete option.
- Choose Delete Audience for permanent removal.

Deactivate an ad account.

Again, you can only deactivate an account not delete them in Business Manager. To do this, proceed to Business Settings and choose Ad Accounts. Pick the ad account you want to edit and click the option to Deactivate.

Control Settings

There are four major things you can do in the Settings page and they are as follows:

- **Change the primary Page.**

You can set the primary Page and edit it at a later time. To start with, proceed to Business Settings. Go to Business Info and choose the option to Edit. Pick a page and Save.

- **Locate a Business ID.**

This is one of the important pieces of information you should know how to access. To find your ID number, Choose Business Info in the Business Settings section. You will find your ID under Business Manager Info.

- **Update your work email address or edit name in Business Manager**

To make changes to your information, access the Business Info section. From there, select the Edit option which you can find under My Info section. Change what you need to update and Save the changes. Facebook will automatically send you an email about the requested change. You will need to verify that the actions were initiated by yourself. Choose Verify Now in the confirmation email to proceed.

- **Adjust the Notifications.**

From Business Settings, go to the Notifications section. There you will find a list of options from the dropdown menu. Adjust it as you prefer.

Apps

In addition to adding ad accounts, you can also add apps to Business Manager. To do this, go to Accounts under Business Settings. Choose Apps. You will find an option to Add New App in this section. You will be given two options. One is to add a completely new one and the other is to request access to an already existing app. In the second option, locate the app by entering the Facebook App ID. If Facebook doesn't allow you to add it, it's likely it has already been added by a Business Manager.

Videos

You can control videos, access to it and actions done by other people.

- **Allow crossposting of videos.**

Remember what we emphasized earlier about the downside of Business Manager? Ads won't be able to run or get boosted unless you publish it manually from your Page settings. To do it the Business Manager way, you can follow the below steps.

- o   Access the Page to be published.
- o   Choose the Settings Tab.
- o   Click on General.
- o   Choose Edit from Page Visibility.
- o   Select Page Published.

You can save it after making your desired changes.

- **Crosspost videos from a Page that isn't owned by Business Manager.**

Pages that are not under your Business Manager can also be granted permission to crosspost your videos. Before this is possible however, both parties are required to give permission. Follow these steps.

- o   Proceed to your Page.
- o   Access Settings tab.
- o   Select Crossposting.
- o   Find the Page by typing the name in the search field or enter the URL corresponding to the Page.
- o   Select the Page to add it. The Page you're trying to add also needs to take similar steps. To make the process easier, include your Page to their settings. Choose Link and a dialog box will appear containing a URL. Copy and share it with the admins of the other Page. This way, the Page admins can access the link which will automatically take them to their Crossposted Videos settings.

After permission from both parties are secured, you can choose specific videos for crossposting. The selected videos will appear in the Page's Video Library and listed in the **Videos You Can Crosspost** section.

- **View Insights.**

In Business Manager, you can also access the Insights for your videos which are crossposted. To access this info, choose Publishing Tools from your business Page. Go to Video Library. Select from the list of videos and you will be able to access the data you're seeking.

System Users

It is important to note that access to System Users is not available for all businesses. For others, this option may not be available. To add a new one, you can start with the following steps.

- Access Business Settings.
- Click on Systems Users.
- Select the option to Add New System User.
- Name the user and choose Create System User.
- Assign assets and corresponding roles to the new system user.
- Generate a new token. One token will be assigned to every new system user so you will have to generate a new one every time you add a new user. You will find the option from the right side of your Page. Copy and save the info.

Instagram

You don't really need a Business Manager account to run Instagram ads. You can do it on a business page. What makes a business manager account great for Instagram ads is that it allows you to review, as well as, answer to comments on the ads. Like we mentioned before, engagement with the audience is crucial in making social media advertising work.

If you have an existing Instagram account, you can link it to your ad account through Business Manager. For this to be possible, you must have both the ad account and Instagram account under the *same* Business Manager to associate the two. Unlike with pages, you can't request access to an Instagram handle that belongs to another Business Manager. It has to be your own. Follow the below steps to link your accounts.

- Access your Business Manager and go to Settings.
- Choose Instagram Accounts and select the one you want to connect to an ad account.
- Choose the option to Assign Ad Accounts.
- You can also grant authorization to multiple ad accounts to access and use the Instagram account. To do this, check the box beside the ad accounts before clicking on Save Changes.

Projects

Another way of organizing your Pages and ad accounts is through Projects. With this option, you can assign ad accounts and Pages to your team. If for instance, your business operates and is organized through various locations, you will find it easier to group and assign your team using Projects. To access this feature, you can follow these steps.

- Go to Business Settings.
- Look for Projects. This will be found in Accounts section.
- Create New Project.
- Name it. Click on Next.
- Check on the Pages you want to include in this newly created project and choose Next.
- Check on the ad accounts you want to include in the project and choose Next.
- Click on Save Changes.

3. Manage Your Data Sources

These include: Catalogs, Pixels, Event Source Groups, Offline Event Sets, Custom Conversions and Shared Audiences

Under the Data Sources of your Business Settings, you will find all these options. You can set them up according to your brand or business needs. Let's go over them one by one and look into how they can be useful.

Catalogs

Organization is key in managing a business. In this section, you can add a new product catalogue, add an existing catalog to your product feed or request access to another catalog.

How to add a new product catalog?

- Go to Business Settings.
- From Data Sources, go to Catalogs.
- Click on the option to **Add New Catalog** and **Create a New Product Catalog**
- Name it. Choose which products to include. Click on **Create Catalog**.
- Choose people to manage the catalog. Click on Save Changes.

You also have the option to assign management roles to your team. You can skip this step if you prefer not to add anyone else.

In addition, you can also link apps and any pixels to your product catalog. All you need to do is tick the boxes next to available apps and pixels. If you don't have any yet, you may add them later and Skip the step in the meantime.

How to add an existing catalog to product feed?

- Select the catalog and click on the option to Add Product feed.
- Enter your name and select the corresponding currency.
- Pick an upload type for the feed.

You can set it up for either Single Upload or Schedule Recurring Uploads.

Single Upload - You will have to manually do the uploading. Every time you make changes to the file, a manual one-time upload will be necessary.

Schedule Recurring Uploads - You can select your preferred intervals for automatic uploading.

After making your choice, proceed to creating the feed by completing the required information. File uploads have to follow the instructions so they can be uploaded correctly.

Column Name	Instructions
id	Type in a unique ID for each item. Note that this will show as "retailer_id" after the product is imported.
availability	Mark if the item's in stock. You can type: "in stock", "available for order", "preorder", "out of stock", or "discontinued". Max 100 characters.
condition	You can type "new", "refurbished", or "used".
description	A short paragraph describing the item. Max 5000 characters.
image_link	Link to item image used in ad. See image resolution guidelines.
link	Link to merchant's site where you can buy the item.
title	Item title. Max 100 characters.
price	Item cost and currency using ISO 4217 currency codes. Ex: 9.99 USD.
sale_price	Discounted price if the item is on sale. Currency should be specified as the ISO 4217 currency code. Required for creative overlays. Ex. 4.99 USD.
sale_price_effective_date	Start and end date and time for the sale, separated by a slash. Required for creative overlays. Ex: 2017-11-01T12:00-0300/2017-12-01T00:00-0300.
gtin, mpn, or brand	GTIN: Global Trade Item Number (UPC, EAN, JAN,ISBN). Mpn - A unique number that identifies a product to its manufacturer. Brand: brand name. Max 70 characters.

- Your file must be saved using a TSV or CSV format. Using 3rd party feed provider is also allowed. In which case, you can use the following file formats: RSS XML, ATOM XML, compressed zip, gzip or bz2 file.
- Choose Next and complete your catalog.

> ## How to request access to a catalog?
> • Go to Business Settings.
> • Go to Catalogs which you will find under the Data Sources section.
> • Choose the option to Add New Catalog.
> • Click Request Access to a Catalog.

Pixels

You need to know whether your advertising efforts are effective or not. Facebook has an analytics tool that measures the effectiveness of your ads. It's called the Pixel. With this tool, you will be able to understand how people respond to your ads and posts through their actions on your website. We'll discuss this in more detail in the coming chapter about Events Manager.

Once you have a pixel set up, you can manage and share it in your Business Manager. An admin can grant access to other team members by adding them. People can also be added through a specific ad account.

Unless a person is a Business Manager Admin, team members will have to be added manually to be able to access pixel. A person who is part of the business with no access to any of the ad accounts in the business will have to be added. Otherwise, that person may have access to ad account but none to the pixels associated with the ad account. Only a Business Manager admin can both view and edit a Facebook pixel. Access to a specific pixel associated to an ad account can be granted by requesting access to the account itself.

How to add people to your Facebook Pixel?

To add an individual or a specific ad account to your Facebook Pixel, you can follow these steps.

- Access Business Settings.
- Go to **People and Assets** section.
- Click on **Pixels**.
- Select one to assign someone to.
- Choose **Add People** to assign a person to a specific pixel or **Assign Ad Accounts** if you want to assign all the people who has access to an ad account to the pixel.
- Select the preferred access.

Add People - You can choose the people and assign them roles which you will find in the dropdown menu.

Assign Ad Accounts - You have to select the account to be assigned to your pixel.

- If you have completed the necessary changes, click on Save Changes.

What roles can you assign to people on your Facebook Pixel?

As a Business Manager Admin, you can specify roles and select people for them. When another admin from a different Business Manager gives you access to their pixel, they can also choose to assign you roles. There are two roles available: Pixel Editor and Pixel Analyst.

Pixel Editor - This person will be able to view pixel information and apply changes as well. Editors are also able to create audiences. In addition, they can use the pixel to create conversion ads. In other words, editors can do as much as admins can except the latter is the only one who can add and remove people from pixel or change their previously assigned roles.

Pixel Analyst - This person will have access to the Facebook Pixel but only for viewing purposes. Unlike admins and editors, analysts won't be able to edit the pixel. They are also unable to create conversion ads or audiences.

Event Source Groups

Every action that are taken by people on your website are recorded as an event in Facebook Analytics. All information is received in the event source. A combination of these is referred to as ESG or Event Source Groups. Through Business Manager and by being an admin, you can create and manage your ESG.

How to create an Event Source Group?

- Proceed to Business Settings.
- Go to **Data Sources** and choose **Event Source Groups**.
- Click on the option **Create Event Source Groups**.
- Enter a name for the group.
- Pick out the data sources to include in the group. Among the choices are **Offline Data Set, Facebook Pixel** and **Mobile App**.
- Wait for the confirmation and click Close.

How to remove event source groups?

- Access Business Manager Settings.
- Choose any of the following: **Pages**, **Pixels** or **Apps**.
- Select the event source you want to remove and click on the X mark at the right side section.
- Choose the option to Remove and confirm the action to delete the event source.

You can also edit permissions to grant access to other Analytics users in the team. They can view the event source group. You can also assign different roles to people. The roles available are Analyst and Limited Analyst.

An Analyst can...
- View and explore event source group data except monetary data
- View as well as explore ESG monetary data
- Create charts and dashboards and save changes

Limited Analyst can...
- View and explore event source group data except monetary data

How to assign roles to people?

- Access Business Settings.
- Go to **Event Source Groups** and choose the one you want to assign people to.
- Click on the option to **Add People**.
- Choose the users from the team you want to assign to the ESG and specify their roles.
- Save the changes.

When users are assigned to an event source group, they will be able to access the data within the event sources. Admins automatically get access to the ESG as Analysts. As an admin yourself, you can change this default setting.

Offline Event Sets

We've talked about how actions taken on a website are tracked and recorded. To make your online ad efforts more inclusive as far as results are concerned, Facebook also allows you to monitor and measure actions taken offline in response to your Facebook ad campaign.

By default, an event set may be automatically created as well as assigned to an ad account. You can access details about it in Events Manager. We'll go into more detail about creating and uploading offline event sets in the coming chapters.

In your Business Manager, you can manage permissions for your existing sets. Data about an offline event can be uploaded by specific users only. This privilege is limited to the following roles.

- Admins of the Business Manager
- Employees who are assigned as Offline Event Set admins
- Business Manager system user

*Offline event set admin roles can be edited or assigned in the Business Settings.

How to add admin to an event set or share it to another business?

- Access Business Settings.
- Go to **Offline Event Sets**
- Choose the set and click on **Add People** if you intend on assigning an admin role to one of your team members.
- Click on **Assign Partner** if you want to share access to an event set with another business. And enter the corresponding **Business ID**

Custom Conversions

Instead of adding conversion pixels to your individual success pages, you can track as well as optimize conversions by using Custom Conversions. In other words, Custom Conversions can make tasks simpler. It can eliminate the need for manually adding codes to your site.

You can create Custom Conversions by accessing Ads manager. You can also edit or remove Custom Conversions through your Business Manager.

How to edit details on your custom conversions in Business Manager?

You can change the name, description as well as the conversion value of custom conversions. To change any of these, you can follow these steps.

- Access your Business Manager.
- Go to the main dropdown which can be found in the upper left section.
- From the **Measure & Report** option, click on **Custom Conversions**.
- Choose which one you want to edit.
- From the dropdown menu, choose **Actions**.
- Click on the option to **Edit Custom Conversion**.
- Apply your changes and choose **Done**.

How to remove your custom conversions?

Before deleting your custom conversions, you can avoid issues with your custom conversion event by changing the way the ad sets are optimized first.

- Access your Business Manager.
- Go to **Custom Conversions** which you will find under the **Measure & Report** section.
- Choose which one you want to delete.
- Click on **Actions**.
- Choose the option to **Delete Custom Conversion**.
- Confirm the action by clicking on **Delete**.

Shared Audiences

After creating audiences for your ads, you can grant access to it to other people. This is called Shared Audiences. It is possible to bulk share Lookalike and Custom Audiences between ad accounts as well as between media agencies provided that the one sharing and receiving are both associated to the same Business Manager. As long as the sharer allows it, the receiver can access insights and use it for targeting strategies and creative planning.

There are a couple of limitations including the following.

- Shared Audiences cannot be used for creating Lookalike Audiences.
- When you're utilizing a particular shared audience for one of your ad sets and the one who owns the audience deletes it, the ad set that you own will become inactive.
  You will have to set a target audience for your ad set.
- Saved Audiences cannot be shared.
- Audiences cannot be sold to other businesses.

How to share an audience?

You can share your audiences with your team or other businesses but you can also choose to prevent other people from accessing Insights about these shared audiences. Choose the levels of permissions to assign to people you're sharing your audiences with.

Access can be granted either for **Targeting Only** or for both **Targeting** and **Insights**.

- Access **Audiences**.
- Click on the boxes for the audiences you intend on sharing.

- Go to the dropdown menu for **Actions**.
- Choose Share.
- Choose or enter the names or ad account IDs you want to share your audiences with.
- From the Permission dropdown menu, decide whether you want to share the audience with either **Targeting Only** or **Targeting and Insights** access.
- Choose Share.

How to view all shared audiences across your business?

- Access **Business Manager**
- Go to **Business Settings**
- Choose **Shared Audiences**

Brand Safety Domains and Block Lists

To preserve content integrity and ensure that only the verified owners are allowed to edit their content and the way it is presented, Facebook has created domain verification. Verified domain owners can overwrite link metadata as an added functionality when they create link page posts. This is an essential free feature that business owners and marketers can take advantage of in order to ensure content security.

What exactly is Domain Verification?

This is among the many features of Business Manager. It provides businesses with a simple way of showing domain ownership without making it necessary for them to edit Open Graph markup tags. Through Business Manager, you can also assign verified domains to your Pages or share your domains with partners. In other words, domain verification allows you to safeguard the integrity of your content and prevent misrepresentation of your brand.

When you verify your domain, you are staking claim to your links and contents. This way, you remain in control and on top of every post, ad or any type of content you put in Facebook.

How to verify domain in Business Manager?

There are two verification methods available in Business Manager. These are DNS TXT record and HTML file upload. You can use either of these methods as part of a streamlined approach. By using these methods, you won't have to manually edit your website's HTML metadata.

What if domain has not been verified?

In an effort to ensure that rightful parties only have the privilege of editing link previews associated to content and reduce the risk of misrepresentation, Facebook encourages businesses and marketers to use domain verification. And as of May 2018, only verified domains are allowed to edit their organic Page post links as well as their unpublished Page post links. If your domain has not been verified yet, you won't have access to this editing privilege.

In addition to domain verification, Facebook also offers other brand safety tools. These tools will allow you to block your content from running with certain kinds of content found within **In-Stream Video, Audience Network** and **Instant Articles** placements.

These brand safety tools include the following.

1. Placement Opt-Out - With this safety tool you can choose to opt-out and prevent your ads from showing in **In-Stream Video, Audience Network** and **Instant Articles** placements.

You can do this by removing these placements in the **ad create flow** under **Edit Placement** section.

2. Category blocking - This is another way of protecting your ads by preventing them from showing side by side with content of certain categories. There is an option in Ads Manager that will allow you to Exclude Categories. You will also find this in the Edit Placements section.

3. Block lists - With this tool, you can prevent your ads from showing on certain apps or websites within the placements.

When you use any of these placement opt-out options, your ads and campaign delivery options become limited. This means fewer people may see your ad. However, it also ensures brand safety, content integrity and prevent any brand misrepresentation.

Integrations Lead Access

Lead generation campaigns for both Instagram and Facebook can best run through lead ads. Lead ads are a way of allowing people to show interest in a certain product or service with the use of a form within an ad that they can fill out with their details. This will allow businesses and marketers to follow up with these leads.

By default, Page admins can access lead information. Also by default, Page roles including analyst and advertiser are allowed to view insights and run lead ads but they are unable to download leads. The settings for lead access can be changed in your Business Manager. Without a Business Manager account, there is no other way to change the settings.

How to control access to your leads?

There is a tool in Business Manager called Lead Access manager that allow admins to customize the level of access for people in the team, partner agency or business and CRM. They may or may not be granted rights to download leads. With this tool, you can grant people with Page roles to download leads. The Lead Access manager is an advanced tool. It must be activated and customized. Otherwise, only Page admins will have the right to access your lead information.

How to enable Leads Access Manager?

A Business Manager admin can activate Leads Access manager. To enable this tool, you can follow these steps.

- Access **Business Manager** settings.
- At the bottom of the page, click on the **Lead Access** icon.
- A message will appear, choose **Customize Access**.

By taking these actions, you will automatically prompt the system to assign permission access to current CRMs and Page admins. Further action is required to customize lead access.

How to assign/ remove leads access?

Go to the **Assigned People and Partner** section found in the middle panel. This will show a list of people, agencies, partners or CRMs who have access to your leads.

From this section, you can edit the settings for any of the following: **People Partner and CRMs.**

How to restore permissions to default settings?

After customizing leads access, you can go back to the default settings at any time. Restoring to default access will remove any changes you've made before.

- Access **Business Manager Settings**.
- Go to the icon list and click on the **Lead Access** icon.
- Choose the page to manage your leads access.
- At the top right corner, choose the option to **Restore Default Access**.
- Confirm the action by clicking on **Restore Default**.

Payment Methods on Business Manager

In order to edit Business Manager payment methods, you must be either a Finance Editor or an admin. All billing details can be managed in Business Manager. After adding a payment method in the account, the same method can be added to an ad account associated with the Business Manager. It can then be set as primary method for all your ads.

How to add a payment method to Business Manager?

- Access Business Manager settings.
- Go to Payments.
- Choose the option to Add Payment Method.
- Click on Continue.

From here, you can follow the indicated instructions for adding your preferred payment method. This will be saved to your Business Manager account.

How to connect a Business Manager payment method to an ad account?

- Access Business Manager.
- Go to Billing.
- Choose the ad account.
- Select Payment Settings.
- Choose the option to Add Payment Method under the Payment Method section.
- Pick your preferred payment method in Business Manager.
- Follow the instructions and save the changes.

If you want to use the method to pay for your ads, you can set it as the primary method for the ad account.

Did You Know?

Eighty-seven percent of active Facebook users access the platform via mobile. (Hootsuite)

Chapter 3 Quiz

Please refer to the Answer Booklet for the solution to this quiz

1. What can a Business Manager admin do that an employee can't?

    A) View business settings
    B) Handle ad accounts, pages and assets
    C) Add or delete employees or partners
    D) Manage permissions

2. What are the roles that can be assigned to ad accounts?

    A) Admin
    B) Advertiser
    C) Analyst
    D) Editor

3. What is the maximum number of ad accounts that a Business Manager can have?

    A) 3
    B) 4
    C) 5
    D) 6

4. What are the different ways to add an ad account in Business Manager?

    A) Add Ad Account
    B) Request Access to an Ad Account
    C) Create a new ad account
    D) Choose an admin

5. Which of the following cannot be done in Business Manager?

    A) Deactivate an ad account
    B) Delete an ad account audience
    C) Delete people from the account
    D) Delete an ad account

6. How many ad accounts does Facebook allow for new Business Manager?

A) 3

B) 4

C) 5

D) 6

7. Which of the following statements is not true?

   A) You can cross-post videos with other Pages not in Business Manager.
   B) You and the admins of the other Page need to give cross-posting permission
   C) All businesses have access to System Users.
   D) You can assign assets and roles to users.

8. When do you need a new token?

   A) When you lose the other one.
   B) When you get permission from admins.
   C) Every time you cross-post
   D) Every time you create a new System User.

9. Which tool in Business Manager allows admins to customize the level of access for people in the team, partner agency or business and CRM?

   A) Lead access manager
   B) Business manager admin
   C) Brand Safety tools
   D) Category Blocking

10. Who can edit Business Manager payment methods?

    A) Finance editor
    B) Analyst
    C) Partners
    D) Business Manager Admin

Chapter 4

Facebook Ads Manager

The starting point of ads and the overall command center for your ad campaign is the Facebook Ads Manager. All the tools you need in order to create and manage your ads, any relevant settings, where and when they run, as well as, monitoring your campaign performance can be found here. At its core, this powerful management tool is designed to assist advertisers no matter their experience level.

Opening the Ads Manager tool will display four sections in the interface. Each tab contains a different set of information that can help you in evaluating the Facebook ads you create.

Account Overview Tab

This section offers a glance on the performance of your Facebook ads. Campaigns can also be filtered and you can switch your view from your active ads to a completely different timeframe.

The Account Overview tab shows at-a-glance information about current ad campaigns.

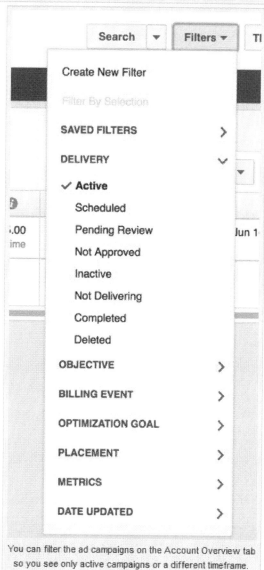

You can filter the ad campaigns on the Account Overview tab
so you see only active campaigns or a different timeframe.

Campaigns, Ads and Ad Sets

Coming up with a strategy to guide the creation of ads can take some time. That being said, understanding how your ad is performing is crucial. It is very important to familiarize yourself with the important metrics and get data for **click-through rates (CTR)** and **cost per conversion (CPC).**

The section dedicated for Campaigns, Ads and Ad Sets is a way for you to analyze your ads. You can choose the tab for the specific grouping you want to analyze. You can also use the **Breakdown and Performance columns** for more details.

Opening the Performance column will display a couple more options. From here, you can access specific aspects of the campaign. You can simply click one of the options to view related metrics.

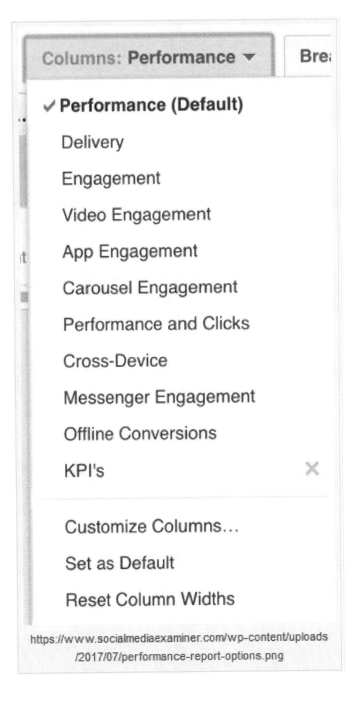

https://www.socialmediaexaminer.com/wp-content/uploads /2017/07/performance-report-options.png

Breakdown column opens up to more data. It can offer you specifics. For instance, if you want to know the specific days when conversions occurred or the device used by people when they clicked on your ad, this is the section that will display the information.

The columns can be further customized to come up with unique reports which you can share with your team. You can use it to analyze the performance and success of key metrics. For instance, when you care about knowing whether or not your ads perform 5% or above on click-through rate, you can set the columns so it shows the higher metrics at the top. After customizing your report, you can save it and use it for future reference. You can click on Save Report, name the report and complete the action by clicking Save in the dialog box.

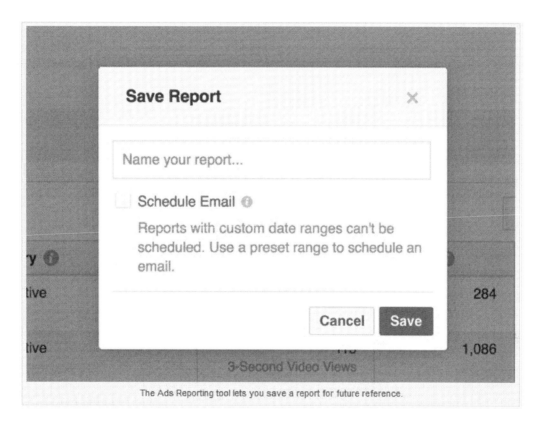

The Ads Reporting tool lets you save a report for future reference.

How to create ads?

Facebook Ads Manager offers two workflows that you can use for creating and managing your ads. You can choose between **Guided Creation** and **Quick Creation**.

Guided Creation

This is a complete walkthrough in the process of creation up to completion of your campaign. It's the perfect workflow for advertisers who are completely new to Facebook ads. The step-by-step instructions are quite easy to follow.

Quick Creation

With this option, you can set your campaign up and proceed to the creation of ads and ad sets at a later time. This workflow is ideal for advertisers who possess a more advances skill set. It will work perfectly with a knowledge of Power Editor workflow.

Your initial choice of workflow will become the default. Every time you click on the button to Create Ad, this option will be set. If you want to change or switch in between the workflows, you can do so by simply clicking on the Switch button which you will find at the top of the section for creation flow.

How to edit ads?

The updated interface of Ads Manager allows you to edit your ads and publish them immediately. You can also make the changes and save the ad for later publishing.

To edit and publish the ads right away, you can follow these steps.

- Choose the **Campaigns, Ads and Ad Sets** you like to edit.
- Click on the **Edit** icon which will open to a side panel.
- Apply the changes you want to make.
- Click on the option to Publish.

If you want to edit but save it for later publishing, you can follow the initial steps above. However, instead of clicking on Publish, click Close.

- Choose the **Campaigns, Ads and Ad Sets** you like to edit.
- Click on the **Edit** icon which will open to a side panel.
- Apply the changes you want to make.
- Click on the option to **Close**.
- To publish the edited ad, access the **Review and Publish section**.
- Select from the list of pending edits and confirm the changes.

How to create and find reports?

You will find the reports in the **Ads Reporting section** which you can access from the **Ads Manager Main Menu**. You can go to the same section to create your reports. You can follow these steps for creating your reports.

- Access the **Ads Reporting section**.
- Choose the option to **Create Report**.

- Select from Account, Campaign, Ad Set or Ad whichever you want to get a report on.
- Click **Apply** after making the choice.
- Save your report by clicking on **Save Changes**.
- Enter the name for the report and Save.

From accessing Ads Manager and exploring the report section, you will come across a couple of ad terms. Below are some of the terms.

Reach

This counts the number of people who have seen your ad at least once.

How it's used - The number of people that are exposed to your ad from your campaign is measured through reach. Although not all of these people may click on the ad itself, reach gives you an idea on how many people have seen your message. And they are more than likely to engage with your brand or business after being exposed to your message. Reach can be affected by several factors including budget, bid and audience targeting.

How it's calculated - Reach is estimated and calculated based on sampled data.

Impressions

Impressions denote how many times your ads were viewed. In contrast to reach that counts how many people are exposed to the ad at least once, impressions may include more than one view of the ads by the same people.

How it's used - This is one of the most common metrics relied upon by advertisers in online marketing. Impressions counts the viewing frequency of your ads or how many times your target audience viewed your ads on screen.

How it's calculated – Impressions counts how many times your ad is on the screen for the first time. In which case, when a person scrolls down and sees your ad and scrolls up again to view the ad, impression counts this as 1. On the other hand, if someone is exposed to the ad twice at different times during the day, this is equivalent to 2 impressions.

Impressions are counted in the same way for all types of ads whether the ads contain videos or images. In which case, a video ad is not required to play before it gets counted as 1 impression. It may not be the most accurate way but this calculation allows for consistency in the reporting of impressions across all ad campaigns that contain images and videos.

In cases of mobile phones where it cannot be determined if the ad is on screen, the impression is counted at the instance the ad is delivered to the device. Invalid traffic such as those that come from non-human sources like detected bots are not counted in the calculation of impressions.

Cost Per Result (CPR)

Result is defined as the number of times an ad was able to achieve the desired outcome depending on the selected settings and objectives. Cost per Result is simply the average of cost for every achieved result from the ads.

How it's used - This metric determines the cost efficiency of your ads. It is indicative of how efficient you were in achieving your ad campaign objectives. The data can be very useful in comparing the performances of your ad campaigns. It can help you in identifying areas of opportunity you can exploit and apply in your future bids for your upcoming ad sets. Cost per result is affected by several factors including target audience, auction bid, ad creative and messaging, schedule and optimization type.

How it's calculated - Cost per result is calculated based on the total of amount spent divided by the total number of results.

Link Clicks

This metric counts how many clicks there were on links within your ad which directed people to experiences or destinations within or outside of Facebook. Link clicks on ads that promote Instagram profile views include the clicks on comments or ad headers leading to the advertiser's profile.

How it's used - Link clicks indicate the interest generated by your ad among your target audience. The most effective way to use link click data is to use it in conjunction with other metrics.

How it's calculated - Clicking on any part of the ad that links to another experience or destination counts. This means a click on a call to action button within an ad or a click on an image within the ad counts equally. Destination and experiences can be in or out of the Facebook platform. Ad links may include any of the following.

- App Stores or App Deep Links
- Click to Message
- Click to Call
- Facebook Marketplace
- Facebook Lead Forms
- Facebook Canvas
- Maps/Directions
- Videos hosted by another website
- Videos launching the Watch & Browse experience
- Websites

Link Clicks For Instagram Profile Visits

Counting link clicks for Instagram ads with a Visit Instagram Profile button is a little different. To be counted, people must click the profile name either in comments or in the header because these will lead them to the same destination as they will be taken to when they click on the **Visit Instagram Profile** button.

Relevance Score

This is a rating of 1 to 10 estimating how well the audience responds to your ad. The relevance score is displayed when the ad has over 500 impressions but this only applies to ads and not to campaigns and ad sets.

How it's used - It lets you know how well your message resonated with your target audience. A higher score is an indication of your ad's performance. An estimated relevance score of 1 means your ad may not be as relevant to your target as you may think and it calls for some changes.

How it's calculated – It's based on numerous factors including the following.

- Positive feedback i.e., clicks, app installs and video views
- Negative feedback i.e., when a person clicks "I don't want to see this" on an ad
- How well your ad performs

Cost Per Click (CPC)

A click can come from various types of interactions. It can include the following.

- Clicks for actions identified as one of your campaign objective i.e., Like to your Page
- Clicks for expanding media to full screen i.e., images
- Clicks for associated business profile picture or Page profile
- Comments or shares
- Link clicks
- Post reactions i.e., likes or loves

Cost Per Click calculates the average cost for each click from multiple types as mentioned above. It is calculated by dividing the total amount spent with the number of clicks.

Post Reactions

This is the total number of reactions received by your ads. Upon viewing your ad, people can use various reaction buttons including Wow, Haha, Angry, Sad, Like or Love.

How it's used - Post reactions are a way for you to tell how relevant your ads are for your target audience, relevant enough for them to post a reaction. You can use this data to make your ads perform much better. You would want people to react to your post because this will move them to start following other reactions and comments. It allows further engagement and encourages ongoing conversation within your business Page. Knowing how the ads help in influencing such reactions is extremely important.

How it's calculated - All reactions whether negative or positive are counted as long as it is in response to your ads as they run.

Click Through Rate (CTR)

This metric counts the number of unique clicks received by your campaign and ads divided by impressions or how many times they're shown.

How it's used - This metric is an indication on how well your ads and keywords are performing. When you're paying your ads through CPM or oCPM, getting a high score for CTR is ideal. It will only mean your ads or campaign are receiving a greater number of clicks for much less money. For instance, when you're getting 1,000 impressions for 1 dollar, you would want to get as many clicks as you can from those impressions because what it costs you won't change whether 1 or 1000 people click.

How it's calculated - CTR is calculated by dividing the total number of clicks with the number of impressions. For instance, if you get 5 clicks and 50 impressions, your CTR is 10%.

Facebook Analytics

Facebook allows business owners and marketers with a variety of actionable data. One of the powerful tools you can take advantage of is Facebook Analytics. It offers a way for you to explore more user interactions with sales funnels and goal paths.

This tool is free and it is designed to be compatible with Facebook Ads. Granted Facebook ads do cost money. However, given the many updates and valuable data you can gather using the tool, it's hard to pass up on. Since the big update, many features and functions were added including the following:

- **Create Event Source Groups** from dashboard, retarget and segment people who took action following specific event path from your page
- Build your **Custom Audience** according to **Omni-channel Insights**.

How to access Facebook Analytics?

For the **Facebook Analytics Dashboard** to work, you must install pixel and allow it to run. After giving it time, it will eventually become populated with data.

- Open the dashboard to get an overview of the data.
- Click on Dashboards from the left sidebar. This will display **Omni-channel and Custom dashboards**.
- Choose Activity to explore data specific to funnels, purchases and active users among others.
- Add relevant charts and move them to your custom dashboard for a much easier access.

Here's how to add/ move relevant chart to your custom dashboard.

- Click on the icon for **Pin to a new dashboard**

- Choose the option to **Create a new dashboard** from the pop-up box
- Or pick from an existing dashboard.
- Add a name for the chart.
- Click on **Add to dashboard**.

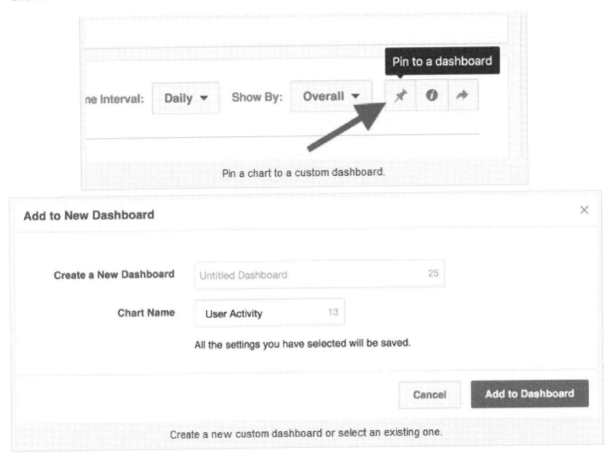

How to review Activity Reports?

Reports are crucial in understanding data. With this data, you are able to make informed decisions according to your specific needs. The good news is that the updated version of Facebook analytics dashboard offers a much more extensive reporting capabilities. It allows you to dig deeper into the available data. You can view micro-conversions combined with events and demographics.

For instance, if you're running an online store and you want to know which of your customers have the best conversion rate from Facebook, you can click on Activity and choose Revenue. This will display purchase-related data.

www.MichaelEzeanaka.com

167

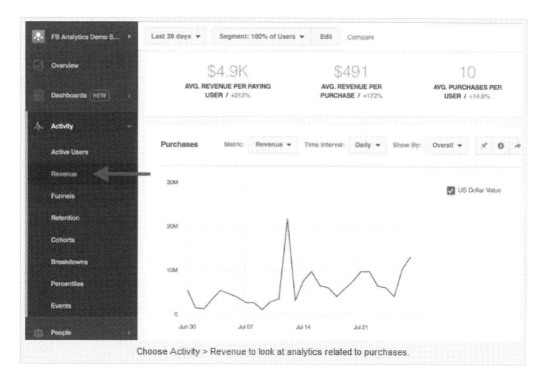

Choose Activity > Revenue to look at analytics related to purchases.

From here, you can narrow down the data even further by picking an option from the drop-down menu.

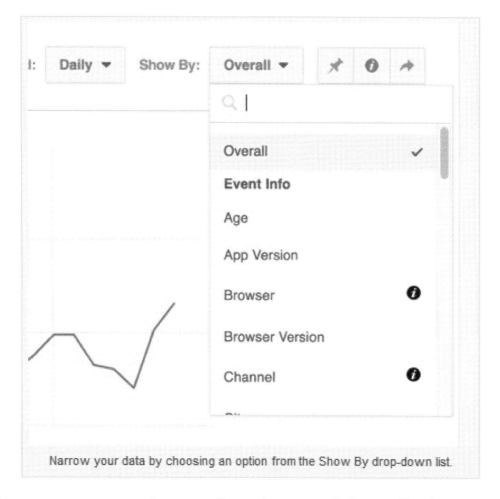

Narrow your data by choosing an option from the Show By drop-down list.

For example, if you want to see conversions according to the source of all the traffic, choose **Traffic Source**

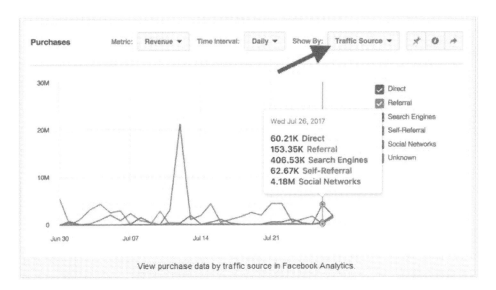

View purchase data by traffic source in Facebook Analytics.

You also have an option for creating cross-channel funnels. Doing so will allow you to test the different interaction paths and find out which ones offer the highest conversion rates.

Here's how to create funnel.

- Access Activity.
- Click on Funnels.
- Choose the option to Create Funnel from the upper-right corner.

Your funnels can be as detailed as you make them to be. Here are a couple of examples.

- Users who sent a message on your Facebook page and purchased from your website
- Users who went for app installation and purchased on your website
- Users who posted a reaction and purchased
- Users who posted a comment on one of your posts and purchased

How to use data from Facebook Analytics?

Facebook Analytics becomes very valuable when you are able to use the data to inform your campaigns. One of the best ways to maximize its use is to pay attention to the funnels that have the best conversion rates and push it further to get more customers from those funnels.

For instance, if the data shows you that people are converting after sending a message, you can take full advantage of this by engaging with people who *Like* your page with the use of Messenger chatbots. On the other hand, if people are converting much better after posting a comment, you should encourage more comments by including questions in your posts.

The bottom line is, if you are able to use the analytics data properly, you can make better decisions for your business and find out the best audience to target, the best placement for your ads, the best channels for driving traffic and the right kind of content to post.

Did You Know?

The best days to post on Instagram are Monday and Thursday. The best times to post are 2 a.m., 8-9 a.m., and 5 p.m. (CoSchedule)

Chapter 4 Quiz

Please refer to the Answer Booklet for the solution to this quiz

1. This section of Ads Manager offers a glance on the performance of your Facebook ads.

    A) Account Overview
    B) Ads
    C) Ad Sets
    D) Campaigns

2. What are the workflows offered in Facebook Ads Manager for creating and managing your ads?

    A) Assisted Creation
    B) Guided Creation
    C) Instant Creation
    D) Quick Creation

3. This workflow is ideal for advertisers who possess a more advances skill set. It will work perfectly with knowledge of Power Editor workflow.

    A) Assisted Creation
    B) Guided Creation
    C) Instant Creation
    D) Quick Creation

4. Which section do you need to go to in order to publish one of your edited ads?

    A) Edit
    B) Publish
    C) Review and Publish
    D) Edit and Publish

5. Where do you need to go to access reports from the Ads manager main menu?

    A) Access Report
    B) Campaign Report
    C) Ad Findings
    D) Ads Reporting

6. This counts the number of people who have seen your ad at least once.

   A) Reach
   B) Impressions
   C) Target
   D) Results

7. This metric counts how many clicks there were on links within your ad which directed people to experiences or destinations within or outside of Facebook.

   A) Reach
   B) Impressions
   C) Link Clicks
   D) Cost Per Result

8. This metric counts how many clicks there were on links within your ad which directed people to experiences or destinations within or outside of Facebook.

   A) Reach
   B) Impressions
   C) Link Clicks
   D) Cost Per Result

9. What are the things you can do with the updated Facebook Analytics?

   A) Create event source groups from dashboard
   B) Build your custom audiences you can base on omni-channel insights
   C) Omni-channel analytics
   D) Advanced machine learning/Artificial Intelligence capabilities

10. What do you need first before the Facebook Analytics dashboard can work?

   A) Customize your dashboard
   B) Install Facebook Pixel
   C) Access Reports
   D) Explore Activity

Chapter 5

Facebook Events Manager

Every click counts as an event as much as engagement and conversions do. And Facebook allows advertisers to measure all these online and offline events.

Events Manager is a feature of Business Manager. In this unified interface, advertisers are provided with an avenue for managing customer data sources both online and offline in a single place. Customer data sources can come from email, Point of Sale (POS), Customer Relationship Management (CRM), apps and websites among other online and offline sources. Access to these data sources can be done under the **Measure and Report Tab**

With Events Manager, you can simplify all tasks related to customer data source handling such as troubleshooting, management, setup and customer data discovery. There are five major aspects of Events Manager and they include the following.

App Events

This is helpful in managing app customer data in Facebook. It comes with a diagnostic tool for standardized custom events from apps and events and they can be used for reporting, audience creation and ad optimization.

Partner Integrations

This is a feature which can be used to connect to other platforms especially those used for customer management, interaction and purchases. Data can be pulled from these platforms into Events Manager. Among the platforms that are integrated into the Facebook events manager system include Shopify, Wix, Magento and Big Commerce.

Custom Conversions Enhancements

This tool paves the way to a much improved rule creation process. It allows businesses and marketers to share their custom conversions between different ad accounts. The enhancement also features an increase in the number of allowed custom conversions for every ad account up to a hundred.

Facebook Pixel Enhancements

The enhancements for Events Manager features a diagnostic tab that offers diagnostics about event errors, location link errors and the corresponding recommended troubleshooting steps.

Offline Events Enhancements

We've briefly mentioned offline events in the previous chapter. This includes events in your business' physical location. In Events Manager, the offline events enhancements now have a more efficient upload functionality. It includes automatic data mapping.

The importance of data sources in Facebook advertising cannot be emphasized enough. With data sources, advertisers can target customers more effectively and efficiently. With the Events Manager, data management has become much simpler. By allowing the tracking of events, measuring the effectiveness of Facebook ads and the value they bring to in-store sales, Facebook significantly increases the chance of success for businesses and marketers.

Facebook Pixel

You need to know whether your advertising efforts are effective or not. Facebook has an analytics tool that measures the effectiveness of your ads. It's called the Pixel. With this tool, you will be able to understand how people respond to your ads and posts through their actions on your website. With a better understanding of their behavior, you are more likely to effectively and efficiently reach a bigger audience.

There are three major ways where Pixel can be really helpful and such include the following:

- Ensure that ads are reaching the right people
- Grow your audiences
- Discover more Facebook advertising tools that can help grow your brand or business

The Facebook Pixel can be incorporated into your website by placing the code in your website's header. When a user pays a visit to your website and takes action during the visit, the pixel is triggered. It will then report the action to you. Not only will you be able to know when someone takes action, you will also be able to connect or reach the same customer in the future using Facebook ads (i.e. retargeting). An action can vary from making a purchase, doing a search or clicking buttons to get more information about a certain product.

What are the perks of using Facebook Pixel?

With the data collected by Pixel, you can refine your marketing strategy. By using this analytics tool effectively, you can reap the following benefits:

Target and reach the right audience

With the Pixel, you can find more customers. It will also allow you to find previous visitors who took the desired action on the website. You can even duplicate your best customers by creating Lookalike Audiences.

Increase your sales

Create automatic bidding so you can target users who are likely to take the desired action on your website. Through Pixel, you can figure out best ways for optimizing your ads for conversions.

Measure the effectiveness of ads

There's no more guess work. Pixel will let you know the direct result of putting out an ad. Useful data such as sales and conversions are accessible.

How to create a Facebook pixel?

Before you can create one, you must have a business website and you should be able to update the code for that website. To proceed, you can follow the below steps.

- Access Events Manager.
- Go to Pixels and click on the option to **Create a Pixel**.
- From the box, click on Create to finish the pixel creation.

- Copy your **Pixel ID or code**.

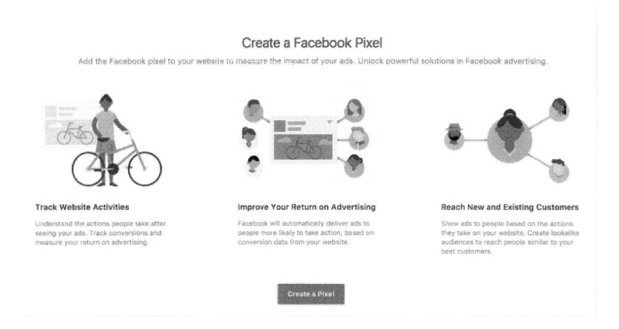

After creating pixel, you can proceed to place the code on your business website. The steps vary according to your specific situation.

How to add Facebook pixel when another person makes changes to your website?

If another person takes care of updating your website's code, you can use the steps here to send them an email of instructions for setting up the pixel on the site.

- Access **Ads Manager**.
- Go to **Facebook Pixels Tab**.
- Choose the option to **Set up pixel**.
- Click on **Email Instructions to a Developer**.
- Add the email address and click on Send.

Choose Installation Option ✕

How do you want to install the pixel code?

To use Facebook pixel, you must first install pixel code on your site. This code sends site visit information back to Facebook so you can measure customer actions and create smarter advertising.

 Install the Code Yourself
We'll walk you through the steps to install the pixel code.

 Email Instructions to a Developer
Send the installation instructions to a developer to install the pixel code for you.

Do you build your website or ecommerce tools on a popular third-party platform? **View pixel integrations** to see if there's an even easier way to install pixel.

Give Feedback

Email Pixel Code ✕

To

Add a recipient

How to update the website code yourself?

If you are updating the code for your website by yourself, you can follow these steps.

- Access the website's code and look for the header.

Find the **<head> </head> tags** in your webpage code, or locate the **header template** in your CMS or web platform. **Learn where to find this template or code** in different web management systems.

```
<!-- Example -->
!DOCTYPE html>
<html lang="en">
  <head>
    <script>...</script>
    insert_pixel_code_here
  </head>
```

- Copy and paste the entire code. Add it in the website's header by pasting it at the very bottom of the header right on top of the closing head tag.
- Make sure the code is working correctly by sending a test. Click on the option to **Send Test Traffic** after successfully adding the code to the website.
- Updating can take a couple of minutes. When the status shows Active, it means you have successfully installed the base code.

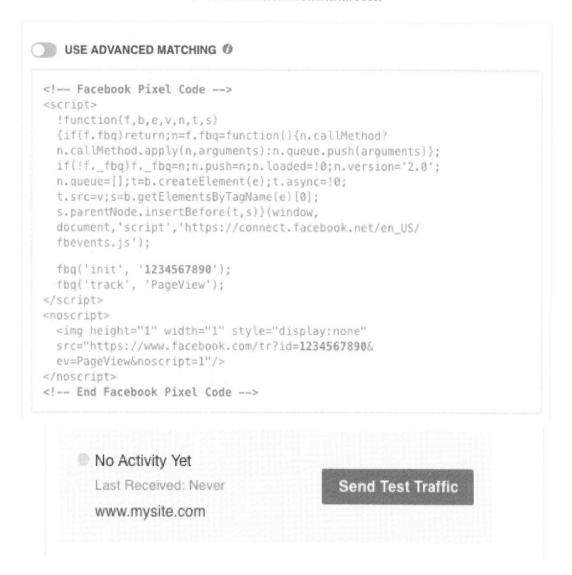

If you're using a tag manager like Adobe, Google Tag Manager, Segment and Tealium or your website is hosted on a web platform like Weebly, Shopify, Wix or Magento, the instructions on adding the pixel code is specific to the tag manager or web platform in use. Other web platforms supported include WooCommerce, Squarespace and BigCommerce.

How to track actions that matter?

After completing the step of placing the pixel on your website, you will have to add events that will allow you to monitor specific actions taken by people on your website. As we mentioned before, events are any actions that occur on your website. You can follow these steps to add events on the site.

- Access your **Events Manager**.
- Go to **Pixels Tab**.
- Proceed to **Set up pixel**.
- Choose the option to **Manually Install the Code Yourself** and Continue.

Install Your Pixel Code   ✕

To use Facebook pixel, you must first install pixel code on your website. This code sends site visit information back to Facebook so you can measure customer actions and create smarter advertising.

Choose an option to install the pixel code. You can change this choice later.

Use an Integration or Tag Manager
Facebook pixel currently integrates with **BigCommerce, Google Tag Manager, Magento, Segment, Shopify, Squarespace, Wix, WooCommerce** and many more. Learn about platform integrations.

Manually Install the Code Yourself
We'll walk you through the steps to install the pixel code.

Email Instructions to a Developer
Send the installation instructions to a developer to install the pixel code for you.

- Select the option to **Install Events**.
- Click on the toggle icon beside the event you want to track.

Purchase

Lead

Complete Registration

Add Payment Info

Initiate Checkout

Add to Cart

Add to Wishlist

Search

View Content

- Choose either of these options: Track Event on Page Load or Track Event on Inline Action

Track Event on Page Load

This option is ideal if you care about an action which is traceable when a user lands on a specific page on your website. A good example is a user reaching the confirmation page after a purchase has been completed.

Track Event on Inline Action

This option is best if you care about tracking an action which requires a user to click on something. For instance, if you want to trace clicks on Add to Cart or clicks on Purchase Button, you should choose this option.

- Add your event parameters such as Currency or Conversion Value. This is a recommended step and will allow you to measure any additional information pertaining to your event.

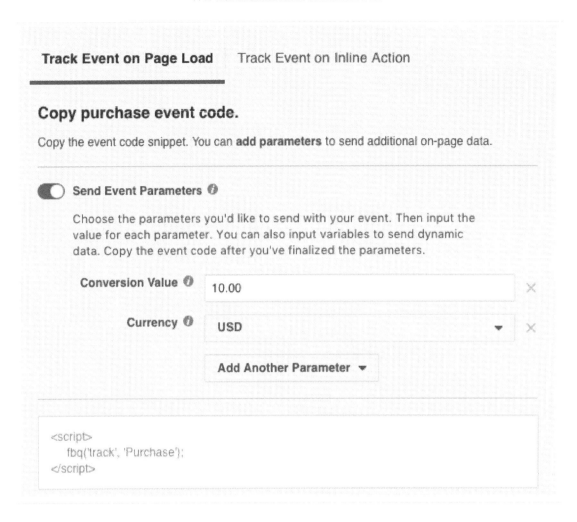

- Copy the event code and add it to your website's relevant page. Do not modify the pixel code that's already in the site's header. The placement of the pixel code shall vary between page load events and inline action events.

Page Load Events

The event code should be placed below the page's closing header section. For most sites, this is the spot after the opening <body> tag.

Inline Action Events

The event code should be placed between the script tags beside the action that you prefer to track. For instance, if you care about tracking a click on the Like button, the event code should be right next to it.

Event codes should be updated if you want to link an event to a specific action. These steps should be repeated for any additional listed events you want to track.

How to check if your pixel is up and running?

To make sure that the pixel you just added is working correctly, you can use a troubleshooting tool called **Facebook Pixel Helper.**

This is a Chrome plugin which you can use to check if the pixel is properly installed on your website. It can also be used to further understand information gathered from pixel as well as check for errors. Here's how to install the tool.

- Access the Chrome web store.
- Search for **Facebook Pixel Helper**.
- Click on **Add to Chrome**.
- Choose the option to **Add extension**.

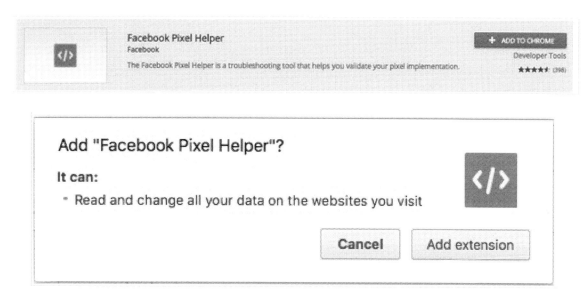

After successfully installing the extension, you will receive a notification indicating the addition of the plugin to Chrome. Also, you will see a small icon in the address bar.

- Click on the icon for Pixel Helper found in the address bar.
- A popup will appear showing the pixels found on the page. It will let you know whether or not the pixel setup was successful.

When the Facebook Pixel Helper is able to locate the pixel on your website and you receive no errors, you can commence creating your ads with the pixel.

What to do if you run into troubleshooting Pixel errors?

If Facebook Pixel Helper detects an error after installing the pixel on your site, you can also use the tool to troubleshoot and fix the issue to get the pixel up and running. There are five common errors that you may run into. These errors include the following.

- No Pixel Found
- Pixel Did Not Load
- Not a Standard Event
- Pixel Activated Multiple Times
- Invalid Pixel ID

Here are a couple of suggestions for fixing these common errors.

No Pixel Found

If you see this error message, the pixel code must be placed on your website. It may not have been added correctly. In this case, go back to setting up the pixel and make sure the steps are done properly.

Pixel Did Not Load

With this error, the Pixel Helper may have found the pixel in the site. However, it may not be able to pass the back data from your website. There are two possible causes for this error. One, this may appear as a result of firing up the pixel for a dynamic event. To fix it, you can try clicking on the button where the code is attached and clicking back on the Pixel Helper. Two, the error may appear as a result of a discrepancy on the pixel base code. You can attempt to remove the code from the site and trying to add it back again.

Not a Standard Event

In this case, Pixel Helper may have found the event code. However, it may not be a match to any of the standard events. It may be caused by a simple typo error. For instance, the event name may have been entered as Purchased instead of Purchase. Check back on the standard event names and make sure that the exact event code is entered correctly.

Pixel Activated Multiple Times

To fix the error, make sure that the pixel code is only used once. Do not place the same event code more than once on a single page to avoid this error.

Invalid Pixel ID

This error means that the pixel base code is not recognizable by Facebook. You can try replacing the pixel ID in the pixel base code with the one assigned to one of your active ad accounts.

Understanding the Pixel Event Data in Your Events Manager

Through Facebook pixel, advertisers can understand the actions taken by people on their website as a response to their Facebook ads. Event data is accessible on Pixel page. Now the next concern is how to understand the data. Here are a couple of factors you need to pay attention to.

High Level Event Metrics

From the Data Sources section, you will find information that allows you to measure and optimize ad campaigns that leverage pixel event data. On this page, you're able to view basic information about the pixel including last activity and status. If you're using multiple pixels, you can simply choose the pixel you want to access. These are a few sections you must get acquainted with.

Events Received

This section tells you the total number of events your pixel was able to receive.

Top Events

This is where you find out how well matched your data is to Facebook users.

Activity

This is a graph showing the number of events that are measured daily for the past 7 days that can be linked to people who viewed the ads. It is a valuable section that allows you to understand the behavior of the most recent visitors to your website. This also helps you identify any issues that may affect your events.

Events

From the summary page of Facebook Pixels, either choose the pixel you want to get information about or click on Details to access detailed insights about the performance of your Facebook ad. Among the key elements in the detail page are the following.

- **Time Frame** - You can use this section to make adjustments to the data's time frame. You can do this by clicking the corresponding button. Choose one of the options from the list in the dropdown menu.
- **Events Tab Graph** - This will display the number as well as the value of the received events, the matched and the attributed events. From here, you will know the amount of traffic received on your website. You can hover over different points in the graph for a view of the metrics breakdown. You can review the table in this section. If you see a dotted line, it only means the data on that section has not been updated for the day yet. You should remember that raw pixel fires are counted. Know the difference between page loads and browser sessions.
- **Events Tab Table** - This is another section that shows a table where you can find out the number and value for received events, matched and attributed events.

There are various reporting metrics and they include the following.

- **Events Received** - This is the total number of events that your pixel received.
- **Total Value** - This is the total value of all of the events within a selected time frame. The value is based on monetary value specific to the uploaded events.
- **Matched Events** - From the total number of events received, matched events is the number of events matched to Facebook users.
- **Matched Value** - This denotes the total value of matched events within a selected time frame.
- **Attributed Value** - From the total number of matched events, attribute events are the number of events that can be attributed to users who either viewed or clicked the ads across all your ad accounts associated to the event set. Events can be attributed with a maximum of 28 days after the occurrence of a click or an impression.
- **Attributed Events** - This counts the total of attributed events within a selected time frame.

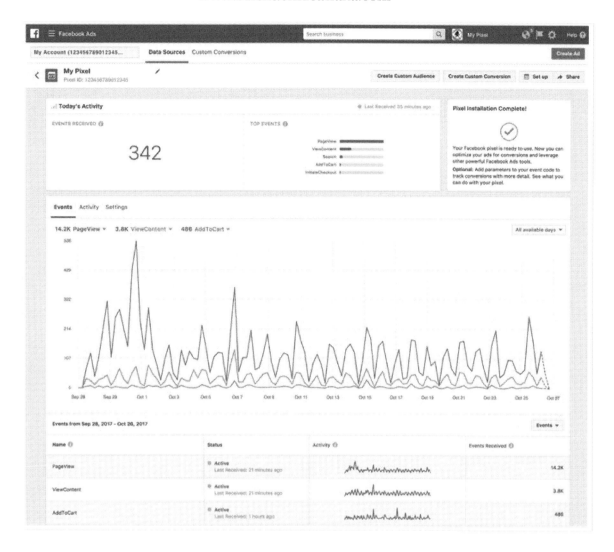

Activity

You refer to this section when you want to access a list of actions people have taken on your site. Choose the event you want to see and the most recent 100 events will be displayed.

> ## You can review the columns and breakdown the information by...
> - Event Category
> - Event Time
> - Device
> - Referring URL
> - Parameters such as currency or value

You will know the amount of traffic received for each of the metrics. You can also use the Activity page if your event setup requires some troubleshooting. It is also useful for making sure the website's event code is working properly.

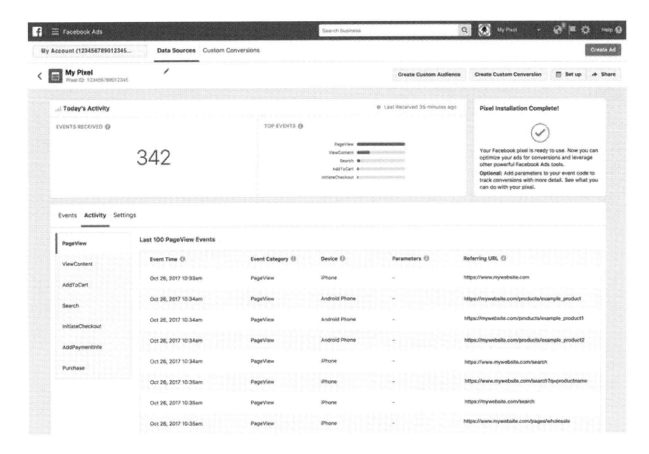

Settings

This section gives you access to the custom conversions and custom audiences associated to your Facebook pixels. This page will show you how they are performing. In addition, you will be able to view and create custom conversions and audiences by volume on this page.

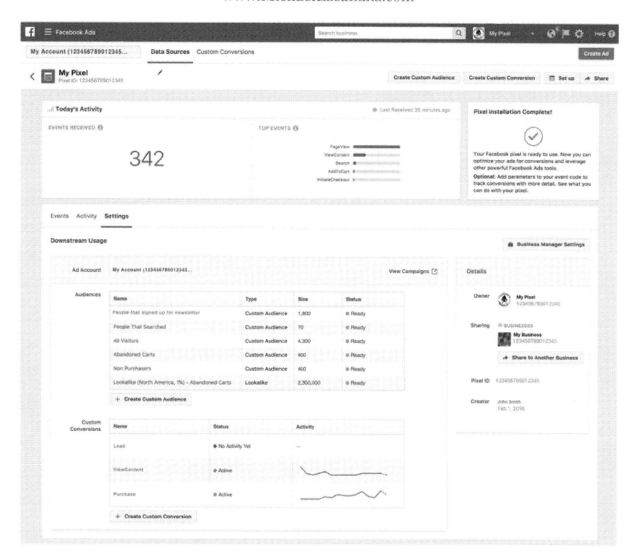

Standard Events versus Custom Conversions

You can use both standard events and custom conversions to track actions and optimize your ads. The major difference between the two is that standard events provide more features. While custom conversions may have less features, it proves to be much simpler to set up. If you do the editing yourself on your website, you may find it easier to use custom conversions. If you want more features, the ability to add parameters and you feel comfortable editing your site's code, then you should consider standard events.

To get a better idea of the differences between the two, refer to the list below.

Standard Events	Custom Conversions
You create it by adding to the pixel base code	You create it in Ads manager with the use of URL rules and there is no need for additional code
You can customize it with parameters	You can customize it using granular URL rules
You get aggregated reporting	You get separate reporting
Compatibility with dynamic product ads	You can't use it with dynamic product ads

How to create custom conversions?

- Access the section for **Custom Conversions**.
- Click on the option to **Create Custom Conversions**.
- Enter the URL or at least a portion of the URL representing the custom conversion. For instance, if you want a thank-you page when a purchase is completed, you can use a URL containing **/thankyou.php**.
- The equivalent of this URL in standard event is **Make Purchase**.

When you use URL Equals, you must include the domain "www" without either "http" or "https." Below are a few examples so you can get a better idea.

URL Option	How you'd set your rule	Equivalent Standard Event
URL Equals	www.mywebsiteurl.com/thankyou.php	Purchase
URL Contains	/thankyou.php	Purchase

Note: When you have other analytics tools, you can make it simpler by copying and pasting the URL from the page views list. This will help you ensure that mistakes and inaccurate numbers are avoided.

- Choose the category and click on Next.

- Enter the name for your custom conversion and add a description.
- Include a conversion value if it applies in the situation. For instance, when you are selling $15 worth of tickets, you must enter "10" as the value. Conversion values are only whole numbers. Additional characters like dollar signs are not accepted. When you include a conversion value, you'll be able to see the report with the return on your ad spend.
- Click on Create and click on Done on the next pop up.

- After completing these steps, you'll be able to create an ad according to your site's conversion objective. Choose the custom conversion to track and optimize for.

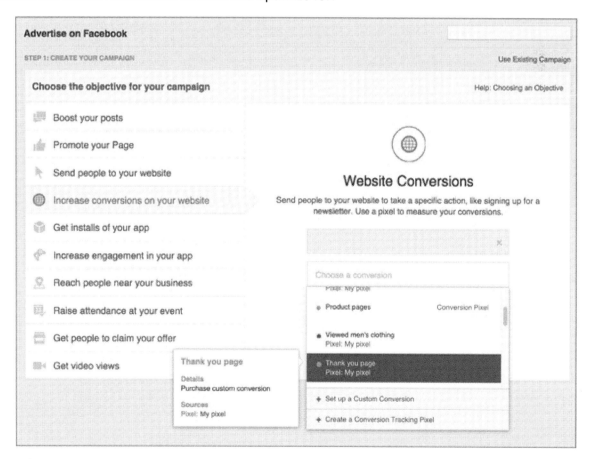

How to use custom conversions for splitting standard events?

After you've started utilizing standard events and found that you require more customization, you can add custom conversions in the mix. For instance, if you're selling ready to wear clothes and been relying on **ViewContent standard events** across all product lines but prefer to optimize them for separate categories, you can do this using custom conversions.

This can be achieved by creating the conversions based on the URL rules for different categories. Here's an example of applying the URL rule to optimize only for those that view clothing for men.

Remember, you are allowed a maximum of 100 custom conversions. You are also allowed to delete previously created ones to make room for new conversions.

Retargeting

Most of the people who would visit your website may not be ready to buy yet. They may drop by, wander around but eventually leave. This does not necessarily mean they are completely uninterested. As a matter of fact, they probably are interested but something came up or got in the way. It's your job to get them back and complete the action that you want them to finish.

Simply put, retargeting is about bringing your previous visitors back to your website. This form of online advertising works by using a cookie. When someone visits your ecommerce site for instance, a cookie is put in the browser. Through this cookie, you will be able to recognize and follow your visitors as they drop by other websites. With this information, you will be able to reach them effectively and efficiently with ads.

Facebook is an excellent tool for retargeting. There is a good chance that the visitors you want to reach again are part of the 2 billion active Facebook users.

To use retargeting effectively and maximize its full potential, your timing is incredibly important. Retargeting is most effective when implemented within 2 weeks of their visit. Here are a couple of tips on how to use retargeting effectively.

Remind them to complete the action.

In most cases, these visitors aren't just highly motivated to buy. Because of this, they need that little push to complete the action you want them to take. Sending them reminders will be of great help in this regard.

Reach them in places where they are most likely to make that purchase.

Here's an interesting finding. Most people use their mobile phones to browse but aren't exactly comfortable making the purchase on mobile. In which case, you may want to consider displaying retargeting ads exclusively for desktop. This is not a hard and fast rule however. Analyze your data and find out whether desktop users outperform mobile visitors or the other way around.

Capture their attention. Remind them of the items they're interested in.

One of the best ways to catch these visitors' attention is through the use of dynamic retargeting ads. This type of ad can be used to automatically show them the products they viewed previously. It is more likely to work because the ad is highly relevant.

Offer them a compelling reason to return and complete their purchase.

A great number of customers click Add to Cart but never get to checkout simply because they're looking to see if there are better options. The great number of cart abandoners can be attributed to a simple change of mind. However, you can change their mind back into completing their purchases by offering them a great deal. One of the best examples is to use a free shipping offer. A freebie or a discount can also work. Explore your options and offer them a little extra.

Consider providing customer service.

According to statistics, 83% of online shoppers require support in order to complete their purchases. The absence of customer support to help them along the way and answer their questions is one of the biggest reasons why add to cart actions do not translate to sales.

Although email and phone support are good, they are not as proactive as some shoppers need it to be. One solution that comes to mind is the use of **Facebook Messenger Destination Ads.**

These are simply ads that encourage customers to get in touch with the website. The ads can also direct them to Facebook Messenger. Through this, a one on one conversation is initiated with the hesitant customer. It's an excellent way to keep them interested and eventually complete the sale.

Stay in touch with them.

The longer you wait to close the sale the harder it gets to actually complete it. However, you can still benefit from staying in touch with them even after 14 days from their first visit. Just because they did not complete their purchase does not necessarily mean they are uninterested. While you have to think about immediate purchases, you also have to consider building long term relationships.

Through **Facebook Lead Ads**, you can entice them to subscribe and be part of your email list so when a great deal comes along, they'd be among the first to know. Simple things like this can help you convert more potential customers to paying customers.

Did You Know?

Customers spend more money (20-40 percent) on brands who engage directly with them on social media.
(Social Media Today)

Chapter 5 Quiz

Please refer to the Answer Booklet for the solution to this quiz

1. Which of the following is a feature which can be used to connect to other platforms especially those used for customer management, interaction and purchases?

    A) App Events
    B) Partner Integrations
    C) Custom Conversions
    D) Offline Events

2. Which of the following is helpful in managing app customer data in Facebook and comes with a diagnostic tool for standardized custom events from apps and events and they can be used for reporting, audience creation and ad optimization.

    A) App Events
    B) Partner Integrations
    C) Custom Conversions
    D) Offline Events

3. What are the benefits of using Facebook Pixel?

    A) Target and reach the right audience
    B) Increase your sales
    C) Measure the effectiveness of your ads
    D) Allow partners and agencies to share audiences

4. Which of the following are standard events?

    A) Purchase
    B) Lead
    C) Complete Registration
    D) Add to Cart

5. What is the troubleshooting tool you can use to check if the pixel is working correctly?

    A) Facebook Pixel Assistant
    B) Facebook Pixel Agent
    C) Facebook Pixel Help
    D) Facebook Pixel Helper

6. Which of these errors will appear when a pixel is found but unable to pass the back data from your website?

    A) Pixel Did Not Load
    B) Invalid Pixel ID
    C) Not a Standard Event
    D) Pixel Activated Multiple Times

7. Which of these reporting metrics pertain to the number of events that can be attributed to users who either viewed or clicked the ads across all your ad accounts associated to the event set?

    A) Events received
    B) Matched events
    C) Attributed events
    D) Attributed value

8. Which of the following statements is false?

    A) You create Standard events by adding to the pixel base code
    B) You don't need an additional code for Custom Conversions
    C) You can customize conversions using parameters
    D) Standard events are compatible with dynamic product ads and custom conversions are not

9. What is the limit of custom conversions you are allowed to have at a time?

    A) 25
    B) 50
    C) 90
    D) 100

10. Which strategies could work in retargeting audiences?

    A) Reach your audience where they are most likely to buy
    B) Remind them of the items they are interested in
    C) Offer them a compelling reason to complete their purchase
    D) Leave them alone

Chapter 6

Customer Avatar and Facebook Audience

A customer avatar is a fictional identity that you can use to guide your decisions about selecting your target audience. It can help you get a better understanding of your customers. Put simply, an avatar is the archetype of who your ideal customers are. Knowing your target audience better will help you create more relevant content and sell more effectively by reaching the right people.

What are the benefits of a customer avatar?

- It can help you create a better connection with your customers when you understand them well enough.
- It will guide you in the process of producing highly targeted messages that can get you better conversion rates.
- It can inspire your ad and content ideas.
- It can help you in driving more sales and increasing customer retention.
- It will allow you to find the audience your product will most likely appeal to.

What are the essentials of creating a customer avatar?

To be more effective, your customer avatar must not be a typical stereotype. It should reflect the persona of real people. You need to really dig deep and get to what makes these people tick. For this to happen, you need to base the creation of your customer avatar according to real data. With this said, you can use the following information to guide you.

Background – This includes basic details about a person like education, employment type, interests and turn-offs among others.

Demographics - Age range, location, gender, income and other demographical info are also essential in determining who they are and where you might find them.

Characteristics - Identify your customer's interests, influences and hobbies. What is it that defines their character? This information is helpful in finding out what can capture their interest.

Pain Points - What are their concerns, challenges or objections? These pain points are very crucial and will help you zero in on how to connect with them effectively. With this information, you can find better ways to engage them.

Gain - Knowing your customers' desires, their preferred results and outcomes are important in determining the best reason why they will buy. It is very helpful information that you can use to increase conversion.

There are many ways to collect these important pieces of information. To be authentic, you need to create your customer avatar based on real and actual customers.

You can utilize your current base of customers for a survey. An offer can be made to compel them to participate in your little survey. Another way is through interviews which you can do via email, phone or even in person.

An interview or a survey will really allow you to go in-depth. However, it can be challenging to get people to participate. An alternative is to utilize resources already available to you. A good example is using analytics systems such as Google Analytics or Facebook Audience Insight.

Facebook Audience Insight

With Audience Insights, you get access to aggregated information about different groups of people starting with Facebook users to users who have connected to your Page and people that belong in Custom Audience.

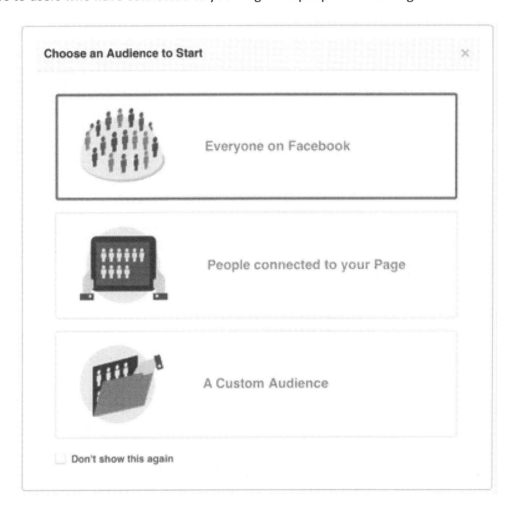

Among the things that you can get from Insights include the following.

Demographics - breakdown of age and gender, job titles, education levels, etc.

Interests and Hobbies - This includes information obtained from third-party giving you an idea about the products your audience may be interested in.

Lifestyles - This is a combination of demographics information and people's interests particularly in your brand or business.

With the options above, you have a good range of audiences to choose from. However, you must be careful about choosing the right one. Accessing data about all users may not necessarily give you a good insight about your target audience while the users connected to your page may not allow you enough room to identify potential niches.

There's also a possibility that some of your followers are not part of your actual customers. To avoid these issues, it will be useful to rely on Audience Insights to determine custom audiences rather than identifying broader audiences.

Custom Audience

From an existing customer list (e.g. email list), a custom audience can be created. And with a custom audience, you can laser focus your Facebook, Instagram and Audience Network Ads to them.

Your hashed customer list can be uploaded, imported or copy and pasted and it will be used to match with Facebook users.

Custom Audiences is an excellent way of reaching customers that you already know using Facebook ads. Your customer list must include contact information such as phone numbers or email addresses. Information you've collected from either an app or your website may also be useful. With this information, Facebook can deliver your ads to the people that match your custom audience from the list.

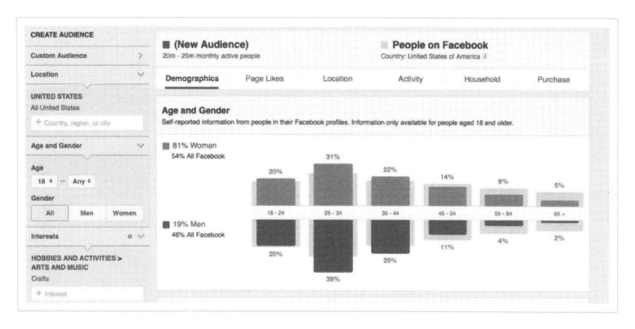

How to create Custom Audience from customer file?

Before you head on to creating a Custom Audience, there are two essential things you have to prepare for. One, you need to get your customer file ready. As you go on creating it, stick to best practices during the process. Two, you have to make sure that you are compliant with the General Data Protection Regulation or GDPR most especially if your customer list includes EU residents. It's an important matter you have to pay attention to. With these two requirements completed, you can follow these steps to start creating your Custom Audience.

- Access **Audiences**.
- With an existing audience, click on the dropdown menu for **Create Audience** and choose **Custom Audience**.

- If you don't have an existing audience, click on the audience creation buttons and choose **Create a Custom Audience**.
- Select the Customer file.
- Choose the option to Add it from your own file.

Adding a Customer File

- Go to the dropdown menu for **Original Data Source**.
- Choose where you want to get the file from. You have an option to either upload it as a .txt or .csv file or copy and paste the information.
- To upload a file, choose the option to **Upload File** and pick the customer file.
- To copy and paste, go to the field that says, **"Paste your content here"**
- Enter a name for your **Custom Audience** and add a description then choose Next.

From the information you obtain about your customers using Custom Audience, you can create a customer avatar that is realistic and truly representative of your target customer. A challenge here is if your Custom Audience is not as large as it should be to get a more comprehensive perspective of your ideal customers.

In this case, you can shift to another group of audience to analyze. You can switch to All Facebook Users and work on segmenting them according to some targeting qualifications. You can segment them based on their interests or any characteristics relevant to your brand or business.

Facebook Live

Facebook Live allows all users including Pages, people and public figures the ability of sharing live video with friends and followers. For businesses and marketers, Facebook live is a way to increase reach and improve audience engagement.

Benefits of Facebook Live

The popularity of social media and online video streaming and the combination of both makes Live a commendable tool. Using Facebook Live for marketing brings a string of benefits.

It can drive engagement.

People are more likely to post a comment on Facebook Live videos. As a matter of fact, Live videos get ten times more comments than regular videos do. People also spend three times longer watching live videos that regular ones.

When you broadcast longer, you present more opportunity for people to share and discover your live video. Facebook allows 90 minutes for Live. By humanizing your brand, you have a bigger opportunity to improve your level of engagement with customers and social followers.

Facebook Live offers a great user experience.

The ability to participate and become involved gives users an exceptional experience. In a world where people are constantly bombarded by ads and announcements, Live video seems like a welcome relief.

Marketers can do a live stream of Q&A sessions, sneak peaks for new products, news sharing or even a behind-the-scenes of a live event. Viewers can provide real time feedback, interact with the broadcaster and other viewers. From the marketing perspective, this is an excellent PR opportunity and is absolutely useful as part of brand strategy.

It can help in boosting organic reach.

One of the most excellent ways of boosting your organic reach is through Facebook Live video. It is quite a distinct type of content. And Facebook algorithm distinguishes between native and Live video with the latter being favored. It means Live Videos have a higher chance of appearing at the top of the News Feed during the broadcast. On top of this, the video is still viewable and discoverable after the broadcast.

There is a unique notification system for Facebook live video. Facebook automatically sends a notification to users who have either recently or frequently interact with the page of the profile broadcasting the live video. This gives such videos more prominence helping brands and businesses reach top-of-mind.

It's affordable.

The cost of live streaming is among its biggest advantages. Sophisticated broadcasting equipment is not a requirement. A little investment on cable, microphone, tripod and lighting can go a long way. Even natural lighting works. People seem to connect better with raw live videos because of their authenticity.

It offers subscription to Live notifications.

People are drawn to dynamic content. With the availability of subscription to Live notifications, interest and a sense of urgency is triggered among followers. The prospect of real time interaction is a compelling enough reason for viewers to join the live broadcast.

The Live Video stays on your Feed.

Even after the live broadcast, the video gets shown on your Facebook page which means followers can still discover and watch the content. This is among the many reasons why advertisers are taking advantage of this opportunity to leverage their videos and boost the effectiveness and efficiency of their online marketing campaigns.

Possible Challenges with Facebook Live

Facebook Live video is not without challenges. In a live broadcast, anything can happen and you must prepare yourself for any possible issues.

Technical Issues

Technical glitches such as blurry videos, lagging, slow streaming or warped sounds can be too obtrusive that viewers may lose interest tuning in to the live broadcast.

Censorship

Facebook Live videos must comply with the Community Standards. You may be in control of the content you broadcast but censoring viewer participation is another challenge.

Controversy

There have been many controversial Live videos and they're not exactly the good kind. In any brand or business, image, confidentiality and conduct are crucial. Boosting your organic reach and building customer engagement should not in any way compromise your brand's image.

Accessibility

If your target audience is within the same time zone, accessibility is not a problem at all. However, if you have a wider target audience, timing can be quite a challenge. It is crucial to catch your viewers at the right time. If you're targeting people across the world, consider the possibility of doing multiple live streams.

Facebook Live Features

Facebook Live is rich in useful features that can help you optimize your brand strategy. Such features include the following.

Notifications

With its very own notification system, Facebook Live can be known to followers in real time. Notifications are also set to on by default which means marketers have a great chance of reaching their audience during their broadcasts. Any person who have recently or frequently interacts with their Page can receive the notification. Other users can also opt to subscribe so they will be notified every time a broadcaster goes Live.

Invite Friends

Broadcasters can reach more people through their viewers. Viewers have the option to send an invite to their friends and watch the broadcast with them.

Facebook Live Map

This map is designed to allow users to discover Live videos easily. All Live videos currently broadcasting will be shown on the map as a blue dot. Popular broadcasts are shown in larger dots. Users can access the map on desktop. When they hover over a dot, they will see a preview of the video.

Live Reactions

Live videos get real time reactions. All the Reactions are shown on the video as the audience clicks on one of the six emoji-like Reactions.

Filters

Live videos can also be filtered which is a great feature for broadcasters. To add a filter, you can follow these steps.

- Start the recording of your live broadcast.
- Tap on the icon for the magic wand.
- Scroll your mouse to the left to access the filter options.
- Tap on a filter to use it.

Snapchat-Like Masks

Masks are also available for broadcasters which can make for a more interesting video. To use a mask during a live broadcast, you can follow these steps.

- Start the recording of your live broadcast.
- Tap on the icon for the magic wand.
- Choose the icon mask from the creative tools tray found at the bottom of the page.
- Scroll your mouse through the options and simply tap on any mask to use it.
- To remove a mask, scroll to the left and click on No mask.

Facebook Live API

An existing broadcasting setup can be incorporated into Live using the Facebook Live API. Instead of streaming from mobile devices, broadcasters can use a professional camera or a sophisticated audio setup. There are other features that come with Live API including special effects, on-screen graphics, instant replay and camera switching. Other sources such as screencasts and games can also be streamed through API. Other possibilities with API include continuous live streaming and scheduled live broadcasts.

Continuous Live Streaming

A continuous live feed is possible with API. The setup is definitely more complex than a mobile broadcast but it's a great option for users who may require a continuous streaming.

Scheduled Live Broadcast

Building up the audience is a good strategy to enforce. This can be done through announcements as posts to your News Feed. One-time notification will be sent as a reminder before the live streaming begins but fans can access a pre-broadcast lobby. It's a way for them to connect and interact. Live broadcasts can be scheduled up to 1 week ahead and fans can enter the lobby 3 minutes before the broadcast.

Share in a Group/Event

Facebook Live has various live streaming options. It allows broadcasting from either a profile or a Page. The Facebook Live Video can also be shared directly in a group or an event.

Metrics

There are different metrics used for measuring the performance of live video broadcasts. Metrics for video in Facebook Insights including number of views, top videos, 30-second videos, viewer engagement and demographic breakdown of minutes viewed among others along with 2 Facebook Live video metrics: peak concurrent viewers and viewers during the live broadcast, are used.

Peak Concurrent Viewers - This records the highest number of viewership during the live broadcast.

Viewers During Live Broadcast - It displays the number of viewers in every moment of the broadcast.

How to start broadcasting a Facebook Live video?

A red icon will show in the top left-hand corner of a live broadcast. **Live** will also appear beside the icon, displaying the number of viewers in real time. To start broadcasting, you can follow these steps.

- Click **Update Status**.
- Tap on the **Live Video** icon.
- Enter a description for the video.
- Select the audience to share the video with.
- Go live.

A broadcaster will be able to see the number of current viewers along with the names of friends watching and the comments in real-time. When the live broadcast ends, a post will be saved on Timeline just like any regular video.

Facebook Live Tips

While there are a lot of things you can do right in Facebook Live so many things can also go wrong. You can ensure the success of your Live videos by following these tips.

Plan the broadcast.

Anything can happen during a live broadcast but this doesn't mean you should just leave everything to chance. Stream with a purpose. Have your objective in mind when planning your content.

You have to think about why the message can be best delivered in a Live stream rather than in another content format. Consider the things you want to say and the topic you want to cover during the broadcast. Be clear about the things you want to say and do.

Tell people when the broadcast is going to happen.

Treat Facebook Live as if you're hosting an event. Because you want people to show up, you should tell them exactly when it's going to happen. Don't just post something about the upcoming broadcast. You may also want to encourage people to enter your Live video subscription. To reach more people, consider promoting your broadcast in other social channels.

Check your connection.

There's nothing more annoying than lagging during a broadcast especially for a viewer. To avoid this issue, make sure to check your connection and that you have a strong signal before going live. Use a speed test app to ensure that your internet speed is fit for live streaming.

Make your description compelling.

Catch your audience's attention with an informative and compelling description. Give them context. Make sure you offer them a good reason to tune in.

Tag your location.

You can reach people through notifications but you can also broaden your reach further by appearing on Facebook Live Map. You can reach new viewers by being discoverable on the Map. All it takes is to tag your location.

Encourage your viewers to follow you.

To ensure the number of your future viewership keeps growing, you can offer your viewers the option to subscribe to your Facebook Live videos. This way, they get automatically notified when you broadcast. They may not be aware of the option so make sure they are informed.

Be responsive to comments.

Engagement is essential in the success of your social content. With Facebook Live video, you have the best chance to engage your viewers. Read and respond to their comments in real time. Mention your viewers by their name. Make them feel involved and included.

Broadcast for extended periods of time.

The longest you can broadcast on mobile is 90 minutes. You don't have to consume that much time but spend at least 10 minutes live. It will give you more time to reach people and interact with them as you get your message across.

Finally, be resourceful and creative with your broadcasts. Do not be afraid to experiment. Explore different kinds of broadcasts. This is the best way to find out what resonates the most with your audience.

When is it best to use Facebook Live?

Depending on your strategy, the requirements of your campaign and your objectives, Facebook Live video can be quite useful. However, there are a couple of situations that call for live streaming and such situations include the following.

- Discuss hot topics
- Do a Q&A session
- Present breaking news
- Broadcast performances and live events
- Show behind-the-scenes
- Product demonstration
- Make announcements or launch campaign

As long as it is relevant and useful to your brand or business, go for it!

Facebook Creative Hub

This is the destination to help with your creative process from learning about, creating a mock up and a preview to testing your Facebook and Instagram ads. The Hub is a resource within Facebook Ads that allows advertisers to explore, share and create.

How exactly can Creative Hub help you in creating more effective Facebook ads?

There are a lot of ways that Creative Hub can be of assistance from learning about the most successful and most creative ad campaigns to sharing ideas that'll help you manage your own ad. Below is a list of the biggest benefits and the best ways to maximize the use of the hub.

Get inspired by big brands.

Access tons of examples of every ad type using the Get Inspired button.

Create a concept and edit your idea with a mockup.

Some people forego the step of creating a mockup for their ads simply because it can be challenging. With this feature in Creative Hub, it's easier to create a mockup and bring your ideas to life until you are able to come up with the most effective and relevant ads for your campaigns.

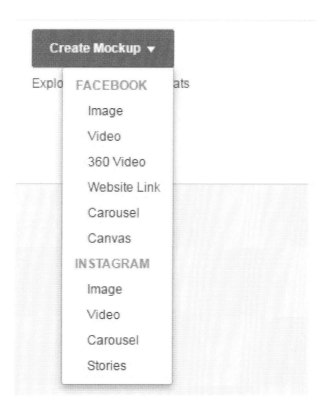

Test your images to make sure they are approved.

Another cool feature of Creative Hub is that it allows you to add images in your mockup ads using a built-in checker. So even before you devote your time to creating your final draft, you have a good idea with regards to whether or not your images will be approved. On top of this, Facebook can also gives you a rough idea on how the use of your image can contribute to the performance of your ad.

Discover new ad formats.

There are tons of things to learn from Creative Hub. You can get creative ideas even with new ad formats. You can get more of this from **Facebook Collections** and **Instagram Stories**.

Discover Instagram.

If you're not using Instagram ads yet, Creative Hub is a good place to start exploring this idea. You can learn from the Instagram pros and create your own mockup too until you are comfortable enough to put it out there and reap the benefits of using this format.

Improve your mobile presentation.

It is undeniable how people rely on their mobile phones for any task possible including browsing and shopping. With Creative Hub, you can get an idea how your content is presented on mobile devices. View the content the way mobile viewers see it and make the necessary adjustments.

You can also use Creative Hub for sharing ideas with your group or clients. You can preview your ads before they go live. Creative Hub also makes it easier to manage, edit and export your content.

Chapter 6 Quiz

Please refer to the Answer Booklet for the solution to this quiz

1. This is a fictional identity that you can use to guide your decisions about selecting your target audience.

   A) Facebook Audience
   B) Facebook Avatar
   C) Custom Audience
   D) Customer Avatar

2. What are the benefits of creating a customer avatar?

   A) It can help you create a better connection with your customers when you understand them well enough
   B) It will guide you in the process of producing highly targeted messages that can get better conversion rates.
   C) It can inspire your ad and content ideas and will allow you to find the audience your product will most likely appeal to
   D) It can help you in driving more sales and increasing customer retention

3. What are the essential information that will help you in the process of creating a customer avater?

   A) Background and Demographics
   B) Characteristics
   C) Pain Point
   D) Gain

4. With this feature, you get access to aggregated information about different groups of people starting with Facebook users to users who have connected to your Page to people that belong in Custom Audience.

   A) Customer Avatar
   B) Lifestyle
   C) Audience Insight
   D) Target Audience

5. What are the two things you need to prepare for before you head on to creating a Custom Audience?

   A) Customer File
   B) GDPR Compliance
   C) Existing Audience
   D) Facebook Users

6. This feature allows all users including Pages, people and public figures the ability of sharing live video with friends and followers.

    A) Facebook Live
    B) Facebook Video
    C) Facebook Streaming
    D) Facebook Messenger

7. Which of the following statements is not true.

    A) Facebook Live has its own notification system
    B) Facebook Live notifications are set to on by default
    C) Any person who have recently or frequently interacts with the broadcaster's Page can receive notification.
    D) There is no subscribe option to Facebook Live notifications.

8. This feature is designed to allow users to discover Live videos easily by displaying all Live videos currently broadcasting.

    A) Facebook Live Notifications
    B) Facebook Live Map
    C) Facebook Live Recording
    D) Facebook Live Filters

9. Which are included in the list of metrics used by Facebook in measuring the success of live video broadcasts?

    A) Peak concurrent viewers
    B) Viewers during the live broadcast
    C) Viewer engagement
    D) Metrics for video through Facebook Insights

10. This is the destination to help with your creative process from learning about, creating a mock up and a preview to testing your Facebook and Instagram ads

    A) Creative Center
    B) Command Center
    C) Creative Hub
    D) Creative Ads

Did You Know?

Video will be more important for social media content marketing than ever. According to Smart Insights, 90 percent of all content shared by users on social media in 2017 was video.

Congratulations!

The fourth character of the password required to unlock the Answer Booklet is letter u.

Chapter 7

Facebook Ad Campaign

There are 3 parts to the Facebook campaign structure and they include the following.

Campaign - A group of ads and ad sets makes a campaign. Each campaign is guided by one advertising objective.

Ad set - A group of ads makes an ad set. Targeting, schedule, budget, placement and bidding are defined at this level.

Ad - Your creative content makes an ad.

By making these components work together, you can run your ads exactly the way you want to run them and reach who you want to reach.

Choosing the Right Objective for Your Ads

Granted, your campaign goals will more likely evolve as your business expands. However, the starting point is always on building awareness for your brand or business and acquiring new customers. You will eventually want to compel people to purchase a product or service. You may also want to encourage them to sign up and join an event you're organizing.

There are various objectives that can go hand in hand with your business goals. Let's explore them one by one.

Goal 1: To raise public awareness of the business

If you want to increase public awareness of your business or brand, you need to tell people what it is that makes your brand or business valuable. People must be made to understand the overall value of your business that makes it unique among others i.e. your unique selling or value proposition.

The complementary advertising objectives to this main goal are Reach and Engagement.

Reach - To achieve this your ad needs to be shown to people either residing nearby or around the general location of your business.

Engagement - To drive engagement, you must connect with people you have already reached and boost your post to further grow your reach.

Goal 2: To find more potential customers

To achieve this objective, you need to find different ways to capture people's interest in your product or service. A couple of things that can work effectively include newsletter sign-ups or attendance in local events hosted by your business.

For instance, a newly opened local grocery delivery service aims to attract customers. To achieve this goal, they created a lead ad and had people sign up in their notification of the delivery service. They had an event launch and awarded attendees by giving them 20% off in their order.

The complementary advertising objectives to this main goal are Conversions and Lead Generation.

Conversions - To improve conversion rates on your website, you will need to run ads that compels people to visit.

Lead generation - To be able to gather leads for the business, you need to run ads that can collect people's information. A good example is a sign up for notifications and newsletters.

Engagement - Increase your event's attendance by creating ads that can promote your event.

Messages - To start communication with your potential customers, you need to run ads that are compelling enough to start a conversation, as well as, encouraging enough for your customers to respond.

Goal 3: To increase sales of the products or services

To measure the success of your campaign, you need to keep track of the number of people who viewed your ad, visited your website and purchased your product or service.

The complementary advertising objectives to this main goal are Engagement and Conversions.

Engagement - When you make an offer, you would want people to sign up and claim it. To do this, you need to create ads with discounts, coupons and other special offers.

Conversions - Interaction and engagement is essential for conversions. Find a way to build communication with your existing audience.

Messages - Connect with your customers by creating ads that can keep them interested and compel them to purchase your products or services.

Setting Your Advertising Objectives

When people see your ads, you want them to respond accordingly. This is why before you create your ad, you need to have a clear objective. Allow this objective to guide your creative process. And this objective should be perfectly aligned with the overall goals for your brand or business. For instance, if you're aiming to get interested people to visit your website, you must create ads that encourage them to go.

Advertising objectives can be grouped into 3 categories. They are awareness, consideration and conversion.

Awareness

These are objectives for generating interest in your brand or business. There are two items in this group: Brand Awareness and Reach.

1. Brand Awareness – This basically entails increasing the awareness of your products or services. As well as, reaching people who are more likely to recall/ remember your ads

Platforms that support this objective	Ad formats to utilize
Facebook	Single image
Instagram	Carousel
Messenger	Single video
	Slideshow

2. Reach – This entails creating ads that can reach as many people from your audience

Platforms that support this objective	Ad formats to utilize
Facebook	Single image
Instagram	Carousel
Messenger	Single video
	Slideshow

Consideration

These are objectives that aim to put your business in the mind of people. When they start thinking about the business, the next goal is to compel them to seek more information about it.

1. Traffic - To increase your website's visits. To have people use your app

With this objective, you can send more people to the website or build their engagement in the app.

Platforms that support this objective	Ad formats to utilize
Facebook	Single image
Instagram	Carousel
Messenger	Single video
Audience Network	Slideshow
	Collection

2. App installs - To direct people to the app store where your app can be downloaded

Platforms that support this objective	Ad formats to utilize
Facebook	Single image
Instagram	Carousel
Messenger	Single video
Audience Network	Slideshow

3. Engagement - To have more people see and engage with your Page and posts

With this objective, you can do the following.

- Boost your post and improve post engagement
- Promote your Page and get more Page Likes
- Have more people claim an offer from your Page and receive more Offer claims
- Increase the attendance for an event on your Page and increase Event responses

Platforms that support this objective	Ad formats to utilize
Facebook	Single image
Instagram (except event ads)	Single video
	Slideshow

4. Video Views - To promote videos for product launches, customer stories raising brand awareness or showing behind-the-scenes footage

Platforms that support this objective	Ad formats to utilize
Facebook	Single image
Instagram	Carousel
Audience Network	Slideshow

5. Lead Generation - To collect lead information from people who are interested in the brand or businesses

Platforms that support this objective	Ad formats to utilize
Facebook	Single image
Instagram	Carousel
Messenger	Slideshow
	Single video

6. Messages - To have more conversations with more people and offer support, answer questions, generate leads and drive transactions

Platforms that support this objective	Ad formats to utilize
Facebook	Single image
Instagram	Carousel
Messenger	Slideshow
	Single video

Conversion

These are objectives encouraging people who expressed interest in your business to use and purchase your product or service.

1. **Conversions** - To have more people use your website, mobile app or Facebook app. To monitor and measure your conversions, use app events and use Facebook pixel

Platforms that support this objective	Ad formats to utilize
Facebook	Single image
Instagram	Carousel
Messenger	Slideshow
Audience Network	Single video
	Collection

2. **Catalog Sales** - To show the products from your catalog to your target audience

Platforms that support this objective	Ad formats to utilize
Facebook	Single image
Instagram	Carousel
Messenger	
Audience Network	

3. **Store Visits** - To promote multiple business locations to nearby people

Platforms that support this objective	Ad formats to utilize
Facebook	Single image
	Carousel
	Single video
	Slideshow
	Carousel

How to Set Up an Ad Account in Business Manager?

- Access your **Business Manager Settings**.
- From the **People and Assets tab**, choose **Ad Accounts**.
- From the right side section, click on **Add New Ad Account**.
- Pick from any of these options: **Create a New Ad Account**, **Claim Ad Account** and **Request Access to an Ad Account**.
- If you pick any of the last two options, you must enter the corresponding **Ad Account ID**.

After setting up the ad account, you are required to provide additional account information and credit card data before you can begin advertising.

How to Add your Ad Account Info?

- From the Business **Manager Main Menu**, go to **Ad Account Settings**.

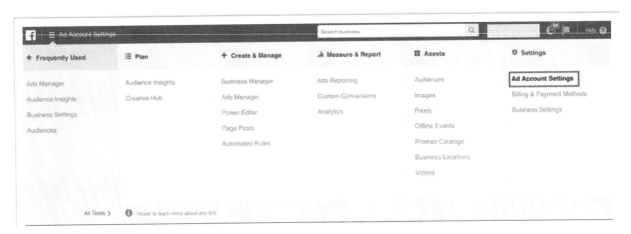

- Enter details including your company's name, address and other pertinent information.

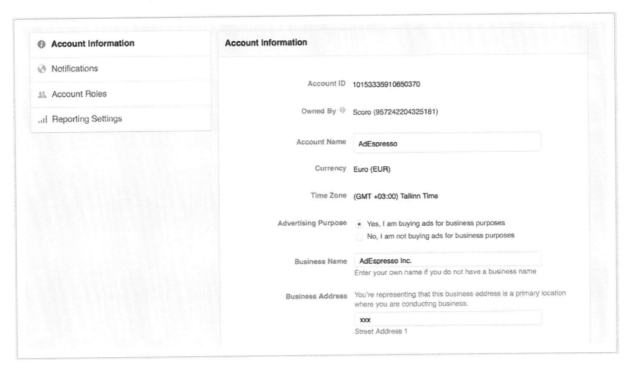

- Under **Payments tab**, choose **Add Payment Method**.
- Fill in your billing information.
- Enter your time zone and select your billing currency.
- After completing your ad account information, click on **Save Changes**.

How to Set Up your Billing and Payment Information?

- From the **Business Manager Menu**, click on **Billing & Payment Methods**.

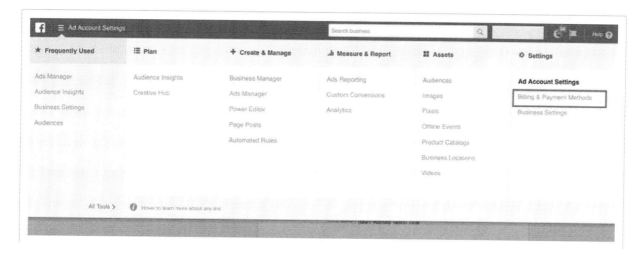

- You can do the following on the Billing page:

> • Add a new payment method.
> • Edit existing payment methods.
> • Set your ad account's spending limit.

How to add new payment method?

- Click the green button for **Add Payment Method**.
- Select your preferred method.

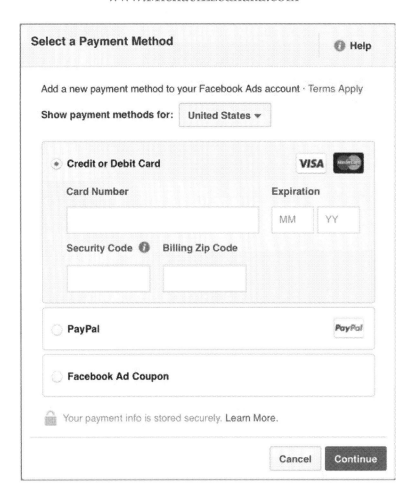

- Enter your information.
- Click Continue.

Adding Multiple Payment Options

There are multiple payment options accepted including Paypal payments and credit card payments. You also have the option to **Add multiple payment options**.

This is not necessary but as you grow your advertising efforts and push through your campaigns, adding a secondary payment method can help you avoid any issues.

This backup method will be useful in certain instances such as your primary card expiring or reaching your monthly limit or your card being blocked for any reason. This way, your advertising campaign won't be jeopardized and you won't be prevented from delivering your message and reaching your potential customers.

If you don't have any backup in place, then in the instance that your primary card fails, your campaign will suffer. Everything will be paused immediately until the outstanding balance is settled. After that, you will have to restart everything in your campaign manually one by one. This can be such a grueling task if you're running multiple campaigns. A secondary payment method can help you avoid the hassle.

How to Set Spending Limit?

You have the option to put a cap on your ad account spending. This way, you can ensure that you don't exceed your monthly advertising budgets.

Setting up an **Ad Account Spending Limit** is especially useful when you're working with agencies. It is important to ensure that your agency won't spend more than you're ready for.

It's quite simple to set your account limit. All you need to do is click on the option to **Set Account Spending Limit**. Enter the amount and you're done.

The key to setting the limit is finding the sweet spot. You don't want to go way beyond but you should also avoid setting the amount too low. When you do, you may face a couple of challenges along the way. Every time you reach the limit, your accounts will be paused. It will stay on pause for 15 minutes or more. Losing time and momentum is not ideal when you want to reach as many people as you want.

Limits on Facebook Ad Accounts

There are certain limitations to your Facebook ad account you need to be mindful of. Among them are the following.

- Each user can manage a maximum of 25 ad accounts.
- Each ad account can manage up to 25 users for every account.
- Each regular ad account is allowed a maximum of 5,000 ads which are not deleted.
- Each regular ad account is allowed a maximum of 1,000 ad set which are not deleted.
- Each regular ad account is allowed a maximum of 1,000 campaigns which are not deleted.
- Each ad account is allowed to have a maximum of 50 ads per ad set which are not deleted.

Note that the limits apply to current and non-deleted campaigns and ads. In which case, when you reach the limit, you can delete your old ads and campaigns to make room for new ones.

Reviewing Your Notification Settings

Facebook Notifications allow you to stay on top of your campaigns. When a lot goes on with your campaigns, your inbox can get flooded very quickly. To avoid this, you can edit the frequency of email notifications.

How to edit your notification settings?

- Access your **Ad Account Settings** page.
- From the left side of the menu, go to Notifications.
- Add or take out the checkmarks next to the notifications according to the ones you want to keep receiving.

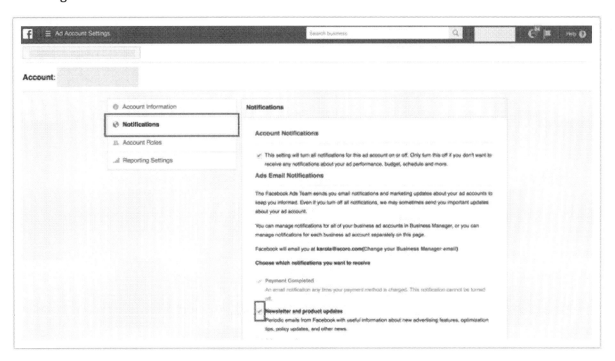

Creating an Effective Ad

Advertising is different for every business. It depends on the nature of the business and each business' specific goals. But the following pointers can help you create an effective ad according to your individual requirements.

Always begin with your goal.

Your goal should always be your starting point. It is crucial that you choose the right objective to guide your ads. Tailor your creative content and format around this objective. There are plenty of ways to increase awareness for your brand. One way of doing it effectively is by telling a story.

Do not just present your products or services the way people usually do. You can try telling a story behind them. It's also a great way of humanizing your business by letting people get to know your brand in a deeper way.

Use your goals to create different audiences.

Use your goal as the driving force in defining your audience. Also consider the possible objectives. Take into account what's important to your audience.

Build a custom ad experience for your audience.

Your approach to new customers should be difference from your existing ones.

Try using less text.

If you decide on using images on top of texts, it may be a good idea to downplay the amount of text you put into the ad. Make the copy short but compelling.

Create a focused message.

Avoid putting too much information in a single ad. Decide from the very beginning what your message will be. Stick and focus on that. If you must display information, you may want to consider using Carousel in order to show multiple images in one ad.

Choose your ad images carefully.

The right image can create a compelling visual message. It is also important to use high-resolution images. Use the size recommendations from the ads guide to make sure your ad images are presented properly. More importantly, it is essential that you follow a consistent theme for your images.

Include call-to-action.

Take advantage of the call-to-action buttons. Use them strategically to drive people to take action upon seeing your ads.

Play around.

Utilize the Creative Hub to explore different formats and images. Create your mock-ups, get as many useful feedbacks as you can and apply them.

Split Testing

This process gives you an opportunity for testing different variations of your ads. This way, you get to find out what works best. You can also learn a thing or two that'll help you improving your future campaigns.

When a split test is created, the audience is divided by ad sets and tested out with one variable to check out which ad set can perform better. The winning version of the ad is determined according to which achieved the lowest cost per result.

Before this, we emphasize on the importance of choosing the right target audience. A customer avatar plays a huge role in this regard. We've looked into the essential things you need to create one in the previous chapter. We will now look further into the process of building this profile essential to your business campaign success.

Here's a step by step guide to the process.

1. Create a profile for your ideal audience.

Whether you've already created one or still in the process of building it, you will find these guide questions useful either to create a new one or improve the one you already have.

- What is the age range of your ideal audience?
- Where do you think they're located?
- Are most of them married?
- Are most of them college educated?

- Is your ideal audience predominantly male or female or both?

These questions pave the way to defining the demographics of your ideal audience. It will help you jumpstart the process of creating a detailed picture of your audience.

2. Develop a series segmented custom audiences that are narrowly defined.

Rather than using big audience segments to create a single custom audience, you actually have the option to build multiple custom audiences.

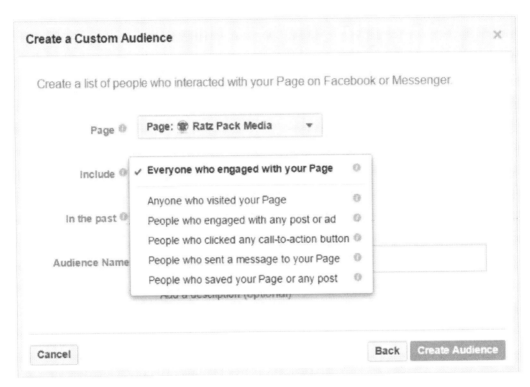

To give you an idea about the custom audience segments to create, here are a couple of examples.

- Video viewers
- Website visitors
- Previous purchasers
- Email subscribers
- People who engaged with posts
- Facebook likes
- 4-5 similar interests
- Lookalikes to any of these audience segments

3. Analyze your custom audience's characteristics using Audience Insights.

At this point, you can check if who you think your audience is aligns with the people that they really are. Compare your impression about them with the data on Audience Insights.

Access **Audience Insights** and go to the **Custom Audience section**.

Choose **Purchasers Audience**. If you have a big enough number like 1,000 in the list, you will have sufficient data to use.

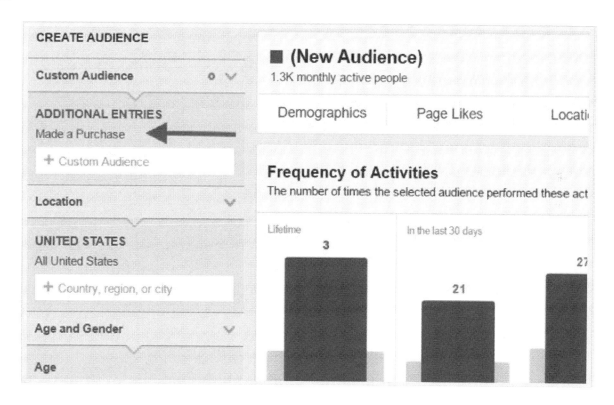

With a smaller number, you can pick another audience big or deep enough from your funnel. If there's not enough purchasers in your list, you may consider choosing **Website visitors** or **Email Subscribers** instead. This may mean the insights you get are not as powerful as those that may come from actual buyers. However, you will still gain some helpful information.

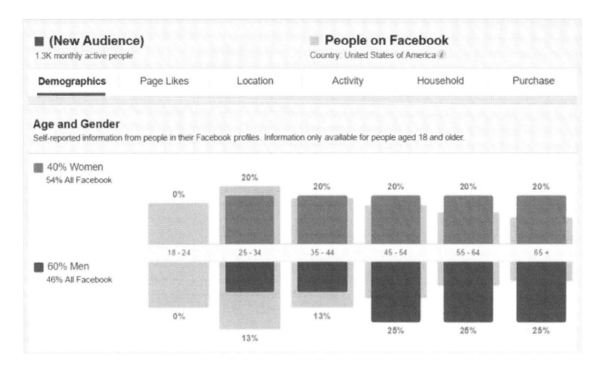

Check out what you have on the **Demographics tab**. Look at how large the audience is. Find out if the information displayed in this section matches your definition of ideal customers.

If you have a match between what you have initially and what audience insight tells you then you're in the right track. Identify any differences if there are any and use what you learn to better define your target audience.

Access the **Activity tab** and check if your buyers are avid Facebook users. If they are regular Facebook users, are they likely to engage with your ads? Do they log in to Facebook using their mobile devices or on desktop?

If your buyers are rarely clicking on ads, then it means that cost per click will not be cost efficient. If they are mobile users, then you need to create an excellent mobile experience for them.

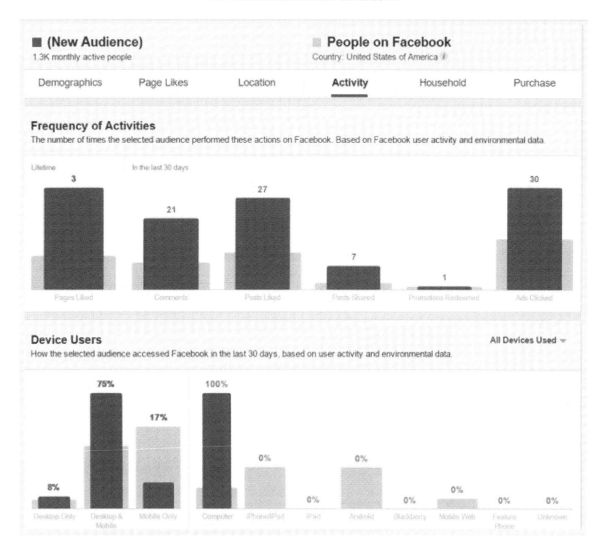

Check out the **Location tab** and find out where your buyers are. Are you thinking of targeting these areas? If you're just starting out, it will make sense to stick with your current target areas and branch out when you're ready.

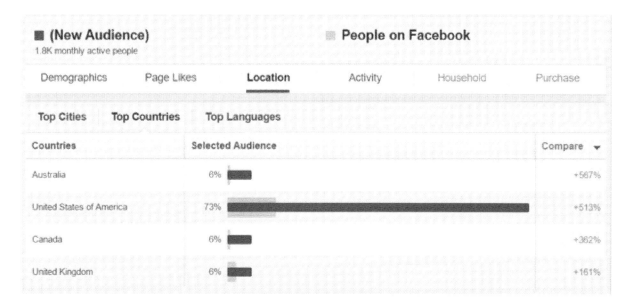

Move next to the section for **Page Likes.**

Does the niche in your ideal audience fit with the pages? You may also want to check out other pages in the same niche as yours. You can learn about the frequency of their posts. And more importantly, you can find out what posts audiences are likely to engage with. This will help you as far as organic reach is concerned.

Page Likes

Facebook Pages that are likely to be relevant to your audience based on Facebook Page likes.

Page	Relevance	Audience	Facebook
Tasty	1	24.9m	83.3m
Walmart	2	23.8m	28.5m
Amazon.com	3	21.2m	25.2m
Target	4	19.2m	21.4m
Facebook	5	19m	48.4m
Family Guy	6	16.3m	40.9m
Eminem	7	16.2m	70.9m
Starbucks	8	15.6m	33.3m
Samsung Mobile USA	9	15.1m	22.6m
Subway	10	14.6m	22.6m

After your analysis of your purchasers, you need to move on to the other custom audiences. Follow the same flow of thought and questioning and get all the much needed information to understand your real target customer better.

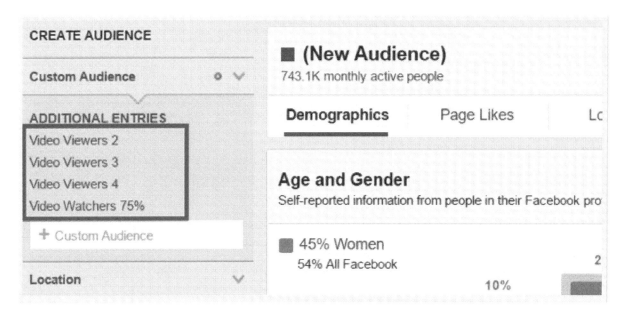

4. Optimize your Facebook targeting by comparing your Custom Audience segment data.

After learning about all the different audience segments, you can now make a full comparison. How close is your audience segment to the actual customers? Are there differences or any disconnect among the types of Facebook users you're targeting, from the people in your email newsletter to your purchasers?

Comparing the data you gathered will allow you to identify the audiences worth targeting. In case of major differences among your actual buyers, Facebook Likes and email subscribers, you may need to rethink your strategy and build a new one.

By the end of this exercise, you should already have found the audience that looks more like your purchasers. You should have already identified other Facebook Pages within your niche. From all this information, you will be able to create ad sets targeted to the right audiences and develop lookalike audiences from your custom audiences who are most like your buying customers.

5. Create multiple ad variations and put them to test.

Create and run ads separately for each of the identified audiences to determine the best-performing groups. Set your daily budget and let that determine the size of your ad sets.

Let's look at the different parts of a Facebook ad. There are 3 areas for your text including the following.

Text Post - This is the area above an image or a video

Headline - Below the image, the headline is that large black bold text.

Description - Below the image, the description is the smaller gray text.

Within the **Power Editor**, start with the ad creation process.

- Write 2 short sentences placed in different locations.
  - Sentence 1 for the Headline
  - Sentence 2 for the Text Post
  - Sentence 3 for the Description
- Choose an image or video.
- Duplicate the ad.
- Change up the placement of the sentences.
- Keep switching the elements until you've come up with multiple combinations of text placements.
- Duplicate your ad set and switch up the targeting.
- Repeat the process until you end up with 5 or about 10 ad sets with 48 ads each.
- Duplicate the combinations and change the image. Use about 4 images or videos or use the same video but use 4 different thumbnails.
- Write 3 new sentences.
- From all these combinations, you should be able to come up with 48 versions. You have a limit of 50 ads for every ad set.

6. Run your ads and track your results.

Give Facebook full 48 hours to run your ads before comparing their performance. For comparison, you can focus on these data points.

Cost per impressions or CPM

A higher CPM for a specific ad set can mean either of these two things.

You have a good content but it's not appealing to the audience. To remedy this issue, you need to try and test out new audiences.

You're targeting the right audience but the content is not good. To remedy this issue, you need to create another content.

Cost per Click or CPC

A higher than average CPC means you need to improve your ads and make them more compelling. Your message and targeting is spot on but your audience is not compelled to take action. Change up the call to action to get more clicks. You can add a phrase like **Click for more information** or write a more compelling **Call to Action** statement.

Time on Site

Getting thousand clicks is good but it can be an issue if the time on site is counted at 12 seconds. This can happen because of the following reasons.

- o   You're focusing too much of your spending on **Audience Network**.
- o   You're not reaching the right audience.
- o   There is no clear connection between the ad and your landing page.

You can remedy the issue by testing out different landing page layouts, images and header text. These changes may help in increasing the time spent on your page. You can also try breaking down your desktop and mobile traffic to check if these visitors behave differently.

Landing Page Conversion Rate

In some cases, you may have a good content, reaching the right audience, getting clicks and people spend time on your landing page but the conversion rate is less than satisfactory. This may happen for the following reasons.

- Your audience may not like your offer. To remedy the issue, try a different offer.
- You ask them to give too much information. To remedy the issue, keep your info requirements to 3-4 fields.
- You ask them for information they are not comfortable sharing.

With these data points, you will be able to compare the performance of your ads and ad sets. The information you obtain from the comparison can be used to fix what needs to be fixed, to adjust your spending and choose which ones to turn off or further optimize.

Ad Budgeting

How much do you want to spend showing your ads to people? Determining a budget is not just about deciding on the amount of money you're ready to spend. It also serves as a cost control tool. Setting a budget keeps you on top of your overall spending.

Here are a couple of reminders.

Your budget isn't about paying for the ability to display your ads. It isn't about buying ad placements. Rather, by setting your budget, you're telling Facebook the amount of money you're willing to spend in showing your ads.

A distinction must be made between budget and amount spent. In some cases, Facebook may not spend all of your budget. When it is determined that your ad set is able to compete in ad auctions consistently, your full budget may be spent. Otherwise, your full budget won't get used. Any unused budget won't be billed to you.

If you're not setting a campaign budget, each of your ad set must have its own budget. In which case, if you have multiple active ad sets, you must individually set a budget for them.

What types of budgets you can avail yourself of?

Budget can be set either at a campaign or ad set level. You can choose any one of the levels and there are two kinds of budgets to choose from.

Daily Budgets - This is the average amount that you're ready to spend on a campaign or an ad set every day.

Lifetime Budgets - This is the amount you're ready to spend for the whole run-time of your campaign or ad set.

Switching budget types is not allowed after the campaign or ad set is created. You can however, duplicate your existing campaign or ad set, switch out your budget type and create a new campaign or ad set.

How to decide on a budget?

When setting your budget, it is helpful to think about what you want to control. Decide on your budget depending on whether you care about controlling cost per optimization event or managing your total spending.

Goal 1 - To control total spending

If this is your main goal, you can set the specific total amount you're ready to spend. Give Facebook the flexibility to target and bid.

For instance, if you want to drive traffic to your website with $1,000, you can set $1,000 as your budget. For your optimization event, choose link clicks. Select a broad target audience, set your bid strategy to the lowest cost and remove the bid cap. This will prompt the delivery system to achieve on your behalf the most number of link clicks at the lowest possible cost while spending your full budget.

Goal 2: To control your cost per optimization event

If this is your goal, you must choose a more constrained bid strategy. You can give Facebook the freedom to spend while meeting your cost goal.

For instance, say purchases are your chosen optimization event. If you make a profit worth $10 and the cost of purchase is at $100 or lower, you can set a higher budget when it's paired with a bid.

When using a cost target for your conversion-optimized ad set or a bid cap, you can set your budget to at a minimum of 5 times as high as your cost target or bid cap. With this strategy, you are more likely to achieve 5 conversions a day at least.

What is the approach used for spending the budget?

The way Facebook spends the budget you set will depend on the delivery type you select. You can choose between standard or accelerated delivery. The latter option is only available when you use a bid cap.

Standard Delivery - In this delivery option, Facebook spends the budget evenly throughout the course of the campaign. This is referred to as pacing. This is the recommended option in most situations.

Accelerated Delivery - In this delivery option, Facebook will spend the budget you set as quickly as possible. This is the recommended option if your campaign is time-sensitive. In this option, your daily budgets may be spent in an hour or less. Your lifetime budget may be spent in a day or less. The spending won't resume until the next day. This is why accelerated delivery must also be used with caution.

How to edit budgets?

You are allowed to apply changes to your previously set budget. And you can do this at any time. To change your budget, you can follow these steps.

- Access the Ads Manager.
- Go to the campaign or ad set you like to edit.
- Choose the option to Edit.
- Change the budget as you please.
- Click on Confirm and Close.

After making changes to your budget, the delivery system will take 15 minutes to update. The Facebook system will need to readjust in order to show your ad in the most effective manner possible.

Budget changes can affect performance.

The changes that can happen in performance after editing your budget depends on how your ad sets or campaign is performing in the first place.

For instance, if your ad set is performing well, increasing the budget is more likely to improve results further. However, if you increase it so much that Facebook can't get enough results that work within the constraints you've set, your budget may not be fully spent. A significant increase in budget with the lowest cost bid strategy may also increase your cost per optimization event. The reason for this is that there's not much low-cost optimization events to use. In order to spend a much higher budget, chasing after higher-cost optimization events will be necessary.

On the other hand, if you lower your budget while getting your desired results, you are likely to continue spending your full budget. However, you are also more likely to achieve fewer results.

What happens if you change the budget while your ad set is not on the right track of spending the full budget? Increasing the budget may not make a lot of difference. However, you may spend a lower percentage of your set budget. On the other hand, reducing your budget may not do much except that a higher percentage of the budget may be spent.

Instagram Advertising

Although Instagram has not kept up with Facebook as far as the number of active users is concerned, it is definitely among the fastest growing apps in the world. Because Instagram users tend to be engaging, the platform also offers plenty of opportunities for advertisers.

Meet your business goals.

From sparking inspiration to driving action, get the business results and customers you care about.

Awareness

Drive awareness of your business, product, app or service.

✔ Reach

✔ Reach & Frequency

✔ Brand Awareness

✔ Local Awareness

Consideration

Have potential customers learn more about your products or services.

✔ Website Clicks

✔ Video Views

✔ Reach & Frequency

Conversion

Increase product sales, mobile app downloads, even visitors to your store.

✔ Website Conversions

✔ Dynamic Ads on Instagram

✔ Mobile App Installs

✔ Mobile App Engagement

What are the advantages of Instagram advertising?

Detailed Targeting - Instagram is under the same wing as Facebook which means you have a great chance of targeting the right audience whether you target them according to their demographics, interests or behaviors.

Definitely Eye-Catching - Among the most visual platforms, Instagram advertising is ideal for both photo and video content. Another advantage is that even low budget advertisers can do well in the platform. Because a huge number of the content uploaded on Instagram are shot on mobile phones, creating an expensive and highly technical content is not necessary.

Increase Sales - Users can make purchases within Instagram itself. Because the platform is highly visual, advertisers can showcase their products and services in a compelling way.

Unique Ad Formats - Brands and businesses can further maximize their content by taking advantage of Instagram's various ad formats including photos and videos, carousel and story ads.

What are the things to consider before getting into Instagram advertising?

This platform does offer great opportunities for advertisers. However, there are a few issues to consider before jumping into it. The following are a few of them.

Limited Audience - With around 800 million active monthly users, Instagram seems like a dream choice for any advertiser. However, for those targeting an older audience, it may not make much sense to use the platform. That's because Instagram users primarily consist of people from ages 18 to 29.

Not Very Text-Friendly - Advertisers can use the platform for tease content or to get users to their sites. For everything else however, it may be a challenge especially for advertisers promoting high engagement products and services that require a lot of written content.

Time Consuming - Instagram ads require time to manage and constantly update. This goes for all advertising efforts on social media but more so for a platform that is so visual.

Consider all these things before you take action.

Facebook Advertising Do's and Don'ts

Facebook Advertising Policies are meant to regulate content and make sure they are appropriate for the users. In this section, we'll look into the do's and don'ts of Facebook advertising.

1. Do stay away from prohibited content.

There's a list of content Facebook doesn't allow. The list is long and it includes the following.

- Ads that violate the Community Standards
- Ads that promote illegal products and services. This includes inappropriate content intended to mislead, exploit and put undue pressure on targeted age groups
- Content promoting discriminatory practices
- Content that either sell or promote the use of tobacco products
- Ads that either sell or promote the use of drugs and related products
- Ads that either sell or promote the use of unsafe supplements
- Content that either sell or promote the use of explosives, ammunition and weapons
- Content that either sell or promote the use of adult products and services
- Ads with adult content including those that depict people in suggestive or explicit positions, nudity or those that are sexually provocative and overly suggestive
- Third-party infringement
- Sensational content
- Content that feature personal attributes
- Misleading or False Content
- Controversial Content
- Content that directs users to non-functional landing pages
- Ads that sell surveillance equipment
- Content with bad grammar and profanity
- Ads with images that depict nonexistent functionality.
- Content that promote negative self-perception such as before and after images
- Ads promoting cash advance and payday loans
- Ads for Multilevel Marketing
- Content that promote penny auctions
- Ads for counterfeit documents
- Low Quality or Disruptive Content
- Ads with Spyware or Malware
- Audio and flash animation that automatically plays without user interaction
- Content promoting unauthorized streaming devices
- Ads using tactics that circumvent Facebook ad review process
- Ads promoting prohibited financial products and services

2. Do exercise caution with restricted content.

The items in the restricted content section requires certain prerequisites. Most of them require prior written permission. Others must absolutely abide by local laws. There are many in this list that are restricted for minors. The restricted section includes ads and content that promote the following.

- Alcohol
- Online Dating Services
- Gambling with real money
- State Lotteries
- Online and Offline Pharmacies promoting prescription pharmaceuticals
- Dietary and Herbal Supplements

- Subscription Services
- Financial Services or credit card applications
- Branded Content
- Student Loan Services
- Political Advertising
- Cryptocurrency Products and Services

3. Don't use video ads with disruptive content.

Video ads are encouraged because they can engage users the way that a *still image* or a plain text can't. However, Facebook doesn't allow videos with disruptive content like flashing screens. Trailers for TV shows, movies, video games and similar content must not target users under the age of 18. Entertainment related video ads that feature excessive depictions of violence, profanity, adult content, drugs and alcohol use are not allowed.

4. Do use targeting options properly.

This means targeting options should not be used for predatory advertising tactics and discrimination. Although Facebook allows you to create an audience, it is important to abide by their terms.

5. Do use positioning accurately.

Your content must be relevant and appropriate to either the product or service you're promoting. All pieces of information must be accurate. Also, the promoted products or services in the ads should match the landing page users are directed to.

6. Don't overdo text in ad images.

Facebook advises against the use of too much text in ad images. It will not only compromise ad reach, it may also get rejected. As much as possible, limit it to a little or zero image text.

7. Don't use lead ads questions.

Content must not contain questions that are intended to obtain sensitive information from users such as the following.

- Account information
- Criminal records
- Financial data
- Government Issued Identifiers
- Health records

- Insurance records
- Political affiliation
- Ethnicity or Race
- Religion
- Sexual orientation
- Membership in trade unions
- Usernames and Passwords

Facebook reserves the right to reject an ad or content that they deem unfit or in violation of their terms and conditions. You will find more information about Facebook advertising policies on their website.

Did You Know?

When asked to choose one social network "if trapped on a deserted island," 44 percent of teenagers chose Snapchat, ahead of Instagram (24 percent) and Facebook (14 percent). (recode)

Chapter 7 Quiz
Please refer to the Answer Booklet for the solution to this quiz

1. What are the parts of a Facebook campaign structure?

    A) Campaign
    B) Ads
    C) Ad Sets
    D) Carousel

2. What are the parts of a Facebook campaign structure?

    A) Awareness
    B) Consideration
    C) Conversion
    D) Purchases

3. These are objectives that aim to put your business in the mind of people. When they start thinking about the business, the next goal is to compel them to seek more information about it.

    A) Awareness
    B) Consideration
    C) Conversion
    D) Purchases

4. These are objectives encouraging people who expressed interest in your business to use and purchase your product or service.

    A) Awareness
    B) Consideration
    C) Conversion
    D) Purchases

5. If you want to collect lead information from people who are interested in the brand or businesses, which advertising objection should you choose?

    A) Traffic
    B) App Installs
    C) Engagement
    D) Lead Generation

6. What are the things you can do with Engagement as your advertising objective?

A) Boost your post and improve post engagement

B) Promote your Page and get more Page Likes

C) Have more people claim an offer from your Page and receive more Offer claims

D) Increase the attendance for an event in your Page and increase Event responses

7. Which of the following statements is not true.

A) Each user can manage a maximum of 25 ad accounts.

B) Each ad account can manage up to 25 users for every account

C) Each regular ad account is allowed a maximum of 5,000 ads which are not deleted

D) Each regular ad account is allowed a maximum of 100 sets which are not deleted

8. Which of the following are examples of custom audience segments?

A) Facebook likes

B) Website visitors

C) Previous buyers

D) Email subscribers

9. How long does the Facebook system need to update after editing your budget?

A) 5 minutes

B) 10 minutes

C) 15 minutes

D) 20 minutes

10. What are the ad formats available on Instagram?

A) Photos and videos

B) Carousels

C) Story ads

D) Canvas story ads

Chapter 8

Sales Funnels and Leads

Capturing your audience's interest is only the beginning. More often than not, most of them are not ready to purchase yet. You need to build goodwill and nurture that relationship until they are ready to give you their business. And you can do this with Facebook sales funnel.

There are various stages to take into consideration. In every step of the way, relevant messages must be used to appeal to these users and bring them a little closer to conversion. Organic posts can do this. However, you can push it further by reinforcing or spearheading Facebook ads that are highly targeted and appeal to these users at various stages of the funnel.

Facebook is used by a lot of people not exactly to purchase random products or avail themselves of services. They log in for recreation and social purposes. Savvy advertisers can leverage sales funnels to generate demand. They can remind Facebook users about needs or pain points they may not have been aware of in the first place. With the help of Facebook sales funnel, you can possibly stand out, get through the noise and obtain the conversions you have been hoping to get.

There are four stages in the Facebook Sales Funnel.

- The user is made aware of your product or service.
- After being introduced to your product or service, the user develops interest and considers a purchase.
- The user is prepared to make the purchase.
- The user has already completed the purchase. The goal now is to nurture the relationship and turn the user from a one-time purchase to a long-term customer.

How to create a Facebook Sales Funnel?

Facebook advertising uses a proactive approach. And you can take advantage of this by creating interest and drive sales. Let's go through the process step-by-step.

1. Generate Awareness

The first step is to get users into the sales funnel. There are different strategies that can be used to generate awareness including the following.

Run Facebook ads - Target users who may be interested in your products or services. You do have to target users that are not yet connected to your business Page. You can revisit your custom audiences and choose the high value ones. Create lookalike audience based on this. When you create your ads, write a quick introduction and tell users why they need your products or services.

Create a referral contest - Hosting a contest or making an offer for extra entries by referring a friend can certainly increase your sign up. You can possibly have second to third degree level of awareness. When you have their email addresses, you will also be able to run retargeting campaigns.

Run engaging posts - Organic posts that are engaging is another way of introducing your brand or business. To do this, you can write posts asking for your audience's opinions. As they respond, the whole post will also show up in their feeds for their friends to check out.

2. Address their pain points and overcome any objections.

Moving from awareness to generating interest, you need to start letting these users know how and why they need your product or service. You need to address their pain points and at the same time, find a way to overcome their objections. There are several ways to do this but you can consider the following strategies too.

Create a retargeting campaign - From the interest you have built in the previous stage, you need to build it up further. This means you need to retarget the users who have previously expressed their interest in your products or services. They need to be reminded about your offers and you must make a more compelling material at this point.

Respond to all comments - With your ads, you can address any comments or hesitations these users may still have. You can also use testimonials to help validate your claims.

Testimonials - You can also use testimonials from satisfied customers to help validate your claims.

Use organic posts and ads - Educate users about the features and benefits of your products and services. You can do this to remind them why they absolutely need what you're offering.

3. Offer incentives for purchases.

If you get the users to the point of considering a purchase, all you need to give them is a little push. You can accomplish this by offering them immediate incentives.

Incentives can come in the form of special discounts. For instance, you can offer 20% off discount on the first purchase. Offer them information for your flash sales in the future. You can also offer free shipping. To make this more compelling, you should create a sense of urgency. For example, add a deadline to the special discount or special promotion. Display the stocks left or put a timer on the sale.

4. Keep your customers engaged by upselling and referral incentives.

After their first purchase, you now have to think about converting these one-time customers to long-term ones. Encourage referrals and drive continuous sales through upselling.

- Retarget customers with loyalty perks
- Remind your customers about your referral programs
- Offer complementary products or services

ClickFunnels on Facebook

ClickFunnels is a software that can help you design and build sales pages and landing pages. It also helps you manage the entire sales funnel. And you can integrate it with your Facebook Page.

Before you can integrate ClickFunnels with your Facebook Page, you need to meet two major requirements.

- Your Facebook Business Page must have at least 2,000 fans (according to Facebook policy).
- You have an existing funnel that's built in ClickFunnels.

Let's begin with creating a sales funnel in ClickFunnels.

How to set up a sales funnel in ClickFunnels?

- Access ClickFunnels and register.
- Click on the option to **Create Funnel**.

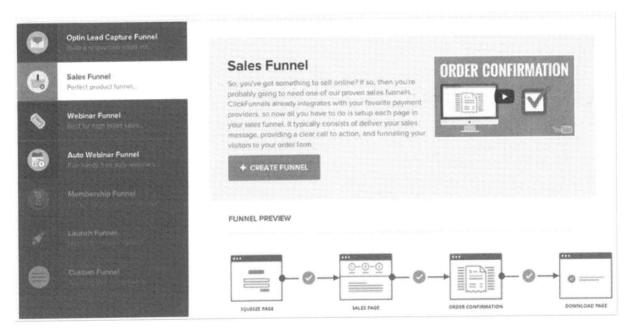

- Choose **Sales Funnel**.
- Click on **Create Funnel**.
- Enter a name for the funnel and add a tag to keep your funnels organized.

- After creating your first sales funnel, choose your template for each page. You can change the template any time but this will make you lose any edits you've applied.

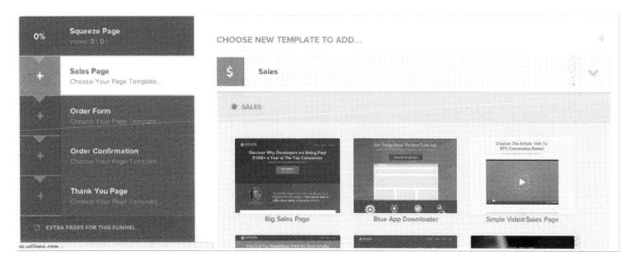

- Use the editor to edit the content and look of your selected templates.

- Go to the **Order Form**, choose the **Product/Sales tab** and click on **Add product**.

- Enter a name for your product, choose your billing integration and set the amount.
- Choose either **Subscription** or **One-time** payment at the bottom of the page.

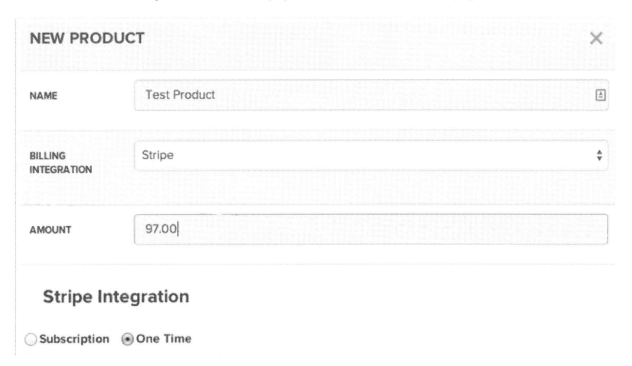

- Create a fulfillment email. This email will be sent to the customer after a purchase. Do not remove the Merge tag below after making your changes.

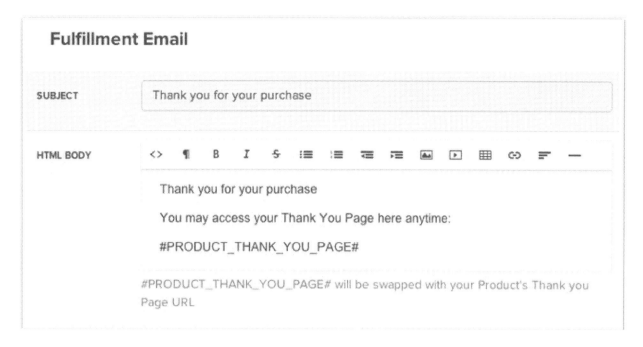

- **Activate the Integrations.** This applies only if you are shipping physical products.
- Click on the **Create Product** button below the page after making the changes.
- This will automatically add the product to your **Order Form**.

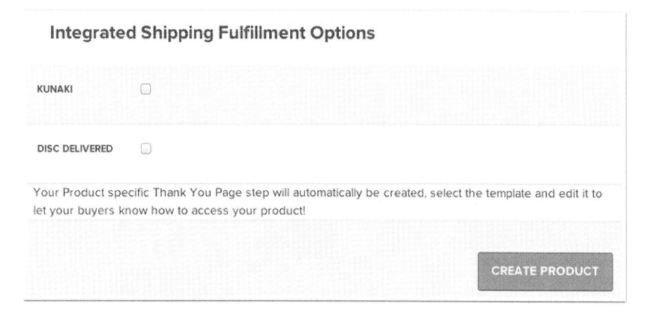

- Get the link for the **Order Form** page.

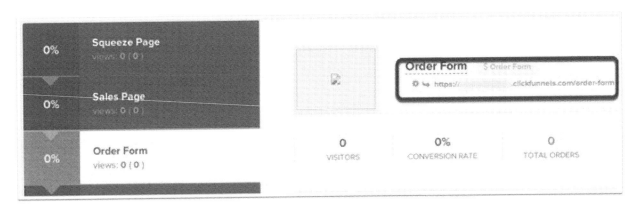

- Go to the Editor of the Sales Page. Access the **Buy Button** settings and attach the link of the Order Form to the **URL/Action** field and save.

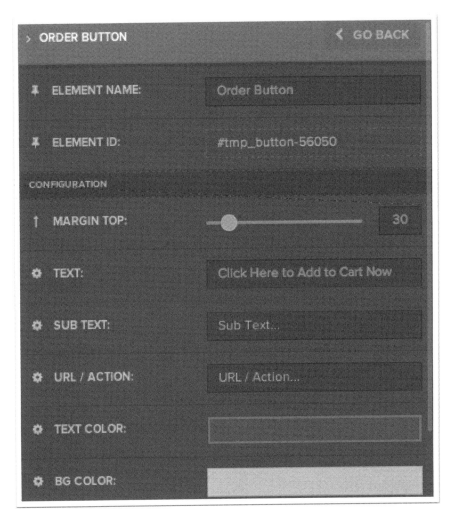

- Adding a product to the Order Form will automatically create a **Product Specific Thank You page**. This will be used for delivering your products. At this point, you can select a template and edit the details on the page. You can allow customers to download what they purchased or receive confirmation for shipping if you're selling a physical product.

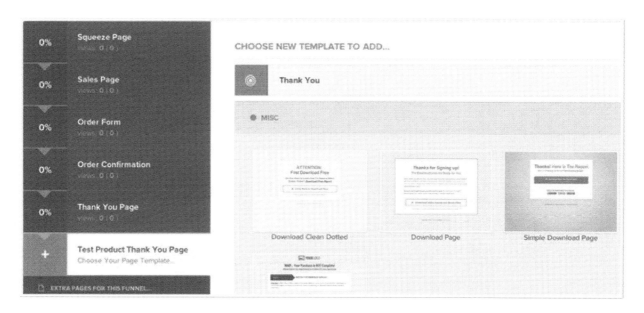

- Test your funnel by going to the **Funnel Settings** page. Edit the Funnel by clicking on the gear icon.

- At the bottom of the newly opened window, **Enable test mode**. This step will allow you to go through each of the pages you have just customized and make sure everything looks ready.

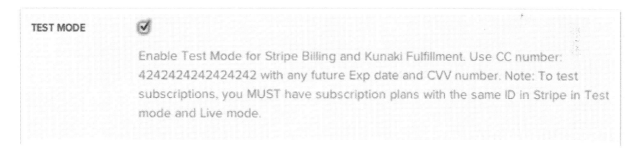

- After this step, disable the test mode so you can start receiving purchases from real customers.

How to add your Funnel to your Facebook business page?

Now that you've created your Funnel in ClickFunnels, you're ready to integrate it with Facebook.

- Access your list of Funnels within **ClickFunnels**.

- Choose the one you want to edit.
- Click on the **Publishing** tab of the funnel.
- Choose the option to **Add to Facebook**.

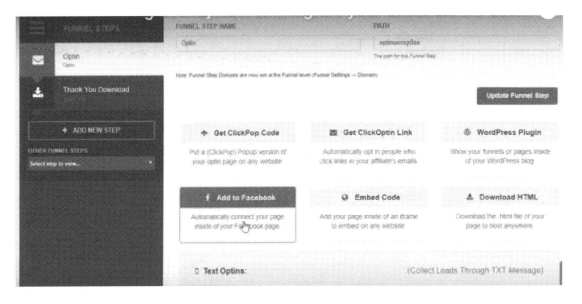

- Click on the dropdown menu to choose your Facebook Business Page.
- Click on Add Page tab.

- Verify that Clickfunnels has been added by opening your Facebook Page.
- Click on **See More**. You should be able to check the addition of ClickFunnels here.
- Edit the Clickfunnels tab by going to Settings.
- Choose the option to Edit Page.

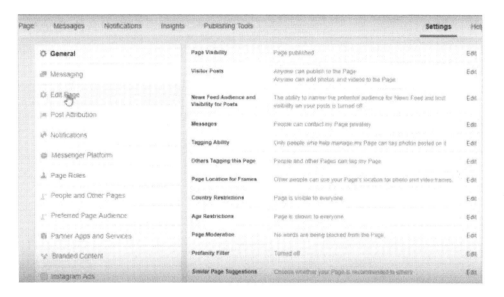

- Scroll down to the bottom and click on Settings.
- Select Edit Settings.

- Add the **Custom Tab Image** you prefer.

- Enter your preferred tab name on the field that says **Custom Tab Name**. Save your changes.

Lead Magnet

We've been talking about creating compelling messages and coming up with irresistible offers to get sign ups from your target audiences. Lead magnet is about offering an incentive for potential buyers to sign up using their email addresses and other contact info. More often than not, marketers usually offer lead magnets in the form of digital content including eBooks, videos, reports, PDF checklists, etc.

Email is a personal thing. This means people are less likely to openly share it. With the right incentive however, they may find a compelling reason to give it to you. And this is why you need a lead magnet. This is essential if you want to generate leads. You can incorporate it to your lead generation campaign.

What will make a lead magnet irresistible?

There are a couple of things you can do to make great lead magnets that attract signups. You can use the following guidelines in coming up with excellent lead magnets.

- Find a real problem and solve it with your lead magnet.
- Help your audience achieve something easily.
- Be as specific as possible to convert leads.
- Offer lead magnets that are easy to digest. If you're offering free reports or eBooks, make it easy to read.
- Offer high-perceived value with high actual value.
- Lead magnets should be instantly accessible.
- Use a lead magnet that demonstrates your expertise or represents your unique selling proposition.

Keep these things in mind when building your lead magnets and you'll achieve great results.

Aweber Email Autoresponder

An autoresponder is a computer program that automatically answers e-mail sent to it. Automating tasks is necessary if you want to handle things more efficiently. When you experience an exponential growth in email subscriptions and your email requirements become a bit more challenging to manage, you will need a tool that allows you to automatically send responses instead of doing them manually and individually.

Aweber is a software that can help you in creating and managing autoresponders. This way, you can communicate with your audience in a timely manner.

Domain Name with GoDaddy

You've chosen your sales funnel and you have your email autoresponder set up. It's now time to think about getting a domain name.

A domain name is a human-readable and recognizable address for your website. While ecommerce sites offer free domain names, you may want to get your own as this will further set you apart. You can choose a domain name that fits your brand or business perfectly. Here are a couple of things to consider when purchasing a domain name.

- A **.com** domain name is among the most prestigious and also among the hardest to find. Most **.com** names are already taken but because it's the most recognizable, you may still want to try just in case the one you have in mind happen to be available.
- Don't be afraid to try other variants of your preferred domain name using other suffixes. If a **.com** name is unavailable, consider other suffixes e.g. **.net, .org, .co.uk** etc.
- Create a domain name that is short and memorable.
- As much as possible, avoid domain names with hyphens.

When it comes to domain names, NameCheap and GoDaddy are great with the later being the most popular. It's a go-to choice for most people for a lot of reasons including the following.

- It's affordable. For $7 a month, you can get a domain name with GoDaddy.
- It has a good integration with products.
- It offers good security.
- GoDaddy provides excellent support with little down-time.

How to register a domain name with GoDaddy?

- Access the GoDaddy website.
- You will be asked if you prefer a .com suffix. A **.com** name is the default but you will be offered other variants too.
- Enter the domain name you want to check for availability.
- Choose the domain type you prefer by clicking on the corresponding checkbox.

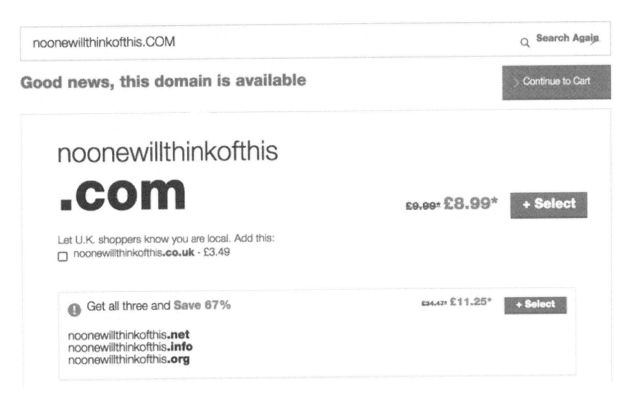

- Decide if you want a domain privacy for additional cost. You will also be offered hosting and email options. If you don't want any, skip them.
- Move on to registration and create an account. Enter the necessary information and click on Submit.

Domain Information

We need a little information from you that will be used for your domain information.

New to GoDaddy?

First Name:*

Last Name:*

Email Address:*

Organization:

☐ By entering a business or organization name, you certify that the Organization specified above is the legal registrant of this domain name.

Country/Region:
Afghanistan

Address 1:*

Address 2: (Suite, Apt #, etc.)

City:*   State: Zip Code:*

Phone:*
UK ∨ +44.

Already have an account?

Username / Customer#:

Password: Forgot Password?

Log In

🛒 Order Summary
2 domains pending registration
x NOONEWILLTHINKO...COM
x NOONEWILLTHINKO...CO.UK

Submit

- Review your purchase and make sure the correct domains are entered.
- You will be asked to register the domain for a certain timeframe. The default is set to 2 years. Other options available are 1, 3, 5 or 10.
- You will get offered other add-ons, skip if you don't want any and proceed to checkout.

Throughout this chapter, we've looked into several ways to improve the effectiveness of your Facebook advertising. To clarify things further, let's list a concise summary of some of the most common mistakes you should avoid and some of the frequently asked questions. We also debunk some common myths about Facebook advertising.

20 Common Facebook Advertising Mistakes

1. Not fully understanding the ad objective

2. Choosing a very broad audience or keeping it too narrow

3. Not targeting the right audience

4. Failing to create compelling headlines

5. Creating ads that are too wordy

6. Missing the mark on the quality of images

7. Failing to make a clear value proposition

8. Ignoring the advantages of using Facebook Pixels

9. Forgetting to add captions for video ads

10. Not delivering the ad at the right time

11. Failing to check in with performance on a daily basis

12. Forgetting to test the landing pages

13. Not maximizing the use of Facebook Insights

14. Failing to optimize the ad creative for clicks and attention

15. Not investing enough or at all in audience research upfront

16. Mismatching the offer with the audience

17. Relying too much on Interest targeting

18. Not using the right ad type for the circumstances

19. Failing to take advantage of optimization rules

20 Being impatient about results.

20 Frequently Asked Questions about Facebook Advertising

1. Where should traffic be directed after a user clicks on the Facebook ad?

Traffic can be sent either to an external website or to an internal Facebook Page. If you have a website capable of tracking actions, it can be used as a landing page for your Facebook ads.

2. How often should one update their Facebook ads?

To keep the audience interested and engaged, keeping content fresh is essential. Monitor your results regularly. When the response rate is becoming stale, your ad is due for an update.

3. How much targeted can ads be?

The biggest advantage of Facebook advertising is its ability to target people in a granular way. With Facebook, you can get as specific as possible with regards to choosing your audience. You can sort them out through demographics, interests, relationship status, income level, employment type, education level and other measures.

4. What is the recommended minimum budget per ad campaign?

This totally depends on your campaign objectives.

5. How should a headline text be written?

Headlines have to be straight to the point. To ensure that your headline text is effective and irresistible, you must keep on testing to see which one gets the most response.

6. How to create real engagement with Facebook ads?

There are several ways to create engagement with the audience. You can use questions, fill-in-the-blanks statements, contests and giveaways. Most importantly, you must have relevant and valuable content.

7. Is it possible to target previous customers using email addresses?

Yes. It is certainly possible to target former customers with their email addresses. This is referred to as Facebook custom audience.

8. Is a narrow audience generally more expensive?

Targeting smaller audience is generally more expensive. What you need to be especially mindful of is frequency because you wouldn't want to keep hitting the same person again and again using the same message.

9. What's the average CTR on Facebook?

The average Click-Through-Rate (CTR) varies according to the market and the industry but the average is somewhere between 0.4 and .5%.

10. Which is better, lifetime budget or daily budget?

One is not exactly better than the other. It all depends on what fits your business best.

11. How do I write better ad copy?

Your ad copy should be short, interesting and to the point. It is important to use the right tone of voice. Focus on the important message. And always write with your target audience in mind.

12. How do I check whether or not my ads design is working?

High quality ads are usually seen as more credible. Ad designs that spark positive emotions are also more likely to perform better. If your ad image is capable of attracting attention in users News Feed then it is more likely to work well. Finally, use split testing to your advantage and find out what works best for your target audience.

13. What are the things to absolutely avoid when writing the ad copy?

Avoid making it too long that it becomes difficult to read. Make sure to proofread and use the right spacing and punctuations. Otherwise, your ad may not seem trustworthy. Always present the unique benefit of your product and make an appealing offer.

14. What are the common bidding mistakes to avoid?

Changing your bidding methods so often that the Facebook system is not given enough time to optimize. You place manual bids that are too low that Facebook is unable to deliver the ads. You choose to bid on impressions when conversion is your objective.

15. How do I find the best target audience on Facebook?

The best way to find the best target audience is to explore different targeting options including: targeting by demographics, custom audiences, lookalike audiences and interest-based targeting.

16. How do I know my ad campaign is relevant to my target audience?

You can analyze the ad metrics relevance score to determine whether or not your ad campaign is relevant to your target audience.

17. How do I check whether or not I've selected the right ad placement for my campaign?

You can always check Facebook Ads Manager and access your campaign results by Placement. Analyze the data to find out if you're using the right ad placement or make changes when necessary.

18. What are the most recommended ad placements?

Your ad placement should be based on your campaign objective. Here are a couple of suggestions.

- For brand awareness, use Facebook and Instagram.
- For engagement, consider Facebook and Instagram.
- For video views, choose among Facebook, Instagram and Audience Network or use a combination
- For app installs, try Facebook, Instagram and Audience Network
- For traffic, consider Facebook and Audience Network
- For product catalog sales, use Facebook and Audience Network
- For conversions, try Facebook and Audience Network.

19. What are the most common landing page mistakes to avoid?

- You're creating a bad first impression.
- You're attempting to target everyone at once.
- Your usage of call-to-actions causes confusion.
- Your value proposition is unclear.
- You're giving your audience a poor mobile experience.
- Your ad designs and the landing page are not congruent e.g. message conveyed, color theme etc.

20. What do I do when my ad frequency is getting too high?

There are several options to consider when frequency is getting too high. Such options include the following.

- Put the ad campaign on a pause.
- Try switching your ad audience and attempt targeting new audiences.
- Edit your ad design and change your offer.

20 Myths about Advertising on Facebook

1. Facebook advertising is not right for Business-to-Business (B2B).

It is actually an effective channel for targeting professionals and businesses where you can specify your audience according to demographics, industry type, employment type, job tittle, income, etc.

2. Investing to get Page Likes is absolutely necessary.

Just because a user liked your page does not mean he or she will become your customer. Invest instead on Facebook ads with a clear objective and a compelling offer.

3. Retargeting all site visitors is essential.

It is indeed important to pay attention to retargeting visitors. However, using a one size fits all approach does not work. Instead of using single ad set to retarget them all, find out their reasons for visiting your website in the first place and retarget them accordingly.

4. Left side ads are more effective than right side ads.

Right side ads can be just as effective as left side ads when used correctly. Separate your right side ads into different ad sets, set them up to pay for link clicks instead of impressions.

5. The most important metric is relevance score.

It is important but what's more important is meeting your Return-on-Investment (ROI) target. Focus on end results and evaluate the cost for every acquired user and ROI.

6. You should always use images of smiling people in your ads.

It's more important to use images that are genuine and can help your audience understand instantly "what's in it for them."

7. You should not have over 20% written text in an ad.

Excessive copy may be shut down by Facebook during the holiday season but can get excellent distribution for the rest of the year. Focus on the quality of the text content instead.

8. A low relevance score will make you pay more for your ads.

Relevance score is only one of the ad metrics used in the auction system. There are other quality indicators considered.

9. Manual bidding is better than automatic bidding.

The algorithm has been designed to provide consistent delivery that yields the best results. More often than not, automatic bidding provides the best results.

10. It's bad to have a high frequency rate.

Although a high frequency rate is one of the signs of a campaign that's performing poorly, there are instances when the frequency may be high but the ROI remains in good standing. This is why advertisers have to look at the data as a whole and focus on ROI, instead of evaluating the performance of a campaign based on a single ad metric only.

11. Facebook ads only work for bottom-of-the-funnel.

Facebook ads can work effectively for every stage of the funnel. When creating your ad campaigns, keep the funnel in mind.

12. Facebook ads are mostly used for increasing followers and engagements in posts.

Facebook advertisers are in fact, creating more and spending more on website conversion ads among other ad types.

13. If you're paying just for clicks, it's perfectly fine to spray and pray you'll get some.

To get most value for what you pay for, it is best to pay attention to ad targeting. It's always important to get your ads in front of the right audience. Otherwise, it will be a total waste of your ad budget.

14. The competition is very fierce for Post engagement ads and page likes.

According to Socialbakers' Facebook ads data, CPC for Page Like ads and Post Engagement ads are actually decreasing. It appears Advertisers are beginning to spend less on these kind of campaigns.

15. Cost per Click on ad types are increasing.

CPC rates for most ad types are relatively steady and has not increased in recent years.

16. Because of Lead Generation ads, website conversion ads have become obsolete.

Advertising budget allocation spent on website conversion ads is steady while advertisers are still hesitant about investing in Lead Generation ads.

17. Advertisers are spending most of their money on video ads.

Video ads certainly have become quite popular. However, video ads still make up only less than 20% of total ad spend for advertisers.

18. Facebook ads are often ignored by users because they are annoying.

When an ad is irrelevant, users will most likely ignore it. This is why targeting is important and showing the ads relevant to your selected audience.

19. You need to spend on professional quality images.

Images on ads have to be attention grabbing and visually appealing but there are plenty of ways to achieve these requirements without spending too much. Striking graphics style can be a great attention grabber. Images with humor work too. Test out different images and see what works best.

20. Facebook advertising is too expensive

Facebook advertising certainly costs money but depending on your objective and available budget, anyone can advertise with as little as $5 a day and achieve great results.

Congratulations!

The sixth character of the password required to unlock the Answer Booklet is letter a.

Chapter 8 Quiz

Please refer to the Answer Booklet for the solution to this quiz

1. What are the steps to creating a Facebook Sales Funnel (in the right order)?

    A) Keep your customers engaged by upselling and referral incentives
    B) Address pain points and objections
    C) Offer incentives for purchases
    D) Generate awareness

2. Which of the following are good examples of generating awareness?

    A) Create a referral contest
    B) Retarget previous buyers
    C) Run Facebook ads for users who may be interested in your product or service
    D) Run engaging posts to introduce your brand or business

3. This is a software that can help you design and build sales pages and landing pages. It also helps you manage the entire sales funnel.

    A) ClicktheFunnel
    B) ClickFunnels
    C) ClickIt
    D) ClickSalesFunnels

4. What are the things you need before you can integrate ClickFunnels with your Facebook page?

    A) An existing funnel in ClickFunnels
    B) Facebook Business Page of at least 500 fans
    C) Facebook Business Page of at least 1500 fans
    D) Facebook Business Page of at least 2000 fans

5. This email will be sent to the customer after a purchase.

    A) Thank You email
    B) Come Again email
    C) Fulfillment email
    D) Subscription email

6. When do you need to activate Integrations in ClickFunnels?

    A) When you're selling ebooks
    B) When you're selling any physical products

C) When you're offering subscriptions

D) When you're offering a service

7. This is about offering an incentive for potential buyers to sign up using their email addresses and other contact info.

A) Lead magnets

B) Incentives

C) Lead ads

D) Lead audience

8. Which of the following statements are true about lead magnets?

A) An effective lead magnet is instantly accessible

B) To get more signups, you should be as specific as possible to convert leads.

C) To maximize lead magnets, you should use one that demonstrates your expertise or represents your unique selling proposition.

D) An excellent lead magnet is one that helps your audience achieve something easily.

9. This is a software that can help you in creating and managing autoresponders so you can communicate with your audience in a timely manner.

A) Aweber Autoresponsive

B) Aweber Auto

C) Aweber Autoresponder

D) Aweber Autorespond

10. This is a human-readable and recognizable address for your website.

A) Domain name

B) Address name

C) Website address

D) Website domain

Did You Know?

Sixty-seven percent of consumers use Facebook and Twitter to find a resolution to issues, and 1 in 3 prefer customer care over social media to telephone or email. (Social Media Today)

Chapter 9

A Case Study

Product: High-Ticket Mastermind Events Valued at $2,000

Target Audience: Small Business Owners, Entrepreneurs and High Level Business Executives looking to grow their business

1. Defining the ideal audience

Kevin Miles is a 30-year-old CEO of Social Media-Marketing Agency – **Kevin Miles Promotions**. He's managed to secure a contract with ABC Ltd to promote one of their high-ticket network events worth $2,000 and he's set to earn 50% commission on each ticket sale. He doesn't have an existing customer base but he has a good idea about his ideal audience. Based on his initial research, he defined his ideal audience as follows.

Age range:

Gender: Men and Women

Education: College level

Job Title: Business owners and entrepreneurs

Interests: Grant Cardone, Rich Dad Poor Dad, Tony Robbins

2. Cross-referencing with Audience Insights

To find out more about his target audience, Kevin used Audience Insights particularly focusing on Interests to find real people that match his ideal audience. This is what he found out.

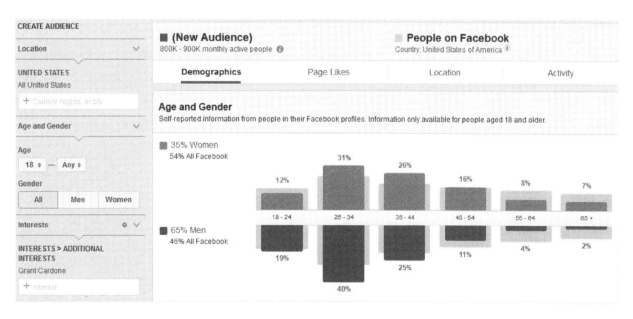

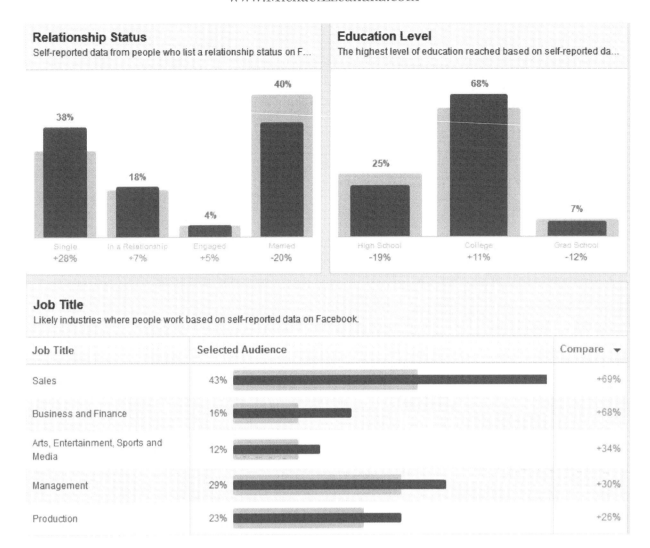

Aside from defining the audience demographics, he further dug in to the research by assessing the Page Likes of his potential audiences. He used this information to list 20+ additional interests that allowed him to narrow down his audience and find the right target.

3. Building the Page

Kevin is fully aware that he needed to build a reputation first in order to get people to buy into his high-ticket event. After defining his target audience well, he began building his page and adding appropriate and relevant content. He applied the knowledge he gathered from his research through Audience Insights to get attention and create awareness for his page.

He made sure that with every post he makes, he is able to add value for the audience. At the same time, he wanted to engage the users who have already liked his page to get information from them. To do this, he would ask his Page fans to rate statements relating to business and the challenges that come with it. He would ask them to give a score for the statements from 1 to 5.

1 - Strongly disagree

2 - Disagree

3 - Can't Say

4 - Agree

5 - Strongly Agree

*Among a few examples of the statements he would use are the following.

- *I have more leads than I can handle.*
- *Every business process is well documented.*
- *I have A-players working for me.*
- *I can run my business stress free.*

With these statements, Kevin puts forward a lot of the pain points of business owners and entrepreneurs. And he would be able to use this information later to position his high-ticket event.

4. Creative Hub

As Kevin was slowly building his page fan base, he explores Facebook Creative Hub to get ideas about content. After getting inspired, he was slowly building his content. He came up with a mockup and used the guidelines provided until he was satisfied with what he had. He created different variations for his ad for split testing later.

5. Buying a domain name.

Kevin knew he wanted a dedicated domain name for promoting the mastermind event so he decided to invest in a domain name. He used GoDaddy to register a domain and opted for the .com suffix which cost more but recognizable. He only needed to buy the domain name so he skipped on any add-ons. After going through the process, he was able to register <**www.jointhemasters.com**>

6. ClickFunnels registration.

Because Kevin did not have the technical skills required to write code or build a website or a sales funnel from scratch, he opted to use ClickFunnels. He would set it up as his landing page for his Facebook ads, the same place where he can add his high-ticket mastermind event as a product where his audience can get a digital ticket for.

He updated his GoDaddy account to add Clickfunnels and integrated the domain name to his funnel.

7. ClickFunnels with aweber

Kevin was slowly building up his customer base and gradually engaging his audience. He knew he would later on need an autoresponder to make email correspondence easier. He needed to automate the process so he signed up with aweber. To manage everything that has to do with his event in one place, he integrated ClickFunnels with Aweber.

8. Creating lead magnets

To create lead magnets, Kevin used the pain points he identified and addressed them, especially for the statements where users either "disagreed" or "strongly disagreed." He wanted to make the lead magnets as instantly accessible as possible. He used samples of topics from the mastermind events itself so he can give people an idea of the things to expect during the event.

Pain Points	Lead Magnet
I have more leads than I can handle.	A Blueprint for Lead Management, downloadable guide
Every business process is well documented.	Business documentation template.
I can run my business stress free.	A guide for automation tools

He used these incentives to position himself as an authority figure, as well as, give people an extra nudge so they would sign up with their email addresses. He offered more incentives for people who referred friends.

9. Integrating sales funnel with Facebook

Kevin had decided that he would be using Facebook primarily for marketing purposes but in order to direct his audience on Facebook to his landing page on ClickFunnels, he had to integrate the platforms together. After the integration, any clicks on his posts or ads will directly bring the users to either his subscription page or the high-ticket event page where they can purchase a ticket.

10. Testing out posts with Facebook Page audience

While his Facebook fan page is growing in numbers, Kevin decided to test out his ads to his existing Page audience. He rolled out a couple of variations and tried out different ad formats including story ads, single image ads and video ads. He took note of the ad content that his audience responded to the most. He used the information he gathered to roll out the event to a wider audience.

11. Lookalike audience.

As his email list was growing, Kevin could already create a lookalike audience. He used the custom audience and ran the best performing ad posts in his page to reach more people.

12. Exclusive Event

With a high-ticket event worth $2,000, Kevin expected plenty of objections. Among them was the high cost. He framed his copies in a way that emphasized the ticket cost is an investment to reach profit goals. For instance, when he asked his Page audience, how much profits they can expect when their pain points are addressed.

One user responded he can potentially earn $100,000 a month if his business operation becomes more efficient. For a $100,000 potential earning, a $2,000 investment doesn't sound that bad. It actually makes a lot of sense from a ROI perspective. Phrased this way, Kevin was able to grow his conversion rates.

He also made the event seem exclusive. To get in to the event, Kevin rolled out application forms. He was careful to keep the form short but sweet with basic info and a maximum of 5 evaluation statements similar to the ones he used for his lead magnets.

With this strategy, Kevin was making an impression about the mastermind event. The idea of applying for attendance to an event effectively invoked a sense of exclusivity among the audience. At the same time, Kevin was able to gather more insight which he can use to address any other possible objections and further grow his conversions.

13. Facebook Group and Email Reminders

Kevin was able to grow the event attendance. To keep the momentum, he decided to create a Facebook Group where only those who have confirmed attendance can have access to. As the event drew closer, he would use Facebook Live to interact with the attendees. He used the interaction to further build confidence in the benefits of the event. He also rolled out email reminders which he automated using aweber.

The event was a success. There was more attendance than Kevin had expected – 68 people attended in total. And with his campaign process well documented in Facebook, ClickFunnels and aweber, he already had valuable data which he can use for promoting other high-ticket mastermind events in the future.

To keep in touch with the attendees, he had automated emails sent through aweber asking them for feedback. He also continued to interact with the Group and Page fans to check with their results after applying the principles they have learned from the mastermind event.

Amount Spent on Marketing = $14,500

Total Revenue = 50% of $2,000 x 68 = $68,000

Net Profit = $68,000 - $14,500 = $53,500

ROI = 53,500/14,500 = 369%

Congratulations!

The eight character of the password required to unlock the Answer Booklet is letter k.

Conclusion II

I hope the above case study has put the entire process into perspective for you. The product marketed could have *anything* e.g. a golf club, an online course, a travel experience etc. The point is that the knowledge you've gained will allow you to effectively market pretty much anything. Now is the time to put into practice what you've learned and further consolidate your knowledge.

When it comes to Facebook, the sky is the limit. You have an opportunity to reach thousands if not millions of people. To get the most bang out of your buck with Facebook advertising, here are a few more reminders to live by.

Be straight with your goal.

What are you trying to achieve? Whether it is to increase traffic, raise awareness for your brand or business or boost your page likes, use this objective to guide your decisions from content creation to targeting to ad placements. Guided by your specific goals, you can create an appropriate call to action which will make your campaign effective.

Try different demographics.

If you're not getting the results you want, consider trying out different demographics. This will give you an idea how they perform until you find the perfect mix of parameters to reach your goals.

Also, don't be constrained by demographics. When using Audience Insight to define your customer avatar, take advantage of utilizing interests, Page likes, etc. Every person has a pain point and something that motivates him or her. You can use this motivation to push your products or services forward.

Be specific with your audience.

It is important to narrow the parameters. This may mean your number of reach decreases. However, it will help make sure that you are indeed targeting the right people.

Don't run ads for too long.

Variation is essential which is why you should not extend the duration of the campaign longer than you should. Once you see the results declining, take it as your cue to switch things around. If you still have budget to spend, choose another ad or ad set. Keep it fresh as much as possible.

Try out different content.

Experiment not just with your demographics but also with the kind of content you're putting out there. You can also choose different variations and audiences. Compare the performance of your ads and campaign.

Facebook gives you access to this data. Take your time to review the information so you can figure out what works best for your business or brand. With this in mind, you will be able to create more effective posts.

You can't expect to get things right the first time. However, as you get the hang of it and apply what you learn, you will be able to improve your results.

You will need to put in all the hard work in the beginning but once you've mastered a formula, you can automate and do less work for more profits.

I want to share with you something that I find terribly sad. Once people start reading a book, they typically only read 10 percent of it before they give up or forget about it. Only 10 percent. What's sad about this is that from this statistic, we can see that very few people actually follow through on what they commit to (at least when it comes to reading). The reason for this is harsh but understandable: most people are not willing to hold themselves accountable. People "want" and "want" all day, but very few actually have the fortitude to put in the work.

So what's my point? First, I am trying to tell you that if you're reading these words, you are a statistical anomaly (and I am grateful for you). But here's the kicker: in order to become successful as a result of this book, you are going to have to be in the 1 percent. You need to take action.

So What's Next?

Now that you are fully aware of the tremendous opportunities available to you with regards to Facebook Advertising, what's the next step? Well, it's time to pull up your sleeves and get to work. It's time to take action. It's time to fire up that laptop and start getting things done. Many aspiring online entrepreneurs will never achieve their goals because they never get started. Don't be one of these dreamers. You have to take action.

I'll tell you right now that getting started is going to be difficult and often confusing. But that is part of the game. As the saying goes, the city of Rome wasn't built in one day. Generating a consistent stream of revenue with Facebook Advertising takes time and hours of hard work. It can take a lot of trial and error before you get the hang of things and begin to see some consistent revenue coming your way. This is why throughout this book, I've gone through the effort of providing simple, step-by-step instructions that'll guide you.

The concepts discussed in this book will assist you immensely whether you're a small business owner looking to grow his or her bottom line and online presence using Facebook Ads or an Affiliate Marketer looking to promote an online course or even the owner of a social media marketing agency who is looking to get into joint partnerships with local businesses in a bid to help promote their brand, a product or an event online. The opportunities are endless!

My last piece of advice for you is this: "Set your goals and don't stop until you achieve them." Don't let anything or anyone try to discourage or bring you down. Just focus on those goals and keep on working and hustling towards them. That's what most successful entrepreneurs would do. Work hard, work smart, and be patient. These are the keys to achieving your goals. It doesn't matter if these are short-term or long-term goals.

I wish you the very best of luck!

The End

Thank you very much for taking the time to read this book. I tried my best to cover as much information as I could without overwhelming you. If you found it useful please let me know by leaving a review on Amazon! Your support really does make a difference and I read all the reviews personally so can I understand what my readers particularly enjoyed and then feature more of that in future books.

I also pride myself on giving my readers the best information out there, being super responsive to them and providing the best customer service. If you feel I have fallen short of this standard in any way, please kindly email me at michael@michaelezeanaka.com so I can get a chance to make it right to you. I wish you all the best with your business!

Other Book(s) By Michael Ezeanaka

Affiliate Marketing: Learn How to Make $10,000+ Each Month On Autopilot

Are you looking for an online business that you can start today? Do you feel like no matter how hard you try - you never seem to make money online? If so, this book has you covered. If you correctly implement the strategies in this book, you can make commissions of up to $10,000 (or more) per month in extra income.

- WITHOUT creating your own products
- WITHOUT any business or management experience
- WITHOUT too much start up capital or investors
- WITHOUT dealing with customers, returns, or fulfillment
- WITHOUT building websites
- WITHOUT selling anything over the phone or in person
- WITHOUT any computer skills at all
- WITHOUT leaving the comfort of your own home

In addition, because I enrolled this book in the kindle matchbook program, **Amazon will make the kindle edition available to you for FREE** after you purchase the paperback edition from Amazon.com, saving you roughly $6.99!!

Available In Kindle, Paperback and Audio

Passive Income Ideas: 50 Ways To Make Money Online Analyzed

How many times have you started a business only to later realise it wasn't what you expected? Would you like to go into business knowing beforehand the potential of the business and what you need to do to scale it? If so, this book can help you

In Passive Income Ideas, you'll discover

- A concise, step-by-step analysis of 50 business models you can leverage to earn passive income (Including one that allows you to earn money watching TV!)
- Strategies that'll help you greatly simplify some of the business models (and in the process make them more passive!)
- What you can do to scale your earnings (regardless of which business you choose)
- Strategies you can implement to minimize the level of competition you face in each marketplace
- Myths that tend to hold people back from succeeding in their business (**we debunk more than 100 such myths!**)
- Well over 150 Insightful tips that'll give you an edge and help you succeed in whichever business you chose to pursue

- More than 100 frequently asked questions (with answers)
- 50 positive vitamins for the mind (in the form of inspirational quotes that'll keep you going during the tough times)
- A business scorecard that neatly summarizes, in alphabetical order, each business models score across 4 criteria i.e. simplicity, passivity, scalability and competitiveness
- ...and much much more!

What's more? Because the book is enrolled in kindle matchbook program, **Amazon will make the kindle edition available to you for FREE** after you purchase the paperback edition from Amazon.com, saving you roughly $6.99!!

Available In <u>Kindle</u>, <u>Paperback</u> and <u>Audio</u>

Work From Home: 50 Ways To Make Money Online Analyzed

This is a **2-in-1 book bundle** consisting of the below books. Amazon will make the kindle edition available to you for FREE when you purchase the print version of this bundle from Amazon.com - **saving you roughly 35%** from the price of the individual books.

- Passive Income Ideas – 50 Ways to Make Money Online Analyzed (Part I)
- Affiliate Marketing – Learn How to Make $10,000+ Each Month on Autopilot (Part 2)

Get this bundle at a 35% discount from Amazon.com

Available In <u>Kindle</u>, <u>Paperback</u> and <u>Audio</u>

Dropshipping: Discover How to Make Money Online, Build Sustainable Streams of Passive Income and Gain Financial Freedom Using The Dropshipping E-Commerce Business Model

How many times have you started a business only to later realise you had to spend a fortune to get the products manufactured, hold inventory and eventually ship the products to customers all over the globe?

Would you like to start your very own e-commerce business that gets right to making money without having to deal with all of these issues? If so, this book can help you

In this book, you'll discover:

- A simple, step-by-step explanation of what the dropshipping business is all about (Chapter 1)
- 8 reasons why you should build a dropshipping business (Chapter 2)
- Disadvantages of the dropshipping business model and what you need to look out for before making a decision (Chapter 3)

- How to start your own dropshipping business including the potential business structure to consider, how to set up a company if you're living outside the US, how much you'll need to start and sources of funding (Chapter 4)
- How the supply chain and fulfilment process works – illustrated with an example transaction (Chapter 5)
- Analysis of 3 potential sales channel for your dropshipping business - including their respective pros and cons (Chapter 6)
- How to do niche research and select winning products – including the tools you need and where to get them (Chapter 7)
- How to find reliable suppliers and manufacturers. As well as 6 things you need to look out for in fake suppliers (Chapter 8)
- How to manage multiple suppliers and the inventory they hold for you (Chapter 9)
- How to deal with security and fraud issues (Chapter 10)
- What you need to do to minimize chargebacks i.e. refund rates (Chapter 11)
- How to price accordingly especially when your supplier offers international shipment (Chapter 12)
- 10 beginner mistakes and how to avoid them (Chapter 13)
- 7 powerful strategies you can leverage to scale up your dropshipping business (Chapter 14)
- 15 practical tips and lessons from successful dropshippers (Chapter 15)

And much, much more!

Finally, because this book is enrolled in Kindle Matchbook Program, the **kindle edition of this book will be available to you for free** when you purchase the paperback version from Amazon.com.

If you're ready to take charge of your financial future, grab your copy of this book today! Start taking control of your life by learning how to create a stream of passive income that'll take care of you and your loved ones.

Available In **Kindle**, Paperback and Audio

Dropshipping and Facebook Advertising: Discover How to Make Money Online and Create Passive Income Streams With Dropshipping and Social Media Marketing

This is a **2-in-1 book bundle** consisting of the below books and split into 2 parts. Amazon will make the kindle edition available to you for FREE when you purchase the print version of this bundle from Amazon.com - **saving you roughly 25%** from the price of the individual paperbacks.

- Dropshipping – Discover How to Make Money Online, Build Sustainable Streams of Passive Income and Gain Financial Freedom Using The Dropshipping E-Commerce Business Model (Part 1)
- Facebook Advertising – Learn How to Make $10,000+ Each Month with Facebook Marketing (Part 2)

Available In **Kindle**, Paperback and Audio

Get this bundle at a 35% discount from Amazon.com

Real Estate Investing For Beginners: Earn Passive Income With Reits, Tax Lien Certificates, Lease, Residential & Commercial Real Estate

In this book, Amazon bestselling author, Michael Ezeanaka, provides a step-by-step analysis of 10 Real Estate business models that have the potential to earn you passive income. A quick overview of each business is presented and their liquidity, scalability, potential return on investment, passivity and simplicity are explored.

In this book, you'll discover:

- How to make money with Real Estate Investment Trusts – including an analysis of the impact of the economy on the income from REITs (Chapter 1)
- A step-by-step description of how a Real Estate Investment Groups works and how to make money with this business model (Chapter 2)
- How to become a limited partner and why stakeholders can influence the running of a Real Estate Limited Partnership even though they have no direct ownership control in it (Chapter 3)
- How to protect yourself as a general partner (Chapter 3)
- Why tax lien certificates are one of the most secure investments you can make and how to diversify your portfolio of tax lien certificates (Chapter 4)
- Strategies you can employ to earn passive income from an empty land (Chapter 5)
- Two critical factors that are currently boosting the industrial real estate market and how you can take advantage of them (Chapter 6)
- Some of the most ideal locations to set up industrial real estate properties in the US, Asia and Europe **(Chapter 6)**
- Why going for long term leases (instead of short term ones) can significantly increase you return on investment from your industrial real estate properties (Chapter 6)
- Why commercial properties can serve as an excellent hedge against inflation – including two ways you can make money with commercial properties (Chapter 7)
- How long term leases and potential 'turnover rents' can earn you significant sums of money from Retail real estate properties and why they are very sensitive to the state of the economy **(Chapter 8)**
- More than 10 zoning rights you need to be aware of when considering investing in Mixed-Use properties **(Chapter 9)**
- 100 Tips for success that will help you minimize risks and maximize returns on your real estate investments

And much, much more!

PLUS, **BONUS MATERIALS**: you can download the author's Real Estate Business Scorecard which neatly summarizes, in alphabetical order, each business model's score across those 5 criteria i.e. liquidity, scalability, potential return on investment, passivity and simplicity!

Finally, because this book is enrolled in Kindle Matchbook Program, the **kindle edition of this book will be available to you for free** when you purchase the paperback version from Amazon.com.

If you're ready to take charge of your financial future, grab your copy of This Book today!

Available In **Kindle**, **Paperback** and **Audio**

Credit Card And Credit Repair Secrets: Discover How To Repair Your Credit, Get A 700+ Credit Score, Access Business Startup Funding, And Travel For Free Using Reward Cards

Are you sick and tired of paying huge interests on loans due to poor credit scores? Are you frustrated with not knowing where or how to get the necessary capital you need to start your business? Would you like to get all these as well as discover how you can travel the world for FREE?

If so, you'll love Credit Card and Credit Repair Secrets.

Imagine knowing simple do-it-yourself strategies you can employ to repair your credit profile, protect it from identity theft, access very cheap and affordable funding for your business and travel the world without any out of pocket expense!

This can be your reality. You can learn how to do all these and more. Moreover, you may be surprised by how simple doing so is.

In this book, you'll discover:

- **3 Types of consumer credit (And How You Can Access Them!)**
- How To Read, Review and Understand Your Credit Report (Including a Sample Letter You Can Send To Dispute Any Inaccuracy In It)
- **How To Achieve a 700+ Credit Score (And What To Do If You Have No FICO Score)**
- How To Monitor Your Credit Score (Including the difference between hard and soft inquiries)
- **What The VantageScore Model Is, It's Purpose, And How It Differs From The FICO Score Model**
- The Factors That Impact Your Credit Rating. Including The Ones That Certainly Don't - Despite What People Say!
- **Which Is More Important: Payment History Or Credit Utilization? (The Answer May Surprise You)**
- Why You Should Always Check Your Credit Report (At least Once A Month!)
- **How Credit Cards Work (From The Business And Consumer Perspective)**
- Factors You Need To Consider When Choosing A Credit Card (Including How To Avoid A Finance Charge on Your Credit Card)
- **How To Climb The Credit Card Ladder And Unlock Reward Points**
- Which Is More Appropriate: A Personal or Business Credit Card? (Find Out!)
- **How to Protect Your Credit Card From Identity Theft**
- Sources of Fund You Can Leverage To Grow Your Business

And much, much more!

An Identity Theft Resource Center (ITRC) report shows that 1,579 data breaches exposed about 179 million identity records in 2017. Being a victim of an identity scam can cause you a lot of problems. One of the worst cases would be the downfall of your credit score. You don't have to fall victim to it.

This book gives you a simple, but incredibly effective, step-by-step process you can use to build, protect and leverage your stellar credit profile to enjoy a financially stress-free life! It's practical. It's actionable. And if you follow it closely, it'll deliver extraordinary results!

PLUS BONUS - because this book is enrolled in Kindle Matchbook Program, the **kindle edition of this book will be available to you for free** when you purchase the paperback version from Amazon.com.

If you're ready to take charge of your financial future, grab your copy of This Book today!

Available In **Kindle**, Paperback and **Audio**

Real Estate Investing And Credit Repair: Discover How To Earn Passive Income With Real Estate, Repair Your Credit, Fund Your Business, And Travel For Free Using Reward Credit Cards

This is a **2-in-1 book bundle** consisting of the below books and split into 2 parts. Amazon will make the kindle edition available to you for FREE when you purchase the print version of this bundle from Amazon.com - **saving you roughly 25%** from the price of the individual paperbacks.

- Real Estate Investing For Beginners – Earn Passive Income With Reits, Tax Lien Certificates, Lease, Residential & Commercial Real Estate (Part 1)
- Credit Card And Credit Repair Secrets – Discover How To Repair Your Credit, Get A 700+ Credit Score, Access Business Startup Funding, And Travel For Free Using Reward Cards (Part 2)

Available In **Kindle**, Paperback and **Audio**

Get this bundle at a 35% discount from Amazon.com

Passive Income With Dividend Investing: Your Step-By-Step Guide To Make Money In The Stock Market Using Dividend Stocks

Have you always wanted to put your money to work in the stock market and earn passive income with dividend stocks?

What would you be able to achieve with a step-by-step guide designed to help you grow your money, navigate the dangers in the stock market and minimize the chance of losing your capital?

Imagine not having to rely solely on a salary or a pension to survive. Imagine having the time, money and freedom to pursue things you're passionate about, whether it's gardening, hiking, reading, restoring a classic car or simply spending time with your loved ones.

This book can help you can create this lifestyle for yourself and your loved ones!

Amazon bestselling author, Michael Ezeanaka, takes you through a proven system that'll help you to build and grow a sustainable stream of passive dividend income. He'll show you, step by step, how to identify stocks to purchase, do accurate due diligence, analyze the impact of the economy on your portfolio and when to consider selling.

In this book, you'll discover:

- Why investing in dividend stocks can position you to benefit tremendously from the "Baby Boomer Boost" (Chapter 1)
- **Which certain industry sectors tend to have a higher dividend payout ratio and why? (Chapter 2)**
- How to time your stock purchase around ex-dividend dates so as to take advantage of discounted share prices (Chapter 2)
- **Why a stock that is showing growth beyond its sustainable rate may indicate some red flags. (Chapter 2)**
- 5 critical questions you need to ask in order to assess if a company's debt volume will affect your dividend payment (Chapter 3)
- **How high dividend yield strategy can result in low capital gain taxes (Chapter 4)**
- Reasons why the average lifespan of a company included in the S&P 500 plummeted from 67 years in the 1920s to just 15 years in 2015. (Chapter 5)
- **A blueprint for selecting good dividend paying stocks (Chapter 6)**
- The vital information you need to look out for when reading company financial statements (Chapter 7)
- **A strategy you can use to remove the emotion from investing, as well as, build wealth cost efficiently (Chapter 8)**
- An affordable way to diversify your portfolio if you have limited funds (Chapter 9)
- **Why you may want to think carefully before selling cyclical stocks with high P/E ratio (Chapter 10)**

And much, much more!

PLUS BONUS - because this book is enrolled in Kindle Matchbook Program, the **kindle edition of this book will be available to you for free** when you purchase the paperback version from Amazon.com.

Whether you're a student, corporate executive, entrepreneur, or stay-at-home parent, the tactics described in this book can set the stage for a financial transformation.

If you're ready to build and grow a steady stream of passive dividend income, Grab your copy of this book today!

Available In <u>Kindle</u>, <u>Paperback</u> and <u>Audio</u>

Made in the USA
Lexington, KY
29 June 2019